Advance Praise for
The Home Energy Diet

The Home Energy Diet is a valuable resource for homeowners and anyone interested in efficient, affordable, and healthy housing. The book balances theoretical understanding with practical wisdom. Paul Scheckel's humorous and down-to-earth-style make the book accessible; it was a pleasure to read.

— JIM GUNSHINAN, managing editor, *Home Energy Magazine*

Although it's addressed to the interested home owner, *The Home Energy Diet* provides enough theory and practice to be extremely useful as a teaching tool and reference guide for tradespeople as well. This book should be required reading for anyone who has anything to do with the care and feeding of a house and any of its components.

— KEN TOHINAKA, senior energy analyst,
Vermont Energy Investment Corporation

The average home causes twice the greenhouse gas emissions of the average car. To help reduce these emissions, improve the comfort of homes, and reduce energy bills, EPA encourages homeowners to make their homes more energy efficient. *The Home Energy Diet* identifies many products and systems in your home that are good opportunities for improved energy efficiency.

— DOUG ANDERSON, ENERGY STAR Program

The Home Energy Diet is comprehensive, complete, and useful — in fact, it's probably the best single volume out there addressing this issue. Buy it, read it, and then put this information to use in your own home.

— RICHARD PEREZ, publisher, *Home Power Magazine*

The Home Energy Diet is an excellent book, clearly showing where energy is used and wasted in the home, and giving excellent guidance on how you can dramatically reduce your energy use, while having a more comfortable, safer, more durable dwelling. I highly recommend it!

— SKIP HAYDEN, senior research scientist,
Advanced Combustion Technologies Laboratory, Ottawa, Canada

The Home Energy Diet does an excellent job conveying every detail of how your home uses — and can potentially save – energy, in an understandable yet comprehensive and *fun* style. Readers will learn plenty through the anecdotes and experiences gleaned from the thousands of homes the author has visited, and through adventures with his own low-energy-diet lifestyle. In fact, even with my own 20 years experience in the energy business, I still learned a lot that I will take away and apply to my own home energy diet.

— RICHARD FAESY, residential energy and green building consultant, LEED Accredited Professional

If you don't have an energy expert in your house, then *The Home Energy Diet* is the next best thing. It has the most up-to-date, reliable and thorough advice you could find anywhere.

— BLAIR HAMILTON, director, Efficiency Vermont

The
HOME ENERGY
DIET

How to Save Money
by Making Your House
Energy-Smart

PAUL SCHECKEL

NEW SOCIETY PUBLISHERS

Dedication

To June, the source of my energy

Cataloging in Publication Data: A catalog record for this publication is available from the National Library of Canada.

Copyright © 2005 by Paul Scheckel. All rights reserved.
Cover design by Diane McIntosh. Cover image: Comstock RF.
Printed in Canada. First printing January 2005.
Paperback ISBN: 0-86571-530-0

Inquiries regarding requests to reprint all or part of *The Home Energy Diet* should be addressed to New Society Publishers at the address below.

To order directly from the publishers, please call toll-free (North America) 1-800-566-6772, or order online at www.newsociety.com

Any other inquiries can be directed by mail to:
New Society Publishers
P.O. Box 189,
Gabriola Island, BC V0R 1X0, Canada

New Society Publishers' mission is to publish books that contribute in fundamental ways to building an ecologically sustainable and just society, and to do so with the least possible impact on the environment, in a manner that models this vision. We are committed to doing this not just through education, but through action. We are acting on our commitment to the world's remaining ancient forests by phasing out our paper supply from ancient forests worldwide. This book is one step towards ending global deforestation and climate change. It is printed on acid-free paper that is 100% old growth forest-free (100% post-consumer recycled), processed chlorine free, and printed with vegetable based, low VOC inks. For further information, or to browse our full list of books and purchase securely, visit our website at: www.newsociety.com

NEW SOCIETY PUBLISHERS   www.newsociety.com

Books for Wiser Living from *Mother Earth News*

Today, more than ever before, our society is seeking ways to live more conscientiously. To help bring you the very best inspiration and information about greener, more sustainable lifestyles, New Society Publishers has joined forces with *Mother Earth News*. For more than 30 years, *Mother Earth News* has been North America's "Original Guide to Living Wisely," creating books and magazines for people with a passion for self-reliance and a desire to live in harmony with nature. Across the countryside and in our cities, New Society Publishers and *Mother Earth News* are leading the way to a wiser, more sustainable world.

Table of Contents

Acknowledgments

NO BOOK IS WRITTEN IN A VACUUM. Vast amounts of time and patience are required by many people, leading to pressures on everyone around the wretched, possessed writer. I liken the writing process to waking up in the morning with a big, gnarly, tangled head of hair — the original notion for this book. Over the course of many months, the hair is washed, brushed, combed and teased until finally it is presentable to the public. I have had many hairdressers working on what once was a tangled knot.

Those to whom I would like to extend my wholehearted thanks and appreciation include: my wife June, for all her patient support; my son Silas for giving me hope for a greener, happier future; my mother for her steadfast trust and support (and for teaching me that electricity doesn't grow on trees); and Josh and Judy Van Houten for countless meals and complex problem solving.

Thanks to the entire staff of the Vermont Energy Investment Corporation — a group of people who live and breathe energy efficiency and with whom I am proud to work. Specifically, I wish to thank Ken Tohinaka, Dave Keefe, Pat Haller, and the entire Residential Services Pod for their time, encouragement, fact-checking, and professional rewards and challenges. I hold much appreciation and respect for Blair Hamilton and Beth Sachs for their lifelong dedication and commitment to efficiency, and for creating a work environment that draws the best out of employees.

Many thanks to Jim Schley, a true "literary architect" whose thorough hand and gentle nature made me a better writer. Thanks also go to my family who put up with all my annoying questions, meters, and probes all around their homes, and to Susan, Mark, and Hilton for encouragement, insights, and technical review.

Many of the figures in this book were supplied by the energy experts of the US Department of Energy's Office of Energy Efficiency and Renewable Energy, and the information gatherers at the Energy Information Administration, many of whom took the time to answer my questions in detail.

The supportive staff at New Society Publishers has been a pleasure to work with. I am proud to be associated with their vision of a better world through books, education and a sustainable business model. Thanks go to Murray Reiss' close and thorough editorial review.

Thanks to all of the people whose homes I have visited over many years of energy auditing — your homes were my playground, my workshop, and my training field (and no, I really didn't see the mess in the teenager's room). Finally, thanks to you, the reader, and everyone who is working personally or professionally towards a sustainable, efficient, and renewable future.

Introduction

WELCOME TO THE REWARDING WORLD OF ENERGY EFFICIENCY! I have done my best to make this book informative, entertaining, and guilt-free, offering something in each chapter for both novice and expert. I think you'll find *The Home Energy Diet* a refreshing approach to what can be a dry subject. I commend you for reading about efficiency, but reading alone will not save energy — *action* will. So I ask that you really *use* this book, and in return I promise you appreciable dividends as you reduce your use of energy and trim your energy bills.

"I'll start tomorrow." How many times have you or someone you know said that about a diet? We know we should do it, we know it's good for us, but we simply don't like change, especially when we think it will hurt. Don't lose another opportunity to save today by waiting until tomorrow! Energy efficiency starts with learning how to recognize a problem, making the right choices, and sometimes changing old habits. This book will help you become more aware of energy use in your home and in the world. I'll help you put your home on an energy diet by showing you how easy it is to make realistic, cost-effective, energy efficient improvements, and by offering you a wealth of ideas to help reduce your use, lower your costs, and increase your comfort. You will succeed with this diet by keeping in mind my "Triple-A" approach to energy efficiency:

- Awareness of all the ways your home uses and loses energy.
- Assessment of your home's energy requirements.
- Action taken to reduce energy consumption to a bare minimum.

Accomplishing these steps can have a positive impact on your lifestyle. I will not ask you to sit alone, shivering in the dark as some readers may remember being asked to do during the "energy crisis" of the 1970s. I think the difference

1

between the 1970s and today is the difference between energy conservation and efficiency. Efficiency is taking advantage of modern technology to do the same thing better. An efficient compact fluorescent bulb can reduce power use by two-thirds and offer better performance over the old-style incandescent light bulb. Conservation is simply turning off the light. Efficiency measures allow you to do more with less, so you come out ahead in terms of cost, savings, and comfort.

Over the past 12 years, I've had the enjoyable job of performing energy audits in thousands of homes, new and old. I've been in all of your attics and basements, probed your flue pipes, and poked around in your refrigerators. I know the kinds of questions you have, I know what your concerns are, I know what kind of beer you drink, and I can put you on the track to energy savings. I've also been involved with renewable energy, having installed many solar electric and hot water systems, and built a half-dozen electric cars, so I can offer some advice about going "off-grid" (or disconnecting from the electric company). You can start a solar energy project as I did, with a single solar panel powering an off-grid room in your house. I now live almost completely dependent upon renewable energy with solar electricity, wood heat, and a biodiesel car. I live an extreme version of the message presented in this book because instead of buying conveniently pre-packaged energy, I am my own energy company, managing my own energy resources. The less I use, the less effort and cost I need to put into energy production.

Just as science continues to prove the health benefits of a proper diet, new forces are motivating us to save energy: dwindling and unpredictable fossil fuel supply, desire for security, stresses on personal and national economies, and pressures on social and natural environments. Energy efficiency is the first step towards a sustainable energy supply and lower pollution levels. Reduced resource consumption at home offers you greater independence, flexibility, and security along with lower energy bills, and will make your house a more comfortable place to live. I can't promise you this will be a painless process, but it will be worth your efforts, and you will feel better as you go along.

Location, amenities, price, schools, and possibly utility costs generally make it to the top of the prospective homebuyer's list. When you bought or rented your home, did you ask about how the heat and hot water worked before you moved in? Was the furnace ductwork checked for costly leaks? Did you have the ventilation system tested to see if it actually moved air? How was the previous occupant's health?

Why are these things important? Energy-related problems are often masked as comfort issues. You may feel cold, dry, stuffy, or even sick inside your home. Indoor air quality is becoming a cause for concern as homes are being built more tight with better construction practices designed to be more energy efficient. Most of us spend up to 90 percent of our time indoors, yet are more aware of outdoor air pollution than of poor indoor air quality. How do you address these issues? We will examine how the systems in your home can work with and against each other to alter your home environment.

If I had to choose only one message to rise like cream to the top of my milk bottle full of advice, it would be that energy efficiency is an investment, not a hardship. The cheapest kilowatt is one you don't have to buy — a concept called *negawatts*. Studies show that the cost of buying efficiency is about half the cost of buying energy. Purchasing a product that uses less energy than another similar product has significant, long-term impacts on your energy consumption and costs. The price you pay to buy a new refrigerator, light bulb, or furnace is a small percentage of the price you will pay to operate it over its lifetime. Many of us look to banks or the stock market for retirement funds, but efficiency improvements offer cost-effective, tax-free returns that are greater than many traditional investments. Compound these returns by re-investing energy cost savings and you can begin building your energy savings account today. As energy prices rise, your savings increase.

This book begins with an overview of energy literacy that presents general information on how energy is measured, where it comes from, where it goes, and its impact on our lives. You can read the book in any order you wish depending on where you want to make improvements, but I recommend that you begin with Chapter 1 to learn the basics and then jump around from there. The chapters are organized in order of what you might find easiest to approach. The electrical use chapter comes first because many electrical efficiency measures are easily addressed. Using energy-efficient lights for example, is an easy thing you can do today that will cost-effectively reduce your electric bill. However, greater overall savings will likely be realized by focusing on areas that cause your home to use more energy for heating, cooling, and hot water. Some improvements may not be worth making unless you were going to replace the item anyway, or perhaps when you are renovating. A heating system is a good example: the cost to replace a properly operating, though perhaps old, furnace would not likely justify the expense unless it has an extremely low efficiency rating. When the time does come to replace it, then the incremental cost to buy an exceptionally efficient model is going to be well worth the energy savings you'll realize over the lifetime of the furnace.

I hope to dispel a few myths about energy use as well. You might be surprised to find that new windows are often at the bottom of the list of efficiency improvements. You'll see why in Chapter 6. Which uses more water, showers or baths? Should you leave your computer on all the time? Does it use more energy to do dishes by hand or in a dishwasher? Can your house be too tight? There are some very common problems built in to many homes, and by the time you're done with this book, you should be able to have an intelligent conversation with any contractor or salesperson who wants to work on your house or sell you a new appliance.

When someone asks me, "Do I use more power than average?" my answer is always: "It depends. Let's try to figure out what *your* average is, and then consider ways to reduce *your* energy consumption." "Average" is better thought of as an estimating tool. The ultimate outcome is for you to be able to detail your own specific energy situation and reduce your overall energy consumption through knowledge, awareness, change of habits, and investments in efficiency. With *The Home Energy Diet*, you will learn to dis-aggregate (pick apart, piece by piece) all your energy uses in order to build an energy profile of your home. This profile may vary seasonally, depending on whether or not you use heat, air conditioning, dehumidifiers, swimming pools, or other seasonal items.

Are you comfortable in your home? If not, try to describe your discomfort in detail: Are you too cold? Too hot? Is the house drafty? If so, where — around windows and doors, or maybe near the heat registers? Is the air too dry? Too humid? Stuffy? How does your house make you feel? Sleepy? Invigorated? (Anxious? Maybe the source of your discomfort is high utility bills). Do you have icicles or ice dams in the winter? Icicles may look quaint, but they are a sure sign of wasted heat energy.

A home inspection by a good energy auditor can help you identify problems and sleuth out the mystery energy users in your home, but there are limits to what an inspection taking only a few hours can accomplish. If you want *all* the answers, the energy guy would need to move in and become intimate with your home, your habits, and your troubles. Short of giving up the spare bed, be prepared for the auditor to get personal with you — and tell the truth! We are not here to judge you or your habits, we are excited energy geeks who really want to know the answers and find solutions to problems. If we want to look in your fridge, it's not because we forgot to eat lunch, but because we want to size it up for potential energy consumption.

Throughout the book are fun short stories based on my years of experience as an energy auditor. There are several characters, but most all of them are named Ken and Connie Sumer (representing the great pastime of consumerism), who generally seem to do everything they can to unknowingly *increase* their energy bills. Like most homeowners, the Sumers don't know very much about energy; why should they? It's a specialty they haven't had time to learn about, and it's not as though houses come with an owner's manual. Yet we all want to lower our energy bills and reduce maintenance costs on our homes. If the technicalities get to be too much for you, read about the Sumers' energy misadventures for a chuckle, or at least for a practical, real-life point of view. These folks really are clueless though. The only reason they know the difference between the cat-box and the water heater is that they actually pay attention to the cat-box! Take the opportunity to really examine how your home operates.

If you have a head for math, the Math Box sidebars are for you. You don't need to read the Math Boxes to understand the point being made; they will just take you deeper into the heart of energy use and savings calculations if that's where you want to go. If you just want to know what to do now to save energy, skip right to the Energy Diet section in the appropriate chapter for a list of energy-efficient action items.

Living with Solar

When I tell people I live off-grid in a solar-powered home, at first they may imagine a hovel — a dark, drafty, old log cabin with a lot of really weird gadgets cobbled together that they could never understand. A look of sympathy comes over their faces as if to empathize with my suffering. "Oh, that's so neat," they say, "but it must be so hard. I mean, how do you live without all the modern conveniences?" They go on about how the kids leave lights on and all that laundry, and they usually end up by concluding that they just can't afford to make the change to solar living. It's far enough out of the norm that they can't picture what it would be like. "And besides, solar power doesn't really work, does it?"

Eventually, some of these people brave the unknown and come for a visit. Immediately they notice that the house looks entirely normal. It's your average home, nothing fancy, just 1,500 square feet of average. Then they notice the 19-cubic foot fridge, the clothes washer, dishwasher, microwave, TV, computer, lights, coffee grinder, hot and cold running water, and so on. "This isn't what I imagined," is the usual comment. "It looks so normal, and everything works!" As if I want to live in the dark ages. I enjoy living in the modern world as much as anyone else — most of all, I want my home and its contents to be simple and affordable, and to work well with a minimum of maintenance, just like everyone else does. My appliance-laden, solar-powered home uses about 80 percent less electricity than the average home, and about a third of this use is the refrigerator! We don't suffer or deny ourselves any modern conveniences because it is getting easier to find very efficient appliances today.

If solar power can work here in cloudy New England, it can work almost anywhere, but you don't have to "go solar" to have a low-energy home. Take advantage of the latest technology to live an energy-efficient, low-impact lifestyle. It gets easier every day, and there are far fewer excuses than there were ten or twenty years ago for being an energy hog.

You can take the concept of "off-grid" even further by heating your home and hot water with renewable fuels (wood) and producing or buying a renewable gasoline (ethanol) or fuel oil (biodiesel) substitute. Alternative energy is not the alternative anymore; it is the practical fuel of choice, and the only fuel we will use in the future.

You may think that individual savings measures are too small to bother with; instead, you're looking for the one magic bullet that will shave a large part of your energy bill. It's fine to go after the big things first, but there will be far more little things to do where the savings really add up. When you are finished reading this book, you will have the tools to determine where to spend your energy-improvement budget for the best savings. And for a comprehensive efficiency resource list, see <www.homeenergydiet.com>.

Follow a strict diet to avoid a fat fuel bill!

CHAPTER 1

Energy Literacy

Energy and Fuel: Where do They Come From; Where do They Go?

THIS CHAPTER INTRODUCES A NUMBER OF IMPORTANT CONCEPTS and definitions regarding energy use. How much energy do we use? Where does it come from? Where does it go? Why does it matter? Where does one start thinking about energy? By the time you are finished reading this chapter, you will be able to grasp global and local energy issues and speak intelligently to your contractors about which fuels you might want to use in your home.

Primary Fuels

Our homes generally consume one or more *primary fuels* in addition to electricity. A primary fuel is one that can be used in a relatively unprocessed form to deliver the energy required for any number of different uses. Examples of primary fuels include oil, coal, uranium, wood, natural gas, propane, water, wind, and solar power.

The most common primary fuels used in homes are natural gas (NG), liquid propane gas (LPG), and oil. Kerosene and coal are also used, though infrequently. Those in more rural regions may add wood to this list. Most homes take advantage of the ultimate primary energy source, the Sun, to some degree, if proper design is considered before construction.

Electricity can be considered a secondary power source as it is not really a fuel, but an energy carrier, bringing to your home the energy embodied in the primary fuels from which it was produced.

We all use fossil fuels; entire societies have been built on their use throughout the past 150 years. We know that they work reliably to bring us warmth and power, and that they're relatively inexpensive, but we now also know that their use has a high environmental cost. All fossil fuels contain the elements carbon and hydrogen. Thus, they are known as *hydrocarbons*. The vast portion of energy available in a fuel comes from its hydrogen content, whereas the carbon generates much of the waste, resulting in pollution. Gasoline, heating oil, and propane are over 80 percent carbon by weight. Natural gas contains 75 percent carbon by weight; the remainder is hydrogen.

Pure hydrogen gas (H_2) is the cleanest energy source and the most abundant element in the universe. Burning pure hydrogen for energy creates only water vapor as a byproduct. Hydrogen fuel cells have received lots of attention lately because they are potentially a very clean source of energy. However it is the *source* of the hydrogen that is at issue. Hydrogen is difficult to find on its own in nature, and needs to be liberated from the substance in which it is found. Most of the hydrogen on the earth is bound up in water (H_2O), and separating water into its constituent hydrogen and oxygen is an energy-intensive process. Fuel cells in use today typically rely on hydrogen-rich fossil fuels for the source of hydrogen.

What we commonly call combustion, or burning, is chemically known as *oxidation*: a reaction between the fuel and oxygen in the air. Both useful heat energy and wasted byproducts — or pollution — are liberated from fuels by oxidation. Combining hydrogen in the fuel with oxygen in the air releases energy, but when oxygen in the air combines with carbon and sulfur in the fuel and nitrogen in the air during the combustion process, the result is air pollution. These pollutants include carbon dioxide (CO_2), carbon monoxide (CO), nitrogen oxides (NO_x), sulfur oxides (SO_x) and particulates.

Before we get too far into a discussion of energy, it would be useful to know how to quantify it.

Measuring Energy

We buy energy in units. The specific unit depends on the type of fuel. Liquid fuels such as oil, gasoline, and liquid petroleum gas (LPG) are sold in gallons, natural gas is sold by the therm or by the cubic foot, and electricity is measured and sold in kilowatt-hours.

When comparing fuels and their energy content, we need to find a common denominator for all energy measurement units regardless of fuel. We need to compare apples to apples. The energy "apple" (at least in the US and Britain) is the British Thermal Unit, or *Btu*. By definition, a Btu is the amount of energy required to raise the temperature of one pound of water (about a pint) by 1°F. For perspective, one Btu is approximately the amount of energy released by completely burning a wooden kitchen match, and there are about 5.8 million Btus in a 42-gallon barrel of oil. Oil is bought and sold on the global market in units called barrels.

A Btu is a fairly small unit of energy. It may take 50 to 100 million Btus or more to heat and/or cool a home over the course of a year. How much energy you use depends on your climate, your home's efficiency, and how you operate your heating and cooling equipment.

Calorie counters may find this relationship helpful: a gallon of gasoline contains the equivalent of about 31,000 food calories (kilo-calories). This is equivalent to the energy in over 50 McDonald's Big Macs!

When large quantities of energy are compared — such as how many Btus are required to heat a home, or when comparing fuel costs — it is common to think in terms of million Btus, or MMBtu. One million Btus is the amount of energy contained in a little over seven gallons of oil.

On a global scale, energy is measured in *quads*, or quadrillion Btus. (One quadrillion is 1 followed by 15 zeros.) There are 172.4 million barrels of oil in a quad. All the energy consumed in the United States amounts to just under 100 quads of energy each year, about one quarter of the world's total energy consumption.

Measuring electrical energy is a little different. While we can still speak in terms of Btus when talking about electricity, the more common units are the *watt* and the *watt-hour*. Electric power usage is measured in watts. We use the term "watts" all the time when we buy light bulbs. How many watts an appliance uses represents its energy demand. Some larger electrical measuring units to know are:

- Kilowatt (kW) = one thousand watts
- Megawatt (mW) = one million watts
- Gigawatt (gW) = one billion watts

When we leave the lights on, power is consumed over time. The way to measure electrical power consumed over time is with the *watt-hour* or more commonly, the *kilowatt-hour*, or kWh. Electric companies bill us in kilowatt-hours.

> A kWh is the consumption of 1,000 watts over a period of one hour, or any product of time and electrical power demand that adds up to 1,000 watt-hours.

For example, a 100-watt light bulb consumes 100 watt-hours when left on for one hour. After ten hours, the same bulb has consumed 1,000 watt-hours, or one kWh. A ten-watt night-light needs to be on for 100 hours to add up to one kWh of power. One kilowatt-hour represents an energy content of 3,413 Btus. An average home might use between 300 and 1,000 kilowatt-hours each month. When speaking of larger electrical production or consumption such as what a power plant produces, we'll need some convenient terms to represent these larger numbers:

- Megawatt-hour (mWh) = one million watt-hours
- Gigawatt-hour (gWh) = one billion watt-hours

A more complete discussion of electrical terms is included in Chapter 2.

The Big Picture

A number of energy sources fuel our lives. We'll take a closer look at each one to discover where each fuel comes from and how it is used. To put things in context, we'll start with a look at the big picture of global and US energy consumption, then examine how energy is used, where it comes from, and where it goes. The remaining chapters will narrow the focus to the energy used in your home.

The annual energy consumption figures used throughout this chapter are based on the most recently available data from the US Energy Information Administration. The years range between 2000 and 2002, which may at first appear confusing, but during that time span the percentages and consumption data changed very little.

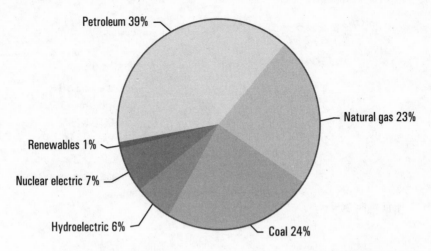

Fig. 1.1: World energy consumption by fuel source, 2002.

Global and US Energy Use

In 2002, the world used 409 quads of energy. Figure 1.1 shows the sources of energy used by the world.

With the world's largest economy, the United States is also the world's biggest producer *and* consumer of energy. In 1950, the US was energy independent, consuming under 35 quads of energy. Fifty years later, our population had increased by 189 percent while energy use grew by 280 percent. One positive spin on US energy consumption is that we are getting more efficient in terms of energy used for each dollar of Gross Domestic Product (GDP), a concept known as *energy intensity*. In 1950, we consumed just over 20,000 Btus for every dollar of GDP. By 2001, that figure declined to just under 10,000 Btus per dollar of GDP and continues to drop. However, one could easily argue that this decrease in energy consumption is tied to the loss of manufacturing facilities, as we become a nation of less energy-intensive service and information providers.

In 2002 the US consumed 97.3 quads of energy — about 24 percent of the world's total annual energy use, equivalent to the energy contained in nearly 17 trillion barrels of oil. This figure is expected to rise to 131 quads by 2020.

Figure 1.2 shows the primary fuel sources that energized the US in 2002.

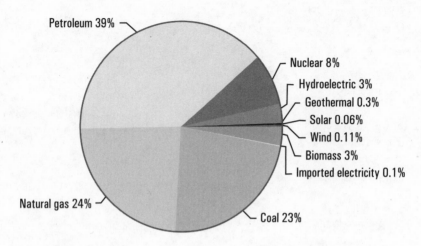

Fig. 1.2: US primary energy source, 2002.

Americans burned up an average of 339 million Btus each in 2002, or the equivalent of about 2,450 gallons of oil. In terms of air pollution, the average American's annual energy-consumption habits produce about 22 tons of the potent greenhouse gas, carbon dioxide (CO_2), a major factor in global warming. In terms of dollars, US consumers spent about $703 billion on energy in 2000, representing about 7.2 percent of the $9.8 trillion GDP for that year.

Some of these primary sources are used in the generation of secondary sources such as gasoline (refined from oil) and electricity (derived from any of these primary sources). Figure 1.3 is a flowchart showing energy flows — inputs, uses, and outputs — in the US in 2002. The chart may at first appear confusing, but if there is one point I want you to grasp here it's that over half the energy we produce is wasted! You'll learn where the majority of this waste comes from in Chapter 2.

Energy Imports

In 2002, US net fossil fuel energy imports totaled 25.4 quads, about 26 percent of total energy consumption, valued at $105 billion. Nearly 60 percent of petroleum products were imported, along with 16 percent of the natural gas we consumed. We imported 81 percent of the uranium used in nuclear reactors,

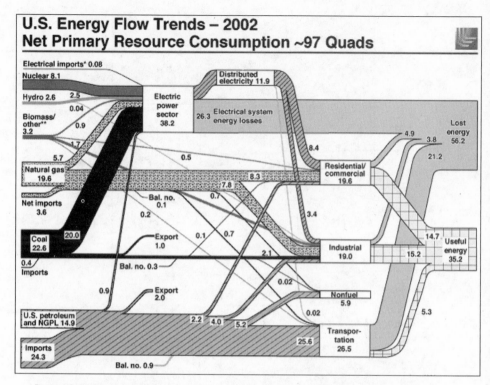

U.S. Energy Flow Trends – 2002
Net Primary Resource Consumption ~97 Quads

Electrical imports* 0.08
Nuclear 8.1
Hydro 2.6 — 2.5
0.04
Biomass/other** 3.2 — 0.9
1.7
5.7
Natural gas 19.6
Net imports 3.6 — 0.2
Coal 22.6 — 20.0
0.4/ Imports
0.9
U.S. petroleum and NGPL 14.9
Imports 24.3

Electric power sector 38.2 — 26.3 Electrical system energy losses
Distributed electricity 11.9
0.5
Bal. no. 0.1
Export 1.0 — 0.1 — 0.7
Bal. no. 0.3
Export 2.0
2.2 — 4.0 — 5.2
Bal. no. 0.9

8.4
8.3
7.8
0.7
3.4
2.1
0.02
0.02

Residential/commercial 19.6
Industrial 19.0
Nonfuel 5.9
Transportation 26.5 — 25.6

4.9 — 3.8
21.2
14.7 — 15.2
5.3

Lost energy 56.2
Useful energy 35.2

Fig. 1.3: US energy inputs by fuel and outputs by sector, 2002. Credit: University of California, Lawrence Livermore National Laboratory, and US Department of Energy.

bringing the total net fuel energy imports up to about 33 percent. Coal is the only primary fuel the US has an abundance of and does not need to import. Energy imports (including enriched uranium) accounted for 24 percent of 2002's $483 billion trade deficit.

Table 1.1 shows energy consumption in several countries compared with population and gross domestic product in 2002. The 37 countries represented consumed 67 percent of the world's energy. Take a look at one of those photos of the earth at night from space — you can tell who the wealthy countries are because they leave the lights on! You can find one of these photos on the web at <http://antwrp.gsfc.nasa.government/apod/image/0011/earthlights_dmsp_big.jpg>.

Table 1.1: Eergy Use Patterns of Selected Countries, 2002.

Country	Population (millions)	Percent of world population	Population rank	Energy consumption rank	Total annual energy use (Quads)	Annual energy consumption/ person/year (MMBTU/capita)
USA	288.0	4.6%	4	1	97.6	339
Canada	31.3	0.5%	37	8	13.1	418
Mexico	102.0	1.6%	12	14	6.6	65
Western Europe	485.1	7.8%	3	2	72.3	149
India	1049.6	16.8%	2	7	14.0	13
China	1294.9	20.7%	1	3	43.1	33
Japan	127.5	2.0%	10	5	22.0	172
Un. Arab Emirates	2.9	0.05%	136	34	2.1	720
Saudi Arabia	23.5	0.4%	47	19	5.1	219

Table 1.1: Eergy Use Patterns of Selected Countries, 2002, continued:

Country	Percent of worlds total energy consumption	Annual Oil Products consumption (m. barrels)	Percent of world oil consumption	Country's energy disparity (Percent of share)	Gross domestic product (billions - 1995 equivalent dollars)	MMBTU/$ GDP
USA	23.7%	7213	25.3%	515%	$9,234	10,575
Canada	3.2%	764	2.7%	634%	$753	17,341
Mexico	1.6%	723	2.5%	99%	$375	17,646
Western Europe	17.6%	5365	18.8%	226%	$10,889	6,637
India	3.4%	798	2.8%	20%	$534	26,198
China	10.5%	1884	6.6%	51%	$1,207	35,714
Japan	5.3%	1935	6.8%	262%	$5,667	3,876
Un. Arab Emirates	9.5%	133	.05%	1094%	$50	41,966
Saudi Arabia	1.3%	553	1.9%	332%	$146	35,344

Western Europe includes: Austria, Belgium, Bosnia and Herzegovina, Croatia, Denmark, Farce Islands, Finland, France, Germany, Gibraltar, Greece, Iceland, Ireland, Italy, Luxembourg, Macedonia, TFRY, Maki, Netherlands, Norway, Portugal, Serbia and Montenegro, Slovenia, Spain, Sweden, Switzerland, Turkey, United Kingdom.

UAE = United Arab Emirates

2002 world oil demand was 78.21 million bbl/day

2002 total world energy consumption was 411.2 quads

Note the high use of energy in the US as compared with population. Associated with this high rate of energy use are a high level of electrification, the world's highest GDP, and extensive land area.

Oil Imports

Oil is our primary energy source and we import over half of what we use. When you think of oil imports, what countries come to mind? It might surprise you to learn that Canada is the United State's primary source of imported oil followed by Saudi Arabia, Venezuela, and Mexico. The actual order varies a bit each year, as each country supplies about 1.5 million barrels to US markets each day. The Persian Gulf region supplies the US with about 22 percent of our oil imports, or about 12 percent of our total oil consumption.

*With the wholesale price of crude oil now rising over $50 per barrel ($1.19 per gallon), every gallon of gasoline or oil you buy sends about 71 cents out of the country. At current rates of consumption and imports, that adds up to a **daily** cash export of about $600,000,000.*

Oil companies are scrounging the globe, pecking away at the earth with deep-drilling oil rigs punching mile-deep holes in anticipation of new oil reserves. It is estimated that 10.3 billion barrels of oil can be extracted from Alaska's Arctic National Wildlife Refuge (ANWR) at a rate of about one million barrels per day. By comparison, the Persian Gulf region was estimated to contain around 672 billion barrels of proven oil reserves in 2000, 65 percent of the world's total proven reserves. In the end, ANWR would supply the US with less than two years worth of oil at current consumption rates. We clearly need to redefine our priorities and strategies for a sustainable and realistic energy future. For an excellent review of the recent history of power, politics, oil, and renewable energy, read *The Party's Over* by Richard Heinberg.

Where Does Energy Come From?

Now that we know what the global and national energy pies look like, let's take a closer look at each slice to learn something about the fuels used to energize our society.

Dirty Coal

Due to its high carbon and sulfur content, burning coal is environmentally very dirty. Coal combustion byproducts are a major contributor to the potent greenhouse gas carbon dioxide (nearly two billion tons each year in the US), along with acid rain-forming nitrogen and sulfur compounds. In addition, a 1999 report *Mercury Falling* by the Environmental Working Group, the Clean Air Network, and the Natural Resources Defense Council, confirmed that about 200,000 pounds of mercury are generated each year from coal power plants. Almost half the mercury is carried into the air, while the remainder results in a solid waste problem to be dealt with during coal processing both on and off the power plant site. It takes only 1/70th of a teaspoon of mercury to contaminate a 25-acre lake to the point where fish would be unsafe to eat.

Coal

Coal is a combustible black or brownish-black rock, formed from plant remains that have been compacted, hardened, chemically altered, and metamorphosed by heat and pressure over geologic time. Standard classifications of coal include (from soft to hard) lignite, sub-bituminous, bituminous, and anthracite. These ranks are based on carbon content, volatile matter, heating value, and agglomerating (caking) properties.

Due to its fairly low cost and domestic abundance, coal remains a very popular industrial fuel. The US imported only about four percent of the coal it used in 2000. About 90 percent of the coal consumed in the US is used to produce over 50 percent of our nation's electricity. On average, a ton of coal contains about 21 million Btus, the equivalent of about 150 gallons of oil. The nation consumed over one billion tons of coal in 2000, representing about a quarter of US energy consumption.

Nuclear

The first nuclear plant in the US was built in Shippingport, Pennsylvania, in 1957. The last order to build a new nuclear plant came in 1977, two years before the Three Mile Island accident. In 2000, 103 nuclear reactors within 66 US nuclear power plants (there are 442 in the world), generated about 20 percent of our nation's electricity. In 2000, 51.5 million pounds of uranium were loaded into nuclear reactors. Seventy-seven percent of this uranium was imported. Our primary foreign sources of uranium are Canada, Russia, Australia, and Uzbekistan.

One pound of enriched uranium contains about 33 billion Btus of energy, the equivalent of approximately 240,000 gallons of oil, 1,500 tons of coal, or 10 megawatt-hours of electricity — enough to power 1,000 homes for a year. However, only about four percent of the fissionable material available in a pound of uranium is used up in a nuclear reactor, and reactors operate at an efficiency of about 31 percent. Adjusting for these factors, the amount of energy converted from a pound of enriched uranium by a nuclear power plant is equivalent to approximately 3,300 gallons of oil, 23 tons of coal, or 134,000 kilowatt-hours of electricity — enough to power about 14 homes for a year.

Nuclear power plants are clean in actual operation, and the fuel is relatively inexpensive (around $11 per pound for wholesale uranium). However, uranium strip mines do terrible environmental and social damage, and there is still no place to put the radioactive waste generated by nuclear reactors. The US Department of Energy's Energy Information Administration (EIA) reports: "A 1982 law required the Department of Energy to dispose of spent fuel as of January 31, 1998; however, feasibility studies have yet to be completed for an underground site in Nevada's Yucca Mountain, located 100 miles north of Las Vegas. Meanwhile, utilities are complaining that they are running out of nuclear waste storage capacity at their nuclear plants."

It is likely that the Yucca Mountain site will eventually accept nuclear waste, but the US General Accounting Office reports that the site will not be ready until 2015. In addition, there are some very real safety concerns associated with the many truck and train trips required to move radioactive waste around the country. There are over 40,000 tons of radioactive waste from US nuclear power plants awaiting permanent storage. This waste is accumulating at a rate of nearly 2,000 tons per year. The Yucca Mountain site has an uncertain capacity, but the assumption is that it will hold about 70,000 tons of waste. At current waste production rates, the facility will be full in fifteen years — by the time the site opens, a new one will be required!

Hydroelectric Power

Hydro power is the largest single renewable energy technology used in the US.

Hydro power represents over 40 percent of our renewable energy consumption, contributing about 2.4 percent (2.3 quads) to the nation's total energy use in 2001.

Actual hydro power contribution to the national electric grid varies between 7 and 12 percent depending on rainfall and water levels.

Hydro power plants convert the energy in flowing water into electricity by using a dam on a river to retain a large reservoir of water. Water can be released under controlled conditions and used for mechanical power, or sent through turbines to generate electrical power. American Rivers, a non-profit conservation organization, notes that there are 75,000 dams greater than six feet in height in the United States, and less than three percent are used to generate electricity. The remainder are used for flood control, municipal and agricultural water supply, or are leftover and unused from mill operations of the past.

One of the drawbacks to hydro power is that some of the projects are so large that many thousands of people, plants, and animals have been displaced from their flooded homes. Hydro-Quebec in Canada (delivering power to the northeastern US and Canada), operates 51 separate hydroelectric generating stations with a capacity of over 30,000 megawatts from 561 dams and 24 large reservoirs. One of these projects, the La Grande dam, flooded 3,822 square miles of land inhabited by the native Cree people. The Three Gorges project on the Yangtze River in China will be the world's largest hydroelectric dam, stretching over 1.4 miles with a generating capacity of over 18 gigawatts. Scheduled for completion in 2009, Three Gorges will create a 375-mile long reservoir, and displace about 1.5 million people.

Natural Gas

Natural gas (NG) is a gaseous mixture of hydrocarbon compounds, primarily methane, found along with oil deposits or on its own. Methane can also be captured from landfills as organic materials decompose, and from animal wastes by a process called *anaerobic digestion* — a breakdown of organic material in the absence of oxygen. Natural gas is somewhat cleaner burning and more versatile than heating oil, and can be used in homes for space and water heating, as well as for cooking and clothes drying. Due to the cost of underground or overland pipelines, and because it is difficult to transport by truck or rail, availability of natural gas is limited to higher population centers where the over 1.1 million miles of pipelines can transport it from 400 thousand wells to power plants, industry, and homes.

Natural gas can also be used to fuel vehicles in slightly modified gasoline burning engines. The gas is stored on board the vehicle in tanks as compressed natural gas (CNG), or cooled to an even more energy-dense liquid state called liquefied natural gas (LNG). The volume of the liquid natural gas is 1/600th that of the gas in its vapor state, increasing its energy density. Unfortunately, it takes quite a lot of energy to compress natural gas, along with specialized handling equipment. This limits our ability to import natural gas from abroad.

Natural gas has received a fair amount of attention lately as a clean-burning fuel that may allow us to transition from fossil fuels altogether. Like all other fossil fuels, there is a finite supply of natural gas, and "clean" is only a relative term. However, because of this clean reputation, the majority of future power plants will likely be fueled by natural gas.

Natural gas has an energy content of approximately 1,000 Btus per cubic foot, depending on the level of purity. It is usually measured and sold in cubic feet (cf), hundreds of cubic feet (Ccf), or units called *therms*. A therm is equivalent to 100,000 Btus, or approximately 100 cubic feet. Homeowners throughout the country pay an average $1.00 per therm to purchase natural gas; the price has been extremely volatile in recent years.

According to the EIA, the US has proven natural gas reserves of 177 trillion cubic feet (Tcf) (about three percent of world reserves), and currently consumes natural gas at a rate of nearly 23 Tcf per year, representing about a quarter of

Production Plateau

The rate at which we can find natural gas and make it available to markets appears to have to reached a plateau. That is, there is still natural gas to be found, but those reserves are shrinking in size. This means that it will become more expensive to find the gas and to deliver it. One of the largest untapped gas fields in North America is on the North Slope of Alaska. This field is estimated to hold about 100 trillion cubic feet of gas, or about four years worth of consumption by the US. A 745-mile pipeline will need to be built for an estimated $6.3 billion to deliver the gas to the nearest port. It is expected to take ten years to build.

US energy consumption. In 2000, 15 percent of natural gas was imported; over 99 percent of this came from Canada via pipeline.

Liquefied Petroleum Gas

Liquefied petroleum gas (LPG) is a petroleum distillate sometimes known as "bottled" gas, and is similar to natural gas. LPG consists of a group of hydrogen-rich gases — propane, butane, ethane, ethylene, propylene, butylene, isobutane, and isobutylene — derived from the process of refining crude oil or natural gas. For convenience of transportation, these gases are liquefied through pressurization. LPG has an energy content of about 91,690 Btus per gallon, or 2,516 Btus per cubic foot. Many people know LPG as the fuel used for the backyard grill.

LPG is commonly used in rural areas where no natural gas pipeline exists, and can be used with natural gas equipment with only minor adjustments. LPG is delivered by truck to where it is needed and dispensed into storage tanks or bottles.

Over 6.5 billion gallons of LPG were used in homes in 2000; 71 percent was used for space heat, 22 percent for hot water, and 7 percent for appliances such as stoves and refrigerators. The price of propane fluctuates wildly depending upon how much of it you use, and if you buy it in bulk (pre-buy for the season)

Rotten Eggs

Both natural gas and liquid propane gas are naturally odor free. Suppliers of these gases add an artificial odorant, ethyl mercaptan, with a distinctive "rotten egg" smell to alert you to possible leaks in the system. It is added at a rate of about one pound per 10,000 gallons of gas. A very slow leak may smell slightly musty — don't ignore that smell. You may also notice this smell when the bottle of LPG is nearing empty. If you notice an odd smell around a gas appliance, it is *not* normal! Call your service person. If you have gas equipment in your home, and are not familiar with this rotten egg smell, your gas company can introduce you to it in a safe way.

or on the spot market (will-call, as needed). You can expect to pay between $1.50 and $3 per gallon to use propane in your home.

Petroleum, or Home Heating Oil

Home heating oils include #2 fuel oil, kerosene (#1 fuel oil), and sometimes diesel motor fuel. Equipment designed for one of these fuels can usually operate acceptably with all of the others. The main difference is the purpose for which they are sold. Home heating oil is nearly identical to diesel motor fuel, but the diesel fuel may have additives to prevent gelling in cold weather. In cold climates, it is necessary to have an indoor space to store home heating oil so that it doesn't thicken, or gel, in cold temperatures. If cold is a problem, kerosene can be mixed with the heating oil to lower the gelling temperature. In addition to having a lower gel temperature, kerosene is slightly lighter in weight and slightly lower in energy content than home heating oil.

Fuel oils have an energy content of approximately 135,000 to 140,000 Btus per gallon, and are generally low-cost fuels due to their high energy density. The price fluctuates, but averages about $1.50 per gallon. Diesel motor fuel is taxed by federal and state government highway departments and is typically a bit more expensive than kerosene and home heating oil. Due to the highway tax imposed on motor fuels, it is illegal to use untaxed kerosene in place of diesel

Buried Sunshine

A report titled "Burning Buried Sunshine: Human Consumption of Ancient Solar Energy" by University of Utah ecologist Jeff Dukes reveals that every gallon of gasoline we burn was produced by 98 tons of ancient, decayed biomass (plants and animals). The report indicates that the 48.5 trillion tons of fossil fuels burned worldwide every year were created by the decomposition of organic matter equal to over 400 times the plant matter that grows on the planet each year.

motor fuel. Red dye is used in kerosene for the purpose of identification for consumers and law enforcement agents.

About 6.1 billion gallons of fuel oil and kerosene were used in our homes in 2000, 84 percent for space heat, the remainder for hot water heating. Over 80 percent of this oil was used in New England and the mid-Atlantic states.

Wood

Wood is a non-fossil, renewable hydrocarbon fuel. While wood fires can be smoky, releasing high quantities of particulate matter, the Environmental Protection Agency has set efficiency guidelines for wood-burning equipment. Wood is burned in an airtight wood stove, allowing for a controlled burn based on how much air is allowed into the combustion chamber. When modern wood-burning appliances are used, wood is generally a more environmentally friendly energy source than fossil fuel. Trees take up carbon dioxide from the atmosphere while they are growing and release it when oxidized in a fire. Thus, there is no *net* carbon dioxide (CO_2) gain in the atmosphere. If left to decay on the forest floor, wood eventually releases the same amount of CO_2 as when burned, albeit over a much longer period of time. Wood is most commonly used in rural areas as a primary or backup fuel for space heating and sometimes for hot water.

The energy content of wood varies by species, but a full cord (a stack measuring 4 feet × 4 feet × 8 feet) of mixed hardwood weighs about two tons and contains about 20 million Btus — the equivalent energy of 145 gallons of fuel oil, or about a ton of coal. Harder woods (such as oak, beech, and maple) have higher energy content than softer woods (pine, hemlock, and aspen). Wood availability and prices vary greatly throughout the country, but the cost per unit of energy is generally about the same as heating oil. A cord of wood costs in the neighborhood of $150, depending on when you buy it, what part of the country you live in, and whether you buy it green or seasoned.

Renewables

Each day more solar energy falls to the Earth than the total amount of energy the planet's six billion inhabitants would consume in 27 years. The desert region of the southwestern United States receives almost twice the sunlight as other regions in the US, making it one of the world's best areas for solar energy. Globally, other areas with high solar intensities include developing nations in Asia, Africa, and Latin America. These countries need education and incentives to foster a sustainable energy future rather than buying into the dirty fossil fuel-based energy we've exploited during the twentieth century.

If you have a suitable house site, solar and/or wind energy can be used to heat your house and your water, or generate electricity; and regardless of where you are on the planet, renewable energy can meet some or all of your energy needs. Many states and utilities offer financial incentives for the purchase and use of renewable energy. These incentives can be in the form of tax credits or cost sharing, and are in a constant state of flux due to budget and other concerns. To see what renewable energy incentives your state offers, visit the website of the Database of State Incentives for Renewable Energy (DSIRE), a comprehensive source of information on state, local, utility, and selected federal incentives that promote renewable energy, at <www.dsireusa.org>

In addition to the sun and wind, efforts are being made to harness thermal and electrical energy from the oceans, biomass — including wood, biodiesel (a vegetable-oil-based diesel fuel substitute), ethanol (an alcohol-based gasoline substitute) — and hydrogen, which can be used in any number of transport-ation and home energy situations.

Local streams can be employed to generate hydroelectric power in quantities that are suitable for an efficient home. Many rural homes use these micro-hydro systems without altering the stream and often without the need for permits. Specific information about solar, wind, and other renewable energy systems for your home can be found in an excellent magazine called *Home Power*, on the web at <www.homepower.org>.

Geothermal energy can be used on a large scale to generate electricity, or at home to help heat your living space or hot water.

There are a few places on the planet where the intense heat from magma or steam from geysers is close enough to the

Deep down at the core of the earth, temperatures reach about 7,600°F. It is estimated that 42 trillion watts of energy is continuously radiated from the earth into space. That adds up to 3.4 quads of energy every day, about three times the daily energy consumption of all humanity.

surface (.5 to 2.5 miles deep) to be used cost-effectively to provide high pressure steam to drive utility-scale electric generators, or to capture the heat for buildings or industrial processes. More practical for home energy use is the top 20 feet or so of the earth's crust where a constant temperature of between 50 and 60°F is maintained depending on climate and depth. It is possible to use this fact to our benefit in transferring heat from the ground to water or air. Geothermal heat can be obtained from the ground or from water in lakes or drilled wells. Because moving heat requires less energy than creating it, geothermal heat pumps can save on home energy costs by delivering more energy than they consume. For more information on geothermal energy, look into the Geothermal Energy Association on the web at <www.geo-energy.org>.

Where Does the Energy Go?

Now that we've reviewed energy supply, let's look at the demand for energy. There are four large categories, or sectors, of energy consumption:

- Residential
- Commercial
- Industrial
- Transportation

Figure 1.4 shows US energy consumption by sector.

Why Renewables?

Each year US coal power plants (50 percent of our electric generation) deposit 100,000 pounds of airborne mercury into our backyards in addition to two billion tons of carbon dioxide.

Each year US nuclear power plants (20 percent of our electric generation) produce 2,000 tons of radioactive waste, in addition to the 40,000 tons already accumulated and waiting for long-term storage. That's 4.5 ounces each to start with and growing by one quarter of an ounce each year.

Much of our energy is imported, sending hundreds of millions of dollars out of our economy every day. Renewable energy is locally produced and locally installed, supporting your community. What would you rather have in your backyard — a blob of mercury and a piece of spent fuel rod for your asthmatic kids to play with, or a clear view of a wind turbine? It's time for us to connect with the realities of our personal energy use and get a good look at what we *don't* want to see in our backyards.

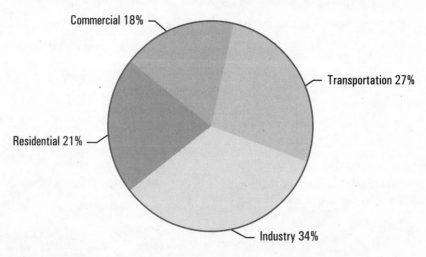

Fig. 1.4: US energy consumption by sector.

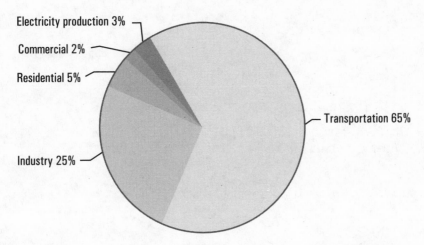

Electricity production 3%

Commercial 2%

Residential 5%

Transportation 65%

Industry 25%

Fig. 1.5: Where the oil goes.

Remember that energy doesn't just go away after we use it. The inherent energy of a fuel is not consumed, but transformed into work, heat, and waste. Every gallon of gasoline you burn in your car's engine produces mechanical energy, heat, and nearly twenty pounds of CO_2, along with other gases such as oxides of sulfur and nitrogen.

Of the fuels used as primary energy sources, nuclear, hydro, wind, and solar power are all used to generate electricity. That leaves us with three giant slices of the energy pie to look more closely at. These are oil, natural gas, and coal. Let's make a pie out of each of these to see what each fuel is used for. Figures 1.5 through 1.7 show the end uses of each of these fuels.

Of the nearly 20 million barrels (840,000,000 gallons) of oil Americans use every day, about 43 percent (361,200,000 gallons) goes straight into our gas tanks; the remaining portion of that shown for "transportation" is primarily diesel, jet fuel, and lubricants. Petroleum refining is the most energy-intensive manufacturing industry in the United States, accounting for about 7.5 percent of total US energy consumption, while supplying about 40 percent of America's energy needs.

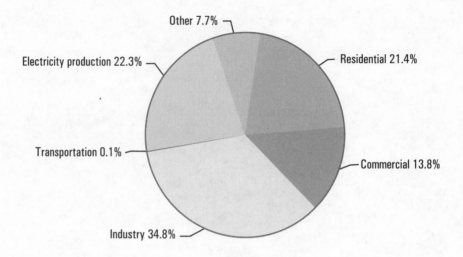

"Other" gas is used in processing natural gas (drilling, plant use, pipeline loss)

Fig. 1.6: Where the gas goes.

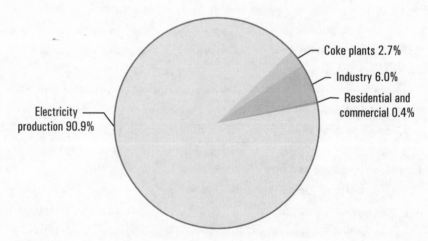

Fig. 1.7: Where the coal goes.

Home Energy Matters

In 2001, the US Department of Energy performed a detailed, nationwide survey of home energy consumption. Figure 1.8 presents the energy consumed by the average American household in 2001 according to end use. In 2001,

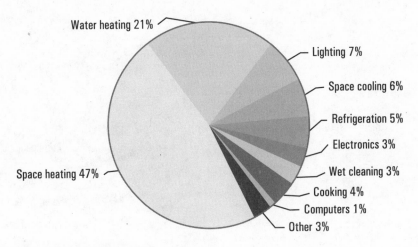

Water heating 21%

Lighting 7%

Space cooling 6%

Refrigeration 5%

Electronics 3%

Wet cleaning 3%

Space heating 47%

Cooking 4%

Computers 1%

Other 3%

"Other" includes clothes washer and dryer, and dishwasher

Fig. 1.8: Typical US household energy consumption by end use, 2001.

each American household spent an average of $1,493 on energy to heat, cool, and power their homes.

We ask a great deal from our homes. They need to shelter us in comfort in addition to providing heat, light, hot water, and all the modern conveniences and entertainments. And we expect all of this to happen economically over a long period of time — without an owner's manual! You probably know more about the operation of your car or VCR than about how your house operates. In fact, we don't really think in terms of the "operation" of our homes at all. We buy a house for price, square footage, location, and amenities. We optimistically assume that the builder and the building codes have taken care of everything else and that the house will "work." Builders and building owners rarely envision the house as a whole, as a living organism with multiple, inter-dependent systems and functions, much like our own bodies. Very often, heating systems are installed almost as an afterthought, and indoor air quality is largely ignored. What you *can't* see in a house sometimes matters more than what you *can* see. I'll show you the inside of your walls later in this book.

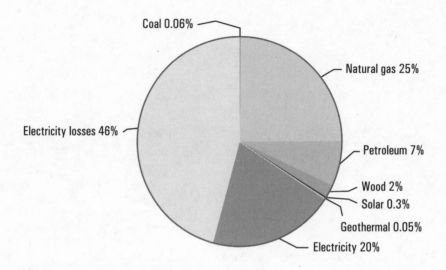

Fig. 1.9: Residential energy consumption by fuel source, 2001

Home Energy Fuels

Figure 1.9 indicates the type and percentage of energy consumed by American households in 2001.

Look at the largest area of energy consumption: electricity *losses*. These losses are due to inefficiency! Electric companies burn fuel to generate electricity. Losses in power generation, transmission, and distribution mean that three units of fuel energy burned at the power plant give you only one unit of energy at the outlet in the wall. This power system (the grid) is only about 30 percent efficient at delivering power to your home. And the problem gets worse inside our homes. The appliances we use are not very efficient either. An incandescent light bulb is only about ten percent efficient at converting electrical energy into light energy — the remaining 90 percent is lost as waste heat. When electricity generation, transmission, and distribution losses are added in, the overall efficiency of the same light bulb at converting the primary energy from the power plant to the actual light that you use in your home has dwindled to just three percent.

One way of addressing the inefficiency of power transmission and distribution is through what power companies call "distributed generation." Distributed generation is where electricity is fed into power lines by small,

What is Efficiency?

Efficiency is the ability to produce a desired effect with a minimum amount of effort or waste. The energy efficiency of an appliance is a comparison, or ratio, of the useful energy output to the total energy input. For example, we want a light bulb to produce light. We all know that after a light bulb has been on for any length of time, it gets hot. Since heat is not what we need from a light bulb, we consider the heat to be a waste product — the heat represents *inefficiency*. A typical incandescent bulb converts about ten percent of the electrical power coursing through its filament into light, and 90 percent into heat. The efficiency ratio of a 100-watt light bulb then is:

10 watts of light output ÷ 100 watts of power input = 10 percent efficiency.

Nothing is 100 percent efficient, so every process has some waste product, or undesired effect. Keep this in mind when you buy new appliances and look for the most efficient products you can find.

scattered power plants such as wind mills, solar electric arrays on roof tops, small-scale hydro power, methane captured at farms or landfills, or fossil fuel-powered turbines. The energy from these decentralized power sources tends to be used on-site by whoever is producing it, with the excess going out onto the grid for everyone else. Energy security analysts think distributed generation is preferable because reducing the demand on a single, central power plant makes widespread power interruptions less likely.

Another way to increase power plant efficiency is by way of *co-generation* (cogen) also known as *combined heat and power* (CHP). Co-generation means producing useful energy for more than one use from the same fuel source. For example, power plants generate enormous amounts of heat. Most of that heat boils water into high-pressure steam, which spins a turbine to produce electricity. Energy is lost in the process via low grade heat left in the water after the steam has passed through the turbine. If that heat energy is captured it can be used to heat the power plant, or even neighboring buildings in the town.

Your car is an excellent example of a co-generation power plant. It uses a single fuel source — gasoline — to produce mechanical power, electrical power, heat, and air conditioning. That still doesn't make the car very efficient — only about 25 percent under ideal conditions. A huge amount of waste heat comes off the engine.

The Right Fuel Choice for Your Home

How do you choose the right fuel for the right task in your home? Is it time to switch fuels? Some questions to ask yourself are:

- Which fuels are locally available and practical to deliver to your home?
- What is the least costly fuel to use?
- What types of equipment provide the greatest efficiency?
- What types of equipment provide the greatest comfort?
- Are some fuels easier to use than others?

How do you begin to think about these issues? Let's use electricity as an example. Electricity is available almost everywhere a house can be built and is probably the most convenient and carefree source of energy for your home. A heating element can be used to heat air by way of electric baseboard heat, radiant heat panels, a hot air furnace, electric clothes dryers, ovens, and toasters. Heating elements are also used to heat water in electric water heaters and dishwashers. Electricity requires no storage tank or monthly deliveries, emits no odor or local pollution, and needs no chimney. Installation of an electric space or water-heating system is far easier, placement more flexible, and is initially cheaper than an equivalent fossil-fuel system. Depending on where you live though, electricity is likely the most costly energy source, making it the least "comfortable" fuel if you can't stay warm without breaking the bank.

Beware of low initial equipment costs when choosing fuels or buying appliances. It is important to consider the lifetime operating cost of an appliance because the initial purchase price is a small percentage of the overall cost of owning and operating almost anything over time (see Chapter 7 to learn

Off-Grid Tip

If you're building a new home at a remote building site where it may be too costly to run power lines, you can go "off-the-grid" and take advantage of renewable energy sources by installing a solar, wind, or micro-hydro power system, or some combination of all of these. Most areas throughout the world can take advantage of some source of renewable energy — even Alaskans enjoy the benefits of solar power! Many off-grid homes use a gasoline, propane, or diesel generator for backup or supplemental power.

Off-grid homes avoid appliances with electric heating elements because it is simply not cost-effective to buy the additional power (more solar electric panels or larger wind generator) required to operate these things. That is to say, no solar-powered home will have electric heat, electric hot water, or an electric dryer. Other fuels are used for these tasks. Smaller, less frequently used items with electric heaters such as toasters or waffle irons may be used in solar-powered homes without any problem.

how to perform a life-cycle cost analysis). Space- and water-heating energy requirements can be substantial, and because electricity is typically the most expensive energy source, performing these tasks with electricity year after year can be more costly than using fossil fuels.

When considering alternatives to electricity, make a list of what fuels are available in your location. In addition to the sun and wind, these fuels are typically natural gas, propane, heating oil, or kerosene. You can find appliances that operate on nearly any of these fuels. Read more about the appliance in question in the appropriate chapter, and then talk to your local fuel dealers for estimates and about the practicality for your home. For the best price, many dealers offer a "pre-buy" plan where you buy all your fuel at once and don't need to worry about price fluctuations during the year.

The next questions to ask are:

- What do you want to use the fuel for? Heating your house and hot water? Cooking?
- Do you only want one fuel in your home? Perhaps you like to cook with gas but heating oil might be cheaper to use to heat your home.
- You might want to consider gas (natural or LP) over oil because it burns more cleanly (less CO_2 and other emissions per unit of energy used). See Appendix B for a CO_2 production profile of fuels.
- Can the fuel be delivered to your home? If there is natural gas in your neighborhood, call the local gas company to find out if it is available to your home. If you need heating oil or propane gas, can a fuel delivery truck get to your home? Sometimes a bridge, steep hill, narrow road, or poor weather can prevent delivery of a fuel to your home.
- Where will the fuel be stored? If you use heating oil, the storage tank (typically 275 gallons) will probably need to be located in your basement or some other place that is out of the weather. A propane storage tank will be outside your home and you'll need to make a space for it that both you and your supplier can live with.

Energy prices vary regionally, seasonally, and annually based on contractual agreements and market forces. The following section will help you determine the delivered energy costs for different fuels.

Comparing Fuel Energy and Costs

Too often I hear homeowners struggling with the question of fuel prices and how to reduce costs. Often, the term "bill" gets in the way. Just because you get two different fuel bills doesn't necessarily mean that you're going to pay more in energy costs than when you only had one bill. In fact, after scrutinizing their energy uses and costs, I often encourage folks to switch fuels for one or more items in their homes. Once you understand how to compare fuel costs and actual, usable energy delivered for that price on an apples-to-apples comparison (using Btus), the mystery clears up.

The Energy Audit

When I visited Ken and Connie Sumer on a hot day last summer, the first thing I noticed pulling into their driveway was that they had underground power lines. The electric meter was on a pole near the driveway, and there was no sign of power cables going into the house. This is not a problem, but it could be a clue to unexplained high use in older homes. More clues turned up.

Connie told me about how they had installed an in-ground pool last year and their power bill really jumped. Not surprisingly, I found out later that the pool filter had a one horsepower pump and they kept it on all day and night. I noticed that the pool was between the house and the power pole and asked them, "How long were you without power after the backhoe started digging?"

"Oh, what a mess — four days! How did you know?"

If your underground lines are damaged due to an excavation project, it is possible that a small amount of current could leak into the ground through a break in the insulation. In such a circumstance, you might notice a spike in your usage when the ground is wet. To help prevent accidental damage, all underground wiring should be encased in properly sized conduit rated for electrical use. If you have underground power lines, it's always a good idea to call the power company before you dig. If you suspect a problem, an electrician can check an underground line with a meter without the need to dig it up.

I took a walk over to the Sumers' meter to get a reading. The meter disk was spinning about as fast as my table saw! Air conditioner I thought. And pool pump. Maybe she's cooking in the electric oven. But, geesh! I could cut wood with that meter dial!

With that in the back of my mind, I met with Connie's husband, Ken Sumer, and continued on my house inspection.

Yes, the central air conditioner was on, the thermostat set for 68°. "Too low," I told Ken. "Are you from the north country?" I teased. "Look, your heat thermostat is set at 72° and if that's good enough in the winter, why not summer too? In fact, if you really want to save energy and money, you should reverse these two settings — 72° or higher in summer, 68° for winter. And I've just solved your high use problem," I boasted.

The heating and air conditioning thermostats were right next to each other. The heat was set higher than the air conditioner. The AC would come on and cool the air off to 68°, and then the heat would kick in trying to keep the place at 72°. You wouldn't think it could get much worse than dueling thermostats.

But it did.

Junior came rollerblading into the living room and looked excitedly at the stranger. I knew that I'd be his next victim.

"Wanna see something cool?" he asked.

I bit. "Sure."

He led me to the playroom with its wall-to-wall aquariums and terrariums. "I collect snakes." He said proudly.

"Cool." I meant the room — it *was* cool, almost cold. "Don't snakes and fish like it hot?"

"Yeah, the tanks all have heaters in them. See those rocks inside? They're really heaters! You just plug 'em in."

I rolled my eyes at the sight of fifty-two little electric rock heaters and twenty fish-tank heaters: 4,100 watts of connected load. I turned to Ken and asked, "Do you want me to do the math for you or do you just want to turn off the air conditioning in this room? You could take the family out to a four-star restaurant with the savings."

"I wanna a cheeseburger!" Junior shouted.

I sought refuge in the basement. Ken followed along.

In the corner of the basement there was a big blue tank — a water pressure tank. They had a drilled well to supply water. I looked at the pressure gauge and watched it slowly descend. I asked Ken if there was water on in the house somewhere. Nope. The gauge bottomed out and then started to rise again. I could hear the pressure switch clicking, switching the well pump on and off.

"Time to call a plumber and have your water system checked out. You could have a bad pressure tank, or an underground water-line leak, or maybe a bad check valve on the pump, causing water to slowly drain out of the system. Maybe the water softener timer's gone haywire. While you're at it, have him check out this gray box. It's for the septic pump, and the light's been on for the last ten minutes. That means you're pumping sewage from the holding tank out to the leach field. You may have a bad float switch in the tank." By the end of this litany, his eyes were *fully* glazed over.

"Call a plumber," I repeated. "Point him over here."

Next, I noticed electric heat tapes on the water pipes. Evidently, the pipes would freeze in the winter and the heat tapes were to keep the pipes warm. They ran along the top of the basement wall and as I looked more closely, I could see daylight through the rim joist at the top of the concrete wall — apparently the remains of an old hose spigot.

"You need to seal up those holes and keep the cold winter air off those pipes. Use expanding foam and then insulate the rim band around the entire basement perimeter. You can then unplug the heat tapes and enjoy lower bills and warmer floors upstairs too."

Turning around, I saw a wood stove and walked towards it.

"Y2K," Ken said sheepishly. "But I do use it occasionally, it's a nice heat you know, but dry." (I side-stepped this comment but readers should see the discussion on heat and air infiltration in Chapter 6.)

"So how many cords do you burn in a season?"

Ken led me to the small room he built in the basement where the wood was stacked. "I just had a cord delivered as back-up in case the power goes out."

In the middle of the wood-room hummed a dehumidifier. I stared. First at the dehumidifier, then at Ken, then at the pile of wet, green wood, then back at the dehumidifier. Ken reached for the tray to empty it out. "Gosh, I can't seem to empty this often enough."

"Smells good in here." I said. "Green wood has quite a lot of moisture in it. And so does your basement. You might want to consider building a small, open-air wood shed outside — just to keep the rain off the wood. Stack the wood in the shed and after a year it will be dry enough to burn. You really don't want to pay extra for your wood by drying it with a dehumidifier. And your basement is so damp that the wood might never really dry out enough to burn well."

The basement was also home to the usual cadre of infrequently used appliances, including an exercise treadmill and an old refrigerator holding a single six-pack of beer and a single can of ginger ale, with a freezer filled with more frost than food. A sump pump sat in a pit in the corner. It was off. Just above it was the circuit breaker box. I looked inside to try to identify the big users in the house. I do this by identifying the 240-volt breakers (the big, fat ones) indicating an especially large electrical load. As I pulled the panel door open, it fell into my hand, revealing a nest of spaghetti-like wiring. Inside the box, I noticed that many of the electrical connections had a chalky white coating on them. One of the breakers was loose in its socket. I tried to push it back in and a few sparks flew.

"Time for an electrician," I said, handing Ken the breaker box door. Bad grounding, poor connections, and corrosion can all lead to inexplicably high electrical use in addition to being a dangerous situation. Ken told me that the basement was prone to flooding and that's why he got the sump pump. That's probably why there was corrosion on the breaker box, too.

Energy Density

The amount of energy contained in a unit of fuel can be described in terms of its *energy density*. Despite their relatively small percentage of hydrogen, hydrocarbon fuels are very energy-dense, meaning that they contain lots of potential energy in relation to their weight or volume. The high energy density of fossil fuels makes them convenient to store and use almost anywhere.

Energy density is expressed as a measure of how much energy is contained in a given unit of a fuel. The units are usually pounds, gallons, or cubic feet. Here are the energy densities by weight of a few energy sources:

- gasoline = 19,000 Btus per pound
- pure hydrogen = 52,000 Btus per pound
- automotive battery (including the lead, electrolyte, and case) = 55 Btus per pound

Expressing energy density in different units reveals other qualities. Using the same fuels, let's switch units from weight to volume:

- gasoline = 935,000 Btus per cubic foot
- hydrogen = 333 Btus per cubic foot
- automotive battery = 5,000 Btus per cubic foot

It's easy to see now what the problem with electric cars is. It takes 345 pounds of batteries to store the equivalent energy of one gallon (just over six pounds) of gasoline. You can also see that 345 pounds of batteries occupies 187 times more space than a gallon of gasoline.

Hydrogen, which can be completely combusted with no waste, is a gas and not very dense. To make hydrogen easy to transport or store in useful quantities would take a very large container. To make the container size more manageable would require that hydrogen gas be compressed, and that takes energy. Natural gas (which is one part carbon to four parts hydrogen or CH_4) comes closest to pure hydrogen of any home energy fuel, but natural gas is only available where pipelines exist to deliver it. Compressing and transporting hydrogen or natural gas has not been found to be cost-effective for home use.

Embodied Energy

When considering the true cost and efficiency of an energy source, the fuel's *embodied energy* should be considered. Embodied energy is a measure of the energy input that goes into producing an end product. For example, it takes a certain amount of energy and resources to extract a gallon of oil from the earth. The well-drilling equipment and processing infrastructure needs to be built, energy is used to extract the oil from its reservoir, then the fuel needs to be transported to and from the refinery (in a fossil fuel-burning truck or train). Finally, the end-user receives the fuel in the form of gasoline, oil, kerosene, jet fuel, liquid propane, diesel fuel, and others.

Embodied energy can be expressed as a ratio of energy output to energy input. This is sometimes called *energy balance* or *energy profit ratio*. For example, if it takes one gallon of oil to get two gallons out of the ground and deliver it to you, the energy balance of that gallon of oil is 2:1. When the energy balance ratio falls below 1:1, then it's time to start looking for another, cheaper fuel source.

However, the actual embodied energy in a gallon of oil is not reflected in its relatively low price. Consider that a gallon of gasoline costs about the same as a gallon of milk, and not much more than water. When you think about the energy that goes into producing a gallon of each, you have to wonder why gasoline is so cheap, or why water is so expensive. Petroleum prices would be quite a bit higher if the industry — rather than the government — were required to pay for the security of its global product transportation routes. That cost is instead reflected in our federal taxes. So you can see that it can be difficult to draw a clean circle around the costs and activities involved in producing fuel to keep our homes warm and economy moving.

Consider the embodied energy involved in supplying a kilowatt-hour of electricity to your home. Energy is used to extract the fuel from the earth (coal, for example), and then to refine, transport, and burn it to produce steam to drive the turbines to create electricity that flows through power lines, switching stations, and transformers. Roughly two thirds of the energy in the original fuel is lost in the generation, transmission, and distribution of electricity. In addition, the electric company expends energy for the operation and maintenance of this infrastructure. Electricity is in fact the most efficient energy source to use once it gets to your home, but it is not very efficient when you consider all of the embodied and lost energy that goes into getting the power to your house. These losses add up to make electricity a very expensive (and wasteful) energy source.

Fuel Energy Content

As we've learned, the Btu is a way of comparing the energy content per unit of fuel (gallons, cubic feet, or therms). Table 1.2 lists common fuels and their energy content per unit. These units represent how the fuels are typically sold. Also included for comparison is the energy content of a typical lead-acid battery as is used in your car and in a solar-powered home, and a pound of enriched uranium as might be used in a nuclear power plant.

As you can see, home heating oil has 50 percent more energy than propane per unit volume. Propane, however, typically costs at least as much or more than heating oil. Figure 1.10 shows the cost per MMBtu of common fuels based on the average price of the fuel, and the Math Box shows you how to make the calculation yourself based on local fuel prices.

Table 1.2: Energy Content of Fuels.

Fuel	BTU/unit	Unit
Home heating oil	138,690	gallon
Natural gas	100,000	therm/Ccf
Liquid petroleum gas (LPG)	91,690	gallon
Gasoline	125,071	gallon
Kerosene	135,000	gallon
Coal	21,000,000	ton
Wood	20,000,000	full cord
Electricity	3,413	kWh
Hydrogen	52,000	pound
Hydrogen	333	cubic foot
Enriched uranium	33 billion	pound
Solar home storage battery	60	pound

Note: Energy content per unit of fuel may vary due to additives, impurities and source.

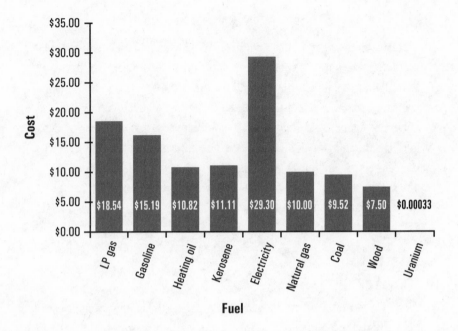

Fig. 1.10: Fuel price per million Btus.

This chart can illustrate why choosing the cheapest fuel per *unit* doesn't guarantee that you will pay the least amount possible for the actual energy delivered. The price per MMBtu of *useful* energy will be affected by the efficiency of the equipment utilizing the fuel. For example, if your heating system is 75 percent efficient at converting fuel input to heat output, you lose 25 percent of your fuel up the chimney along with 25 percent of your fuel dollars.

Figure 1.11 shows the fuel price per MMBtu after adjusting for average equipment efficiency, and the Math Box shows you how to make the calculation yourself based on local fuel prices and your equipment's rated efficiency.

As you can see, when equipment efficiency is taken into account, the net energy converted into useful work is reduced, and the effective price of the fuel rises.

The assumptions for fuel price and equipment efficiency in Figure 1.10 and Figure 1.11 are shown in Table 1.3. I have included the energy content of uranium here to illustrate both its incredible energy content by weight, and its

Math Box: Determining Price per Million Btus of a Fuel

To determine the fuel cost per million Btus you need to know the price you pay per unit of fuel, and the number of Btus per unit of fuel.

For example: what is the price per MMBtu of home heating oil? Looking at Table 1.2, you find that oil contains 138,690 Btus per gallon. Let's assume that you pay $1.35 per gallon. First you need to determine how many units of the fuel make up 1 million Btus.

1,000,000 Btus ÷ 138,690 Btus per gallon = 7.2 gallons
Now multiply by the price per unit:
7.2 gallons × $1.35 per gallon = $9.72 per MMBtu

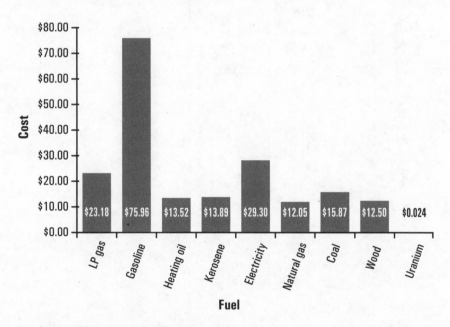

Note: Gasoline is included assuming a 20% efficient gasoline car engine

Fig. 1.11: Fuel price per million Btus adjusted for efficiency.

Table 1.3: Fuel Cost Comparison Assumptions.

Fuel	LP gas	Gasoline	Heating oil	Kerosene	Electricity	Natural gas	Coal	Wood	Enriched uranium
$/unit	$1.70	$1.90	$1.50	$1.50	$0.10	$1.00	$200.00	$150.00	$11.00
BTU/unit	91,690	125,071	138,690	135,000	3,413	100,000	21,000,000	##	33,000,000,000
Unit	gallon	gallon	gallon	gallon	kWh	therm	ton	full cord	pound
$/MMBTU	$18.54	$15.19	$10.82	$11.11	$29.30	$10.00	$9.52	$7.50	$0.00033
Typical combustion on efficiency	80%	20%	80%	80%	100%	83%	60%	60%	1.4%
Net $/MMBTU	$23.18	$75.96	$13.52	$13.89	$29.30	$12.05	$15.87	$12.50	$0.024

Gasoline is used only for illustration. The efficiency shown is for that of an internal combustion engine. Other efficiency figures are typical for heating equipment

Math Box: Determining Price per Million Btus of a Fuel Adjusted for Efficiency

To determine the price per MMBtu of fuel adjusted for equipment efficiency, you will need to divide the purchase price per MMBtu by the equipment's efficiency rating.

Let's use natural gas in this example. We'll assume that you pay $0.98 per therm and your furnace is 80 percent efficient. First find the number of therms in 1 MMBtu:

1,000,000 Btus ÷ 100,000 Btus per therm = 10 therms

Next, find the price per MMBtu:

10 therms × $0.98 per therm = $9.80 per MMBtu

Now adjust for efficiency:

$9.80 per MMBtu ÷ 80-percent = $12.25

If you increase the efficiency of your equipment, your fuel price will be correspondingly reduced. For example, if you buy a new high efficiency ENERGY STAR® rated gas heating system that is 90 percent efficient to replace your old 80 percent efficient system, your net price per MMBtu would be:

$9.80 ÷ 90-percent = $10.89

This savings of $1.36 per MMBtu really adds up year after year if you pour 75 MMBtus of heat energy into your home each winter.

overall inefficiency as a fuel. This inefficiency is primarily due to the fact that only about four percent of the fissionable material in the uranium loaded into reactors is converted into energy. Still, enriched uranium is incredibly energy-dense.

Efficiency and Cost-Effectiveness

Let's take a few minutes here to clear up any confusion between efficiency and cost. Efficiency is the ability to produce a desired result with a minimum of effort or waste. Mathematically, efficiency is the relationship of energy output divided by energy input, and is usually expressed in percentage. Nothing is more than 100 percent efficient. An electric water heater is very efficient (nearly 100 percent) at converting its electrical energy input into hot water output, and it is likely the cheapest kind of water heater to buy and install. This does *not* mean that the electric water heater is the most *cost-effective* way to heat water over the long term. Because electricity is an expensive energy source compared to most other fuels you can use to heat your water, a more expensive fossil fuel or solar water heater can cost less to buy, install, and operate over time.

To determine overall cost-effectiveness, you must consider efficiency (which affects operating costs), initial cost of the equipment, maintenance costs, and the lifetime of the equipment. To learn more about performing a *life-cycle cost analysis* for any energy using appliance in your home, see Chapter 7.

The efficiency of fuel-burning heating equipment depends on:

- How thoroughly the fuel is burned which is called *combustion efficiency*.
- How well heat is transferred from the flame to the air in a furnace or water in a water heater which is called *transfer efficiency*.
- How much heat is lost through the jacket, or housing, of the equipment which is called *standby loss*.
- How much heat goes up the chimney while the burner is firing which is called *flue loss*.
- Heat lost up the chimney while the burner is *not* firing is called *off-cycle loss*. This includes heat lost from the heating appliance along with heated air from the house.

The *net* price (after accounting for conversion efficiency) per MMBtu of gasoline burned in a typical (very inefficient) internal combustion engine is much higher than the purchase price. Most of the fuel energy consumed by your car is wasted as heat, a byproduct of combustion. The same is true for a gasoline-powered generator, a very expensive way to make electricity.

Math Box: Fuel-Switch Savings Calculations

To figure your own fuel-switch savings scenarios, follow these steps.

1. Decide what appliance you want to consider for a fuel switch and what fuel you want to use for the new appliance.
2. Determine that appliance's energy consumption in fuel units (gallons, kWh, Ccf or therms) by looking at your bills, having an energy audit, or reading the rest of this book to learn to make a reasonable estimate.
3. Determine the operating cost of the appliance by multiplying the fuel units by the price per unit.
4. Convert fuel units to equivalent Btus of energy consumption.
5. Multiply the Btus consumed by the old equipment by its efficiency.
6. Divide the adjusted Btus (from #5) by the efficiency of the new equipment. This is how many Btus the new equipment will consume.
7. Convert Btus to units of the fuel under consideration.
8. Multiply the number of fuel units by the price per unit.
9. Subtract new from original fuel costs to determine energy cost savings.

For example: I want to know if it is worth while to switch my electric water heater to a natural gas water heater. I have read the chapter on electricity use and determined that my water heater uses 5,250 kWh per year (including standby losses) to heat water. The local utility charges $0.095 per kWh, so it costs me:

5,250 × $0.095 = $498.75 per year to heat my water

There are 3,413 Btus in a kWh (from Table 1.2), so my water heater uses:

5,250 kWh × 3,413 = 17,918,250 Btus per year

The efficiency of the electric water heater (in this case called *energy factor*, read more about this in Chapter 4) is 0.89. Multiplying total consumption by the energy factor removes the effect of standby losses and offers a level ground for comparison to the new water heater, with its own energy factor.

$$17,918,250 \times .89 = 15,947,243 \text{ Btus hot water demand}$$

The new gas water heater has an energy factor of 0.63. Dividing demand by the new energy factor gives us total Btus required to heat the water, including standby losses.

$$15,947,243 \div .63 = 25,313,084 \text{ Btus total energy consumption}$$

You probably noticed that the energy consumption has increased compared with that of the electric water heater. This is because the efficiency of the gas water heater is lower than that of the electric. Let's see how this works out in terms of cost by first converting from Btus to new fuel units. Table 1.2 shows that there are 100,000 Btus in a therm.

$$25,313,084 \div 100,000 = 253 \text{ therms}$$

I'll need to buy 253 therms of natural gas instead of 5,250 kilowatt-hours to keep my family in hot water. The local gas utility charges $0.98 per therm, so to operate the gas water heater would cost:

$$253 \times \$0.98 = \$247.94$$

By switching from an electric water heater to a gas unit, we will save:

$$\$567 - \$248 = \$319 \text{ per year}$$

With an installed cost of $900 (it's a high quality, sealed-combustion model), the gas water heater will pay for itself in under three years.

Changing Fuels, Changing Habits

I told Ken Sumer that he might want to remove the electric baseboard heaters from the two back bedrooms (which were an addition to the original home) and instead run some ductwork from the gas furnace to supply heat to those rooms.

"That's too expensive. I can't really afford to do it now, that's why I put the electric heat in when we built the addition. It's cheap and convenient."

"You can't afford *not* to," I said, pulling out my handy price-per-MMBtu comparison chart. "Look, you're spending about $400 to heat those rooms with electricity every year. By switching to gas, you would save two thirds of that. It might cost you $600 for the ductwork, so with a $267 per year savings, the fuel switch would pay for itself in less than two years!"

In fact, not only would his bills drop, but the family's comfort level would increase. More heat, less money. Can't lose!

Fuel Switching Savings Scenarios

Once you know what fuels are locally available, their costs, their appropriateness for specific jobs, and your needs, you can determine the most efficient equipment and the least costly fuel options for any task in any home. You can simply reference Figure 1.10 to get an idea of what the lowest cost fuels are, although these costs will vary widely throughout the country. To learn the intricacies of fuel-switch savings calculations, work through the exercises in the fuel-switch savings Math Box on pages 49 and 50.

Increase Efficiency, Reduce Waste

Refer back to Figure 1.9. The biggest slice of the home-energy-use pie is electrical energy waste. There is little you can do about this at the power plant, but you can make a big difference at home, and you will see your efforts reflected in lower energy bills. Many small efforts add up to big change. One of the easiest things to do is to simply be aware of what is using energy at any given time and why. Our homes have many *phantom loads*, using energy that we may

Math Box: Pilot Lights

How much does it cost you to leave your furnace pilot on throughout the summer?

1,000 Btus × 24 hours = 24,000 Btus per day

That amounts to almost eight gallons of LPG, or 7.2 therms of natural gas every month. Multiply those numbers by the price you pay per unit of fuel.

be unaware of. As you will read in the chapter on electricity, a phantom load is an item that consumes energy even when it appears to be off. This is true not only for electric appliances, but for gas equipment as well.

If you have a gas oven, water heater, or space heater with a standing pilot light, you may be burning more money than you need to. The pilot light on your oven might use 400 Btus, your water heater's pilot light might burn at a rate of 700 Btus, and a gas furnace could be as high as 1,000 Btus. Many new gas appliances have electronic ignition, eliminating wasteful pilot lights. If you're shopping for new fossil fuel equipment, look for those with electronic ignition. If you'd like to figure out just how much a pilot light is costing you, see the Math Box above.

How Heat Moves

Heat is energy. The faster a substance's molecules move, the more energy it contains and the hotter the object. As long as there are temperature differences, heat will move — always from hot to cold (from high energy to low-energy). The universe wants to be at equilibrium and until that happens, everything will be in some kind of chaotic motion, desperate for balance. In your home, this means that air you paid to heat is frantically trying to get outside and be at one with the cold.

There are three ways, or paths, by which heat can be transmitted. Your house exhibits all three of these types of heat loss, as does a tea kettle heating on a stovetop. Reducing heat transmission cost-effectively is the key to energy savings and increased personal comfort. These three heat transfer paths are:

Conduction

Heat conducts *through* solid objects in contact with each other. The flame from the stove heats the tea kettle and heat is conducted through the metal and into the water. The hot handle will conduct its heat to your hand. More dense materials (such as metal) conduct heat better than less dense materials (such as air or insulation).

Convection

Heat transfer by a moving fluid like air or water is called convection. Convection happens because of density differences between warmer and cooler parts of the fluid. The hotter the fluid, the less dense it is. In the tea kettle, the water on the bottom heats up first and becomes less dense as its molecules begin moving faster and expand. These lighter molecules rise to the top of the kettle, forcing cooler, heavier molecules down. This motion is called convection. When you blow on a hot drink, convective heat loss occurs between the drink and the air. A cool wind causes convective heat loss from your skin.

Radiation

Heat passing through space from one object to another is said to radiate. The sun radiates heat that you can feel on your skin. When you stand next to a cold window, your body radiates heat towards the window and that is why you feel cold — heat is being removed from your body. The window doesn't radiate cold towards you because heat always moves from hot to cold. The tea kettle will radiate heat to the air and objects around it until there is no temperature difference between them.

Specific, Sensible, and Latent Heat

Air and moisture are the two biggest components in our living environment affecting our comfort level. Each absorbs and gives up heat predictably, but differently.

The number of Btus required to raise the temperature of one pound of a material by 1°F is called its *specific heat*.

When one Btu of heat energy is added to one pound of water, its temperature rises 1°F. The specific heat of water then is 1. This relationship holds true while water is in its liquid phase, between 32°F and 212°F. For air, the relationship says that raising one pound of air one degree requires 0.24 Btu.

As we add Btus to a material, its temperature rises according to its specific heat. This relationship is called *sensible* heat.

Things get more complicated when materials change phase such as when water changes from liquid to vapor. When one pound of water reaches 212°F it boils, remaining at 212° while it slowly vaporizes into steam. With a specific heat of 1, the pound of water absorbed 162 Btus to go from 50°F to 212°F (212 – 50 = 162), but will absorb 970 more Btus to completely turn to steam. The pound of water requires six times more energy to allow it to change phase. The heat energy required for water to change phase — that is to boil or freeze, condense from the air or evaporate into the air — is called *latent heat*.

As you can see, there is a lot of energy in water vapor. If you can get water to evaporate, it will absorb lots of heat energy from where it is evaporating, effectively cooling the object. This is why we sweat. The heat released or absorbed when a material changes from liquid to vapor is called *latent heat of vaporization* and is a very efficient way of removing heat from our bodies. To get that water vapor to condense again releases the same amount of energy. If you want to freeze that pound of water, you would need to remove 18 Btus to cool it from 50°F to 32°F (50 – 32), and another 144 Btus to change its phase to a frozen block. This is called *latent heat of fusion*.

Latent heat of vaporization is the basic principle behind evaporative coolers and heat pumps (air conditioners are heat pumps). Evaporation removes heat from the source, while condensation releases the heat in the water vapor onto a cooler object. Think of your eyeglasses (if you wear them). When you come in from the cold, the eyeglasses fog up as moisture condenses out of the warm air and onto the cold surface, warming up the glasses (heat travels from hot to cold). Stepping outside again reverses the process as heat from the glasses along with the moisture now condensed on their surface is released into the cold air.

This is the same idea behind high efficiency "condensing" boilers or furnaces — they capture the latent heat of vaporization, which would otherwise be lost up the chimney along with hot flue gasses. Twelve percent of the heat generated by combustion of natural gas is water's latent heat, so a condensing furnace can theoretically be 12 percent more efficient than a conventional furnace.

Next Steps

Now that you know how to think critically about energy use, you can apply this knowledge to reducing energy use in your own home. In the coming chapters, we will examine ways to reduce home energy use, increase occupant comfort, and also learn about how the systems within your home may interact with each other to support the individuals living in the home. We'll do this by looking into the following areas:

- Electric appliance efficiency
- Hot water use
- Heating and air conditioning equipment
- Thermal performance of the home
- Occupant behavior

Understanding how these components work individually and in combination will lead to a more intimate understanding of your home. You already know that your house has a distinct personality with its sometimes mysterious creaks and groans and its particular spaces — each offering a unique feeling.

Your home may be asking for attention. Do you understand its language? Can you make your home happy? If you do, it will return the favor!

CHAPTER 2

Electricity

Where It Comes From, How It's Used, and How to Use Less of It

Introduction to Using Electricity in Your Home

WITHIN A YEAR OF OPENING NEW YORK'S PEARL STREET Generating Station in 1882, there were 11,000 bulbs lighting up the New York night. Edison's reported goal was to "make electric lights so cheap that only the rich will be able to burn candles."

By 1900, homeowners were introduced to a myriad of electric appliances designed to make life easier by doing our dishes and laundry, providing entertainment by radio and TV, and offering rural families an alternative to cooking on the wood stove. Thus began our devotion to power and appliances designed to allow us more leisure time. With millions of appliances, gadgets and toys to plug in, electricity use accounts for 27 percent of the average home's annual energy consumption.

By using the information in this chapter, you can reduce your electrical consumption to the point where you will hardly notice your electric bills. You'll learn some of the technical terminology used when discussing electrical use, explore where electricity comes from, where it goes, and how it is measured and quantified. I'll show you how to decipher your electric bill, and introduce some tools to measure electricity use in your home. These tools will help you perform an electrical energy audit of your home so that you can identify some of your big power users, and help you sleuth out some of the mysterious things that can make your power bills higher. You'll learn why electricity is the most expensive energy you can buy, how to determine the operating cost of any appliance in your home, and when it might be worthwhile to replace an appliance with a new, more efficient one. A broad electrical diet offers generalized ways to reduce electrical consumption at home, and a section on electrical safety helps you decide when it's time to call the electrician.

Chapter 3 follows with brief discussions of many high-use electrical items, and more extensive "diets" to help you trim the consumption of these bigger users. Savings tables will help to clarify the impacts of reducing energy consumption. Sometimes simple changes in habits and usage patterns are all that is needed.

The "Appliance Use Chart" in Appendix C lists the power use of many common household appliances. This chart will serve as a reference for your home energy audit.

Terms

Before getting started on a discussion of electricity, it will be helpful to explore some of the terms used to describe how production and consumption of electricity is measured.

Supply and demand are familiar concepts. Electrical *demand* is simply how much energy is demanded each moment by the appliances in your home from the power company. A typical home has a demand of approximately 10,000 to 15,000 watts.

Electrical *supply* is called "capacity" and describes the amount of instantaneous power that can be produced by a power plant at any given time. A typical utility-scale generating station may have a capacity of between fifty million and several hundred million watts. A solar electric system powering a single home might have a capacity between a few hundred and a few thousand watts, while a commonly used gasoline-powered generator has a capacity of about five thousand watts.

Capacity and demand are both measured in the same units of power we are used to seeing on light bulbs — watts (after 18th century inventor, James Watt).

The Elements of Electricity

The following four related elements of electricity describe an electrical circuit and can help you determine the power demand and consumption of any appliance in your home. These terms can also be used when talking about the capacity of your home's electrical service, or the capacity of a power plant.

Volts are a measure of electrical pressure, or how much force is pushing the electrons through the wire. Household appliances commonly found in the US require electricity to be supplied at a pressure of 120 volts. Some larger appliances might require 240 volts.

Amps are a measure of the flow of electrons, or current.

Power is the product of volts and amps. Power is measured in *watts*, and can be thought of as energy consumed over time.

Resistance or *load* is the opposition to the flow of current and is measured in *ohms*. Anything you plug into an electrical outlet accepts some power, but resists accepting *all* the power available to it from the power outlet. If you (foolishly) stuck each end of a paper clip into an electrical outlet, there would be little resistance and it would heat up and glow like the filament in a light bulb, but only briefly before it melted. There would not be enough resistance in the clip to create enough opposition to the flow of current to prevent the clip's destruction. The filament in a light bulb is carefully designed to have enough resistance to glow, but not too much (it would not glow) or too little (it would burn itself up).

Because the amount of power produced by an electric company and consumed by all the buildings on the power company's distribution network of wires, transformers, switches, and the like (otherwise known as the *grid*) are quite large, we'll need larger figures to work with:

- *Kilowatt* (kW) = one thousand watts
- *Megawatt* (mW) = one million watts
- *Gigawatt* (gW) = one billion watts.

Like Water in a Hose

Think of the elements of electricity like water in a hose. More pressure in the hose translates to more volts. A fatter hose will carry more water — or current — meaning that more amps can flow through a fatter wire. The combination of pressure and flow produces power. Now imagine a sprinkler head nozzle on the hose. Changing the flow of water coming out of the nozzle is like adjusting the resistance, changing the current flow but not affecting the pressure within the hose. Changing pressure or flow while the other value remains constant, results in a proportional change in the power.

Kilowatt-Hours: Measuring Electricity Consumption over Time

When I do an energy audit for someone, there is a big difference between how I look at the electric bill and how the homeowner looks at the same bill. The owner is concerned about dollars, while I look only at power consumption and, as importantly, any seasonal patterns of consumption. I often begin an audit with a review of the past year's power bills and explain how power consumption is measured and billed. The power company bills you for the power you use over the course of time, usually one month. When we add time to electrical demand, we need a new definition.

Consumption is how much power is consumed by an appliance or a whole house over time, and is measured in watt-hours, or more conveniently, kilowatt-hours (kWh). A kWh is the consumption of 1,000 watts over a period of one hour, or any mathematical product of time and electrical power demand that adds up to 1,000-watt-hours.

Math Box: Ohm's Law

There is a mathematical relationship between volts, amps, and watts. It is known as *Ohm's Law* (after the 19th century German physicist, G.S. Ohm).

amps × volts = watts

If we know any two of these quantities, we can find the third. For example, you might see stamped on the back or bottom of your TV: 120V /0.75A How many watts does it use? Ohm's Law can tell us:

0.75 amps × 120 volts = 90 watts

Using a 100-watt light bulb as another example, we know two things: the voltage (120) and the wattage (100). To determine the amperage flowing through the light bulb's filament, the formula needs to be rearranged:

watts ÷ volts = amps
100 watts ÷ 120 volts = 0.83 amps

To discover the resistance of the bulb's filament, a different iteration of Ohm's Law is needed:

volts ÷ amps = ohms
120 volts ÷ 0.83 amps = 144.6 ohms

Here are two easy formula circles to use with Ohm's Law. Cover up the unit you are looking for, and do the math. The value on the top is divided by the value on the bottom. For example, using formula circle #2, if you know the volts and amps of an electrical device, and you want to find the resistance in ohms, put your thumb over the word "ohms" and it shows that you need to divide volts by amps to get the answer.

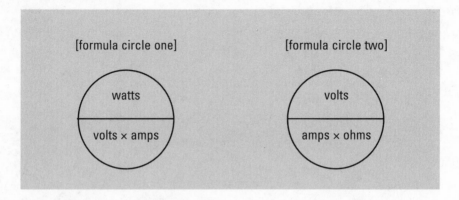

What does a kWh "Feel" Like?

Here are a few comparisons to give you a feel for what a kilowatt-hour is.

- A gallon of gasoline contains the energy equivalent of over 36 kWh.
- A car battery stores less than one kilowatt-hour of power.
- It takes 861 food calories (more than one quarter pound of butter) to supply the energy equivalent of one kWh — about the energy you'd burn up during two solid hours of high impact aerobics.

If you like math, you'll like what James Watt did back in the 1700s. He determined that an average horse could lift a 550-pound weight one vertical foot in one second. This rate of work is now known as the *horsepower* (HP) and can also be expressed as 550 foot-pounds. A horse can perform work, and so can electricity. Horsepower can therefore be expressed in terms of electrical power. Electric motors are often rated in horsepower. In an ideal world:

$$1 \text{ HP} = 746 \text{ watts}$$

or

$$1 \text{ HP} = 0.746 \text{ kilowatts}$$

Math Box: Consumption and Watt-hours

Consumption = demand × time.

A 100-watt light bulb left on for three hours uses:

100 watts × 3 hours = 300-watt-hours

A 100-watt light bulb consumes 100-watt-hours when left on for one hour. After ten hours, the same bulb has consumed 1,000-watt-hours, or one kWh. A ten-watt night-light needs to be on for 100 hours to add up to one kWh of power.

In reality, because no activity or process is 100 percent efficient, a 1 HP motor will demand about 1,000 watts, more or less, depending on the motor's efficiency and how hard it is working. This is a helpful relationship to know when determining the power consumption of the various motors around your home.

Human Limits

I read somewhere that a human in decent physical condition can only generate about one quarter of a horsepower — or around 200 watts of energy — for any length of time. I got a chance to prove this for a school demonstration project when I built a bicycle-powered generator. The bicycle drove a generator that could power four light bulbs. First, I screwed in four 100-watt bulbs and jumped on. I could barely move the pedals. The load was too much for my legs; it was like trying to bike up a vertical incline. I unscrewed three of the four bulbs and pedaled happily for a couple of minutes before breaking a sweat. Then a second bulb was switched on, and after a minute of producing 200 watts, I was beat. To generate one kWh, I would need to pedal for five hours with two 100-watt light bulbs switched on (2 × 100-watts × 5 hours = 1 kWh). At a cost of only ten cents from the power company, a kWh is a pretty good deal!

The instructor currently using this bicycle generator lays down a $10 bill and offers it to any student who can produce ten cents worth of electricity (one kilowatt-hour). After several years, not even the cockiest jock has earned the prize. When those four 100-watt bulbs are replaced with four high efficiency, 25-watt compact fluorescent bulbs, all four light up with equivalent light and minimal complaint from the rider — but he still wasn't willing to ride for long enough to take home the $10.

Awareness: The Big Picture

All of the fuels used for electricity production represented 41 percent of the total US energy consumption in 2000. Electric generating capacity in the US grew by only ten percent between 1990 and 2000, but power plants generated 26 percent more power. That means that power plants are working harder and longer to keep up with demand. This concept is known as *capacity factor*. An increased capacity factor means that power plants are in full operation for more hours to keep up with power demand.

Generating capacity in 2000 was 811,625 megawatts, and power plants generated over 3.8 trillion kWh of electricity. The US Department of Energy's Energy Information Administration (EIA) forecasts a 1.8 percent average annual growth in electricity sales from 2000 through 2020, requiring 1,300 new power plants to meet demand. That's more than one new power plant built every week for twenty years!

Where Does Electricity Come From?

The typical power plant boils water by burning a fossil fuel or by nuclear fission. The force of the steam generated by the boiling water spins a turbine attached to an electrical generator, which produces electricity.

Figure 2.1 shows the primary energy sources used to generate electricity in the US in 2000.

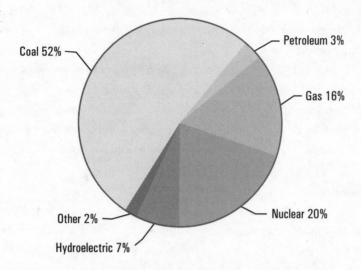

Fig 2.1: US electricity generation by source, 2002.

Coal

In 2000, coal-fired electric generating plants produced 1,968 billion kWh, with a capacity of 315.2 gigawatts, consuming 991 million tons of coal — over 90 percent of the coal used in the US that year. Coal is such a major fuel source for electricity generation due to its relatively low cost and domestic abundance.

Nuclear

In 2000, 103 nuclear reactors within 66 nuclear power plants operating in the US (there are 442 in the world), produced 754 billion kWh of electricity with a capacity of 97.6 gigawatts. The largest nuclear power plant in the US is at Palo Verde, AZ, with three units totaling 3,733 megawatts of capacity.

Hydroelectric Power

The National Hydropower Association reports that total US hydroelectric capacity in 2001 was about 104 gigawatts. The EIA reported a hydroelectric power production of 232,950 gigawatt-hours in 2001 down from 379,982 gigawatt-hours in 1997, and the lowest level since 1967 due to generally lower water levels. Hydroelectric power contribution fluctuates depending on rainfall and water levels.

The Grand Coulee Dam on the Columbia River in Washington is the largest power plant in the country with a generating capacity of 7,079 megawatts. The US Department of Energy's Hydropower Program estimates that electricity generated by US hydropower plants averages 2.4 cents per kWh on the wholesale power market — about half that of electricity produced from coal.

Natural Gas

In 2000, over 6.3 trillion cubic feet of natural gas (22 percent of total natural gas consumption) were used to generate 612 billion kWh of electricity. Natural gas power plants had a capacity of about 100 gigawatts (12 percent of total generating capacity) in 2000 and growth is rapid.

Petroleum

Oil-fired electrical generators are typically more expensive to operate than those of other fuel types. They are used primarily for meeting peak demand in times of high power use; 173 million barrels of oil were used to generate 109 billion kWh of electricity in 2000, with a capacity of 39.3 gigawatts, or three percent of total generation. Many petroleum-burning power plants can also be fueled by natural gas. Thus, they can take advantage of either fuel based on market price. These dual-fired plants had a capacity of 145.5 gigawatts. Their production in megawatt-hours is included in the figures for each fuel.

Wind

Wind doesn't show as a distinct resource on the national scale of electricity production yet, but the American Wind Energy Association reports that there were 2.5 gigawatts of wind-energy capacity in the US in 2000, 0.3 percent of total electrical generating capacity. Offshore and land-based "wind farms" show great potential for future wind energy growth. Wind-generated electricity has been found to be very cost-competitive with traditional electrical generating sources. The use of wind power is growing rapidly with large off-shore wind projects on the coasts, while midwest farms harvest vast amounts of energy on the plains alongside more traditional crops. Debate over wind energy is

generally limited to concerns over aesthetics, cost, and resource reliability —
only three drawbacks out of the many inherent to fossil fuel usage as well.

Solar

The Solar Energy Industries Association indicates that US solar electric
generating capacity in 2001 was 350 million watts, and the National Center for
Photovoltaics reports that 75 megawatts of solar electric generating capacity was
installed in 2000. Both wind and solar technologies are improving while costs are
dropping, and both industries are growing quite rapidly. While solar electric
power is growing quickly, it is more costly to install than wind power equipment.

Other Renewable Electricity Sources

Geothermal, biomass, wind, and solar electricity combined produced 84
billion kWh in 2000 (about two percent of total electric generation), with a
combined capacity of 17.4 gigawatts. Geothermal and hydro resources are well
exploited, and unlikely to grow much in the future. Electricity generated from
biomass is primarily the result of burning woodchips.

Electricity Imports

Once electricity is produced, its energy can be transported across state or
international borders where it is then sold. US electricity imports in 2000 were
just under 49 billion kWh, but exports totaled almost 15 billion kWh. Net
electricity imports amount to 0.9 percent of consumption. Over 99 percent of
US electricity imports are from Canada, the remainder from Mexico. However,
in 2000 the US imported about 20 percent of the primary fuels required to
produce electricity.

Where Does Electricity Go?

All the electricity sold in 2000 was consumed largely by three main sectors as
indicated by Figure 2.2.

Just over four quadrillion Btus (quads) of electricity were consumed in
American homes in 2000, or 1.2 trillion kWh. On average, each household in
the US used in the neighborhood of 11,700 kWh (the equivalent of 40.2 million
Btus). Motors consume about 60 percent of all the electricity used in

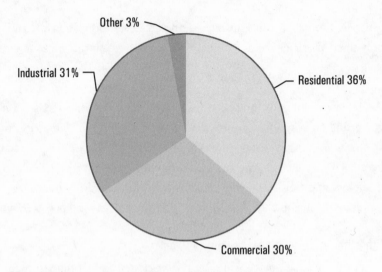

Other 3%

Industrial 31%

Residential 36%

Commercial 30%

"Other" includes public street and highway lighting, public authorities and railroad use

Fig 2.2: US electricity use by sector.

the US. Much of this is in the commercial and industrial sector, but consider all the motors in your home: in blenders, coffee grinders, refrigerator and air conditioner compressors, vacuum cleaners, water pumps, furnace blowers, circulator pumps, VCRs, CD and tape players, and so on.

Powerful Impacts

Electricity sales totaled $228 billion in 2000, with the average price for a kWh at around 6.7 cents. It might interest you to know that as a homeowner, you are paying top dollar for electricity. On average, residential customers paid 8.22 cents per kWh while commercial customers paid 7.22 cents per kWh, and industrial rates averaged 4.46 cents per kWh.

Pollution Generation

But what are we paying for besides the commodity of an invisible kilowatt-hour? Electricity originates from sources with a myriad of environmental, social, political, and monetary liabilities.

Back in 1992, California's Pacific Gas and Electric's Public Relations director, Larry Simi, noted:

"In order to supply the electricity needs of California, we burn fossil fuels, we discharge hot water into the San Francisco and Monterey bays and the Pacific Ocean, we cover open hillsides with noisy, ugly windmills, we dam wild and scenic rivers, we drill geothermal wells that release arsenic, our power lines emit electromagnetic fields — and we run a nuclear power plant. And you think your clients have image problems?"

Following are a few more reasons to invest in an electrically efficient lifestyle.

Nothing is 100 percent efficient, and with inefficiency comes trouble. The trouble with fossil-fueled power plants is that the fuels burned to create the electricity do not burn completely. There are chemical components — chiefly carbon and sulfur that combine with components in the atmosphere to create what we know as air pollution. Nationwide, electric power industry emissions in 2000 produced 2.6 billion tons of the potent greenhouse gas carbon dioxide (CO_2), about 41 percent of the total US CO_2 emissions for 2000. This figure corresponds to nearly 9.2 tons of CO_2 per year from each of us. CO_2 and other pollutants such as sulfur dioxide are carried on the wind and mix with other atmospheric gases to produce acid rain and holes in the ozone layer of Earth's upper atmosphere. See Appendix B for CO_2 production information and to determine your personal CO_2 production.

Electricity is Inherently Wasteful

Electricity isn't really a fuel; it is an energy carrier, the result of converting one energy source (the primary fuel) into another form of energy. Because nothing is 100 percent efficient, every conversion of energy introduces a loss in the form of heat.

Refer back to Figure 1.3 showing energy flow trends in the US. Note the box toward the top left of the figure that says "Electric power sector." The box indicates that over 40 quads of energy went into generating electricity, but only about 12 quads (30 percent) of electrical energy were actually used. The remaining 70 percent was wasted! It's not that you wasted it at home, but because that's the nature of electrical generation. What this inefficiency means is that anything that uses electricity is going to be relatively costly to operate.

Why the huge waste? Power plants burn fuel and convert it into electricity with a thermal efficiency of around 33 percent. The remaining energy embodied in the fuel is released into the atmosphere as waste heat. Power plants need large cooling systems to deal with this waste heat. Those big hourglass shaped towers you see at power plants are cooling towers, and that's steam coming out the top, not smoke. Some power plants capture a portion of this waste heat and use it for heating buildings, or for industrial processes.

The electricity is then transported through many miles of cable, multiple transformers, and switching stations before it finally gets to the circuit breaker box in your basement. Each cable, connection, and transformation introduces a little bit of energy loss. These inefficiencies are known as transmission and distribution losses, and they can account for a loss of ten percent or more of the generated power. By the time the electricity gets to your home, 70 percent of the energy that went into making it has dissipated as heat, making the national electric generation and distribution system about 30 percent efficient. What this means is that for every three units of fuel put into a power plant, only one unit makes it to your home in the form of usable electrical power. For every kWh of electricity you save at home, you're really saving over three times more in total primary fuel consumption.

If the power plant were located next door, as in the case of a local or home-based solar, hydro or wind generator, the transmission, distribution, and conversion losses would be much lower. The widespread use of small power plants scattered throughout the region is what utilities call *distributed generation*.

Why the High Cost

All the inefficiencies in the generation and distribution of electricity add up to a very costly source of energy. In fact, in most parts of the country, electricity is the most expensive form of energy. Electric *resistance heating* is one of the costliest offenders you will find in your home. This category of appliances includes those that produce heat from electricity such as electric baseboard and portable space heaters, toasters, electric dryers, water heaters, and ovens. If you have any of these electric-resistant heating appliances, you would do well to investigate other fuel options to reduce your overall energy costs.

Incandescent light bulbs (the "regular," old-style light bulbs) fall into the resistance heat category as well. An incandescent light bulb has an electrically resistive filament that converts about ten percent of the power supplied to it into usable light, which makes it a 90 percent efficient electric heater! If you feel heat coming from an energy-using device (anything from a light bulb to a car engine), it is less than 100 percent efficient — unless it was designed to be a heater!

Is Electricity Efficient?

The answer to this question depends on how far back you want to follow the electrons moving through the wires. An electric water heater is nearly 100 percent efficient at converting the electricity going into it into heated water. But when you factor in the *inefficiency* of the power grid, the electric water heater is only about 30 percent efficient. An efficient gas or oil water heater converts about 60 percent of the fossil fuel's energy into hot water. The remaining 40 percent of the energy embodied in the fuel goes out the chimney as waste heat and combustion byproducts such as oxides of carbon, sulfur, and nitrogen. But the fossil fuel-fired water heater is still twice as efficient *overall* as the electric water heater.

Using an incandescent light bulb as an example, if the bulb is ten percent efficient, and the power grid is 30 percent efficient, the overall efficiency of the bulb is only three percent.

Is Electricity Cost-Effective?

An item that is *cost-effective* produces good results for the amount of money you spend. To be cost-effective, the device should be reasonably priced, economical to operate, do its job well, and last a long time.

Just because your electric heater is 100 percent efficient and didn't cost very much to buy, doesn't mean that it is the cheapest, most cost-effective way to provide heat. It might be cheap to buy and install, and it might last twenty years or more, but because electricity is so expensive you will pay a steep premium to operate the heater over its lifetime. A heater operated by gas or oil may cost a bit more to buy and maintain, but the operating costs will likely be quite a bit lower than the electric heater. To determine cost-effectiveness, a life-cycle cost

Math Box: Efficiency

When determining the total efficiency of a *system*, the efficiencies of each component making up the system are multiplied together. As an example, I'll use national electric grid average efficiency figures. Generation efficiency is about 33 percent (66 percent of the energy embodied in the primary fuel is lost), while power transmission and distribution efficiencies are each about 95 percent efficient (5 percent of the generated electricity is lost).

Generation Efficiency × Transmission Efficiency × Distribution Efficiency
= Total Grid Efficiency or:

$$0.33 \times 0.95 \times 0.95 = 0.30 \text{ or } 30 \text{ percent}$$

analysis should be performed to compare the lifetime operation and maintenance costs of the equipment you are considering. See Chapter 7 to learn about life-cycle costing.

Assessing Electric Use of Appliances

Three very common questions I hear while doing an energy audit are: "How much electricity do I use? How much *should* I use? Is my usage average?" As usual, the answer is, "It depends." What "it" depends on is exactly what things you have plugged into your electrical outlets, how much power each one uses, and how you use these items.

An examination of your electric bill will show you how much power (in kilowatt-hours) you use each month. Many bills even show your average daily kWh. On average, American households consume about 30 kilowatt-hours of electricity per day. In my energy efficient off-grid home with two adults and one child, we use about four kilowatt-hours per day. We are able to do this by careful energy management and the use of only the most energy-efficient lights and appliances. We have all the modern conveniences so we don't suffer. We

Off-Grid Tip: Heat From Water or Electricity?

Every spring, we raise two dozen or so chicks on our homestead. When they are young, they need to be kept quite warm. Many people use a 100-watt (or more) light bulb to act as a brood heater. Because we live off-grid using solar power and a finite amount of stored energy, we don't use wasteful incandescent light bulbs for heaters — we don't even use them for lights! Instead of the electric light (a load that would drain our batteries overnight), we use a few one-gallon jugs of very hot water wrapped in a dishtowel. The water stays hot overnight, radiating heat out to the chicks, and the towel acts as insulation while preventing the chicks from overheating. As the water in the jug cools, the chicks move closer. By morning, it's time to refill the jug with hot water. The hot water we use is heated by our gas water heater and maybe the little left in the tea kettle, and the chicks grow up happy and healthy. This is a very cost-effective alternative to heating a small space with electricity.

choose and use our appliances carefully, keeping in mind low-energy and resource consumption, which add up to lower energy cost. The benefits of low-energy consumption also include greater independence, security, and the ability to choose where your electricity comes from. In my case, solar energy meets about 80 percent of our family's annual power needs. If we used 30 kWh every day, a solar system would need to be quite large and expensive to provide us with the same percentage of our power. With today's technology and a few good habits, there is really no need to use so much electricity in the home anymore.

How Appliances Use Electricity

What happens when you plug something into a power outlet in your home? If you think about the water hose example, plugging something into an outlet and flipping the switch is like opening the water valve. Electrons flow from the outlet into the device. In fact, at first they literally gush into the circuit or appliance. This is known as *surge current*, and this surge is the reason why light bulbs usually blow out the instant you switch them on (maybe your mother knew that when she told you not to keep flipping the switch on and off all the time). And yes, your light bulbs will last longer if you keep them on all the time, but it's far cheaper to buy new bulbs than to pay for the electricity to run them continuously. Surge current in light bulbs (fluorescent or incandescent) is only a few percent of the rated wattage, and only lasts for a second. If you're coming back into the room within 15 minutes, leave the light on, otherwise turn it off.

Light bulbs blow because of this self-induced surge. After the bulb heats up, its resistance increases, and less current flows. That's why a bulb will rarely burn out after it's already on. Surge current is why the computer salesman tells you to keep your computer on all the time — it lengthens the lifetime of the power supply inside by reducing the number of surge current cycles within the electronics. I have to say, though, that I don't know anybody who's had a computer long enough for this failure to occur, and I strongly encourage you to turn it off if you'll be away from the computer for more than an hour.

Surge current occurs on nearly all electrical devices. If it's a big enough load (such as a refrigerator or furnace), it saps the juice from everywhere in the house to satisfy the surge, resulting in a momentary dimming of lights. The dimming is worse if your house wiring is substandard or if you're at the end of the power line.

You might think that all these extra power surges would cause your electric bill to rise, but in most cases it does not. The duration of the surge is so short that it does not generally add anything noticeable to your electric consumption. Motors are the one exception; they can take from two to ten times more power to start compared to the amount of power they use once they are up and running. If you have a furnace that short-cycles, or a private water system with a leak or a faulty or undersized pressure tank, their motors will cycle on and off more frequently, noticeably increasing your electric bill.

Once past the surge current phase, the appliance settles down to do its job at its rated power demand. The electrons can be manipulated by the circuitry in an appliance in hundreds of ways to turn motors, light bulbs, calculate formulas, play music, record movies, or project an image. The list of uses for electricity is endless and nearly miraculous.

Know Your Loads

Only you know how much time each appliance in your home operates on a daily basis. This is one half of knowing your loads; the other half is knowing the electrical demand of the appliance. The electrical ratings of an appliance can be found on a tag or stamp on the item, usually near where the power cord enters the appliance, and may include the model and serial numbers. Also listed on the stamp will be the required voltage (a number followed by a V), along with the amp rating (a number followed by an A), and/or the wattage rating (a number followed by a W). Sometimes wattage is shown as a number followed by VA, referring to volt-amps (power is the product of volts and amps); for our purposes this simply means watts. Most household appliances in the US require 120 volts, but larger appliances like electric dryers, stoves, water pumps, water heaters, and welders might need 240 volts. If amps are listed but watts are not, watts can be calculated by using the Ohm's Law equation: watts = volts × amps.

Determining Appliance Power Consumption

Once you have found the power demand of your appliance in watts, add up the number of hours the appliance is used each month. Maybe your TV is on four hours a day. That's 120 hours a month, and you've found the tag on the back that says it uses 90 watts. Now multiply the watts by the hours to get monthly watt-hours (Wh) consumed.

In this example, the television uses 10.8 kWh per month. Take an inventory of all your appliances and record the wattage and daily operating time of each. Now you can figure out how much each is costing you. Once you know that, you can make an informed decision as to what action to take. Your choices include:

- You are satisfied with this cost and won't make any changes.
- It's time to implement conservation measures to reduce power use.
- You want to invest in a more efficient appliance (see the chapter on buying new appliances).

Math Box: Appliance Power Consumption

You can determine the power consumption of any appliance in your home by knowing how many watts the appliance uses and for how much time it is on. Here is the equation to use:

watt-hours = appliance watts × run time (hours)

From the example using the television:

90 watts × 120 hours = 10,800 Wh per month.

Next, you'll need to divide this number by 1,000. You do this because that's how the electric company bills you – in *kilo* watt-hours

10,800 ÷ 1,000 = 10.8 kWh

Determining Appliance Operating Costs

Once you know the wattage and run-time of the appliance, it is a simple task to determine its operating cost. The only missing number is the price you pay for each kilowatt-hour and you can get that from your electric bill.

From the previous example, the TV uses 10.8 kWh per month, and let's say you pay 8.2 cents per kWh. Simply multiply your monthly kWh by the price you pay for each kWh.

Some appliances defy this simple method of determining operating cost because either their wattage or their run-time will vary under their own control (see the sidebar on cycle factor). A refrigerator is a good example of both of these exceptions and because a refrigerator is usually one of the top five energy users in your home, it is well worth studying its power use. Under normal operating conditions, your fridge may demand 250 watts for five hours a day. Then it goes into defrost cycle and suddenly draws 400 watts for 15 minutes. Its operating time might vary with the ambient temperature, how much warm

Cycle Factor

Some appliances cycle on and off while in use and you may never know it. The appliance appears to be operating normally, and it is, but something about its operation has changed. *Cycle factor* is the percentage of time the appliance is actually operating at full capacity. Cycle factor is usually a consideration in items that have a thermostat — anything that heats or cools. These appliances include refrigerators, ovens, dryers, air conditioners, dehumidifiers, coffee makers, and any kind of oven. For example: while a coffee maker is keeping a pot of coffee warm, the burner is not on 100 percent of the time. It cycles on and off to keep the coffee at the right temperature. In most cases, the cycle factor is difficult to ascertain. It all depends on the thermostat setting, as the cycling is the result of the action of the thermostat. An electric dryer, for example, may have a cycle factor of 0.75, meaning that the heating element is actually on only 75 percent of the total drying time as the thermostat cycles the heating element on and off based on the temperature inside. The clothes keep on spinning, but the heating element turns on and off.

Math Box: Appliance Operating Cost

Kilowatt-hours × price per kilowatt-hour = operating cost

10.8 kWh × $0.082 per kWh = 88 cents a month.

food you put into it, and how often the door is open. The best way to determine the power consumption and operating costs of these types of appliances is to use a meter that records power consumption over time (Read more about meters in the "Tools" section later in this chapter). If you don't have a meter, there are some resources that allow you to make a reasonable guess at your power consumption. One resource is the "Appliance Use Chart" in Appendix C. If your fridge was manufactured between 1979 and 1992, you can access a database of refrigerator power consumption on the web at <www.waptac.com>. New refrigerators are supplied with yellow Energy Guide tags indicating their power consumption (more about this in Chapter 7).

Phantom Loads

Turning things off is one way to avoid using electricity — or is it? Ever wonder if there were ghosts running around your house at night turning everything on and running up your power bill? What you have is the modern technology equivalent of ghosts — *phantom loads*, or leaking electricity. Phantom loads are much like a leaky faucet, only you can't see leaking electrons. This is a growing problem with many of the new electronic gadgets filling our homes today. These things appear to be off, but are really still using power. Because of this unwelcome, unadvertised habit, they are called "phantom," "ghost," "parasitic," or simply "standby" loads.

> *Reducing phantom loads from 50 watts to 25 watts would save 219 kWh or $17.96 a year.*

Take a look behind your TV. If you're like most people, there's a tangled spaghetti of power cords there, underneath the dust balls. These cords come from electronic components such as stereos, VCRs, satellite receivers, cable tuner boxes, video games, lava lamps, fish tanks, and so forth. Some of these things use a little power even when they are turned off. Your cable or satellite tuner box, for example, draws about 15 watts (or more) all the time! It doesn't matter if you've turned it off. If a device with a phantom load is plugged in, it's like having an automatic withdrawal from your checking account each month that you didn't sign up for.

Many phantom loads are not obvious. A search for phantom loads in your house might start at your TV or entertainment center, then the computer center, and then kitchen gadgets including the coffee maker and microwave. Find everything with a remote control, a clock, or a little red light that's always on. Look around your wall outlets and count up all the little black boxes (power cubes) that are plugged into them — they are power converters, battery chargers, or standby circuits and each one draws a little power regardless of how the power switch is set. Another test is to put your hand on the unit a few hours after you have turned it off. Is it warm? If so, it is using power and is a phantom load. Anything that works without your thinking much about it, is a potential problem. These items include doorbells, timers, and heating system controls. The best test to determine how much power is being used by a phantom load is to measure the wattage drawn by the appliance. More on this soon.

The US Department of Energy's Lawrence Berkeley National Laboratory (LBNL) estimates that standby power may account for five percent of the electricity used in US homes, totaling more than $4 billion per year in electricity costs. The actual dollar cost to you of phantom loads may not add up to much, but enough so that an inexpensive switched power-strip can pay for itself in less than a year by allowing you to eliminate those phantom loads (see "Off-Grid Tip" sidebar). Small details like eliminating phantom loads make a big difference if you ever want to go off-grid. In my home, just two power strips (one for the TV and VCR and one for the microwave) save the equivalent of three weeks of power consumed by everything else in the house over the course of a year.

Off-Grid Tip: Power Strips

One way to rein in your power consumption is to plug all your phantom loads into a power strip with a switch. The cost is usually under $10. Make the switch accessible so that it isn't a chore to use. Turn the power strip on only when you use the appliance, and be diligent about turning it off. Eliminating phantom loads may sound like small potatoes, but why pay for power that will ultimately be wasted? If you go solar, you will need to purchase additional solar panels to meet those waste needs, and every little detail adds up to big savings.

Off-Grid Phantom Loads

Invisible phantom loads rob power and cost you money; 50 watts of phantom load over 24 hours a day, every day, adds up to 1.2 kWh per day. In a location with an average of four hours of sun per day, you'll need an additional 300 watts (1,200 watt-hours ÷ 4 hours) of solar modules. At a cost of $6 per watt, your phantom loads will add over $1,800 to the system cost. Better to buy a few power strips, or invest in a more efficient appliance.

Here's another way to look at it. My microwave oven uses five watts of power when it is "off.' That is, it presents a constant drain on my system of five watts. That works out to 120 watt-hours per day, or 44 kWh per year. Since I only use four kWh per day, that's 11 days of power consumption. With an average of four hours of sun per day, I'd need to buy 30 additional watts of solar electric power to meet the microwave's phantom need. At $6 per watt, that's $180. A $5 power strip has a 3,600 percent return on its investment!

Tools for Measuring Electricity Use

How do you know if the heating element is on or off? Unless you have a meter, you won't know.

The only way to be absolutely sure of how many watts an appliance actually demands is to plug the unit into a meter that measures watts (demand) and watt-hours (consumption). Power companies call this *sub-metering*. You may be able to borrow a meter from your electric company, much like the kWh meter out on the side of your house, but with a power cord on each end. This allows you to plug an appliance into it, let it run for a few days, and record the readings to determine the average daily power consumption. Two popular digital meters that can tell you the watts and watt-hours of any 120-volt appliance are the "Watts-Up?" (Figure 2.3) and the "Kill-A-Watt" meters. You can find these meters on the Internet (try <www.efi.org>, among others) or from catalog stores like Gaiam for under $100. This handy device lets you see exactly how much power each item in your home uses, while recording power consumption over time in watt-hours.

Another circumstance that makes metering the only true test of consumption is that the amp and watt ratings printed on electrical equipment are sometimes higher than what they may use in actual operation. This is especially true of devices with motors. Often the manufacturer lists the maximum power the appliance will draw. For example, a fan spinning normally will draw less power than a fan that has a stick jammed in it preventing the blades from turning.

The only limitation of commonly available household power meters is that they measure only 120-volt equipment and not higher powered 240-volt

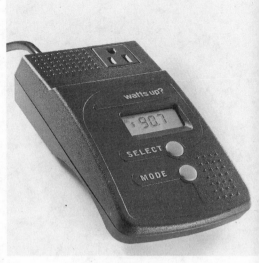

Fig. 2.3: Digital power meter for home appliances.
Credit: Electronic Education Devices <www.doubleed.com>.

appliances such as dryers and electric ranges. In addition, it is difficult to meter those items that don't have a cord that plugs into an outlet. Equipment such as electric water heaters and furnace blowers are usually wired directly to their own circuit breaker. You'll need a professional energy auditor with the right knowledge and equipment to determine the usage of these larger items.

Some electric companies are starting to show their customers real-time power use on the Web. This service allows you to see how much power your home is currently using. You can then turn things on and off to see what the effect is. Even if your power company doesn't offer an online or sub-metering service, or you don't have a digital meter, the power company's meter outside your house can provide you with some very useful information.

Your Electric Meter

My older neighbors tell me that people once read their own electric meters and paid their bill by the honor system. Then came the meter reader, and now electric companies can install meters that send power data back to corporate headquarters by way of electronic communication.

Fig. 2.4: Odometer kilowatt-hour meter.

Fig. 2.5: Dial kilowatt-hour meter.

The power meter is a tool, just like the odometer or speedometer in a car. Like an odometer, it keeps track of usage over time — not in miles but in kilowatt-hours. The electric meter also has a kind of speedometer function — it tells you how fast you're using that power. I recommend reading your meter on a daily or weekly basis because it gives you a current picture of your household power use. This is much more useful than studying an electric bill that reflects a month's usage from long ago when you may not remember what you did to use so much power. To read your meter, you'll first need to find it. There are several types and yours probably looks like one in Figure 2.4, 2.5 or 2.6

The meter is probably either on the side of the house or out on a power pole or pedestal near the house. Sometimes it's inside the house. You may have more than one meter for your home — including one for a specific use (electric heat, for example) that might be billed at a different rate. If this is the case, you might want to talk to your power company to see if it's worthwhile to continue this double-rate schedule. Household usage patterns change, and so do rate structures. If the meter was put in thirty years ago to take advantage of a lower electric heat rate in effect at that time, you may be paying extra for that use today.

If you live in a multi-family house, your meter will be grouped with one or more other meters. If there are multiple meters on your dwelling, you'll need the meter number to identify yours. The meter number is usually printed or stamped on the bottom of the meter, behind the glass cover. The same number should appear somewhere on your electric bill. If you can't find your meter or your meter number, call the electric company.

Each meter style allows you to read kilowatt-hours directly off the dial. You will need to determine if the last digit (the one farthest to the right) of your meter is

Fig. 2.6: Combination digital/dial kilowatt-hour meter.

a "one" or a "ten" digit. If it's blacked out, or always shows "0," or if your bills always show a kWh number that ends in 0, then the meter probably rounds off your kWh consumption to the nearest ten. This makes it harder to tell exactly what's happening on a daily basis, but checking the meter is still useful to watch for general consumption and usage patterns.

You may have a newer, digital meter. If so, the readings may be obvious, showing a number followed by a "kWh," or they may be somewhat cryptic, using codes that only the power company can decipher. If you have one of these meters, you may need to ask the electric company for advice on how to read it.

How to Read Your Electric Meter

There are two readings you can take off your electric meter. The first is the kilowatt-hour reading.

The odometer style of meter is easy to read. The numbers represent kilowatt-hours, and turn over as you use power. Write them down as you see them.

The dial style requires a closer look. Refer to Figure 2.5. Each of the four or five dials spin in the opposite direction of the next. Look at the leftmost dial first, and write down the number the needle points to. If the pointer is in between two numbers, record the lower number. Figure 2.5 reads 01759.

Now go back inside and have a normal day. Tomorrow at the same time, go out and read the meter again. Subtract yesterday's number from today's, and you have your first useful number: kWh per day. Think about what you've used power for — lights, laundry, refrigerator, space and water heating, air conditioning, and so on. Do this every day for a week and see if the daily total changes significantly. Maybe you use more power on the weekends when you're home, or maybe your consumption is highest when you do laundry. Maybe you plugged in a dehumidifier in the basement this week. Once you have an idea of your average daily power use, you can start assessing where that power is going. Unplug something or plug something in, then resume your daily meter reading. The difference in the reading is how much power the item uses, assuming everything else has remained the same. You can even try this on an hourly basis to determine, for example, how many kWh a dryer load consumes. Try this during different seasons. Winter and summer usage may be higher than spring and fall due to seasonal loads such as heat, fans, pools, etc.

The second number you will record off your electric meter is the power demand of the entire house, or how much electricity your house is using at the moment. When you look at your power meter, you will notice a spinning horizontal disk. The faster the disk spins the more power you're using. You can think of demand as "miles-per-hour" or how fast you're racking up the kilowatt-hours.

In order to record a demand reading, you will need the "Kh" value, usually located somewhere on the face of the meter. The Kh number is the factor used to convert disk rotations into watt-hours. So if you see "Kh 7.2" printed on the meter, it means that each rotation of the disk represents the consumption of 7.2 watt-hours. All you need to do is time the number of seconds it takes for one revolution of the disk, and then apply a simple formula.

Your job now is to figure out what is using power in the house. The "Appliance Use Chart" in Appendix C can give you an idea of the kinds of items to look for, but the best thing to do is identify everything that is plugged in, determine whether or not it's on or if it's a phantom load, and decide what action to take.

Math Box: Power Demand From Your Electric Meter

Here's the formula to determine watts being used by your whole house at any given time. This example assumes that you have timed one revolution of the spinning disc at 20 seconds:

Kh (watt-hours per revolution) × 3,600 (seconds per hour)
÷ time (in seconds) per revolution

7.2 × 3,600 ÷ 20 seconds = 1,296 watts, or 1.296 kW

Your house has a power demand of 1,296 watts. After an hour of consumption at this rate, you will have used just under 1.3 kWh.

High Bill Complaints

Many of the energy audits I perform are generated by high bill complaints from customers. They say things like "I can't be using that much power. There must be something wrong with the meter!"

A big part of the problem here is that by the time you see your electric bill, as much as six weeks could have passed since the time of the meter reading. One needs an excellent memory to recall all the activities that might have occurred during the period that raised concern. I show up for an electrical audit, and usually after poking around for long enough and asking personal, probing questions, the culprit makes itself known. Sometimes though, despite a thorough sleuthing of both the house and the owner's memory, I sometimes end up guessing at the cause of the unexpectedly high power use.

Electric meters are very simple electromechanical instruments that operate on basic laws of physics. The meter is calibrated before it is installed and it may drift a little over time, but (barring physical damage) not drastically. Sometimes the power company can do a side-by-side test with another meter. In the few instances I'm aware of where meters were tested, they were found to be off by less than five percent, with a 50-percent chance of being off in the customer's favor. The meter will not be functioning correctly one month and drastically off the next unless it's been physically damaged. The meter's accuracy may indeed worsen with age, but it will show small, gradual changes over a long period.

If you receive a high bill, don't immediately suspect that something is wrong with your meter. Instead, think about things that you may have done differently. The most likely things to cause a spike in your bill are:

- The addition of occupants in your home
- The addition of appliances
- Faulty appliances
- The use of electric resistance heating
- Use of appliances with large motors (pumps, compressors, air conditioners)
- Seasonal appliances
- An estimated bill or one that reflects a longer billing period

Did you plug in an electric blanket or small electric space heater? Did you turn on the dehumidifier, or get a new (or worse, used) freezer? Did you start a new hobby that requires an air compressor or lots of shop lighting? Do you use grow lights in the spring? Heat tapes in the winter? If you have a private water system, you may have a well pump or pressure tank problem causing the pump to run more than it should. Maybe your electric water heater thermostat has gone bad and is on all the time. If so, the symptom would be scalding hot water. Not enough hot water could be a sign of sediment in the tank, a problem that can also cause the heating element to run more often. Think about occupancy changes. Were the kids home from college for vacation bringing with them all their laundry? Did grandma turn up the heat in her bedroom?

Your eyes and ears can be the best tools you have to reduce your electrical use. Noticing what is plugged into electrical outlets and being aware of things that are on sounds easy, but we tend to get used to things such as the humming refrigerator or the bathroom light that's always on. When I do an energy audit, it begins before I turn into the driveway. I give the house a broad view from the street and look for clues. I once spotted an obvious cause of a high bill complaint before I even got out of the car — there were two 300-watt halogen flood lights on in broad daylight on the side of the garage. When I asked the owner why the lights were on, the answer was "the switch broke." The lights had been on for the past several months. How much was that costing him? You know the math now and it can be broken down into two parts — consumption, then cost:

$$300 \text{ watts} \times 2 \text{ lights} \times 730 \text{ hours run time each month}$$
$$\div\ 1{,}000 = 438 \text{ kWh per month}$$
$$438 \text{ kWh} \times \$0.10 \text{ per kWh} = \$43.80$$

The homeowner was paying nearly $44 a month for several months when all that was required to repair the problem was a one-dollar switch! Even after paying the electrician for an hour's time, the repair has about a one-month payback. An even more cost-effective fix would be to replace the switch with a motion sensor, and to replace the 300-watt bulbs with new, 27-watt fluorescent fixtures designed for outdoor use.

A bad connection somewhere in the power distribution system of the house — somewhere between the power meter outside and any electrical outlet in the house — can also lead to abnormally high power consumption. The strangest thing I have ever seen cause an unexplained high electric bill was a bird's nest in a box housing a power company's equipment. The bird's nest apparently acted as a load on the circuit, causing power consumption to increase.

As you can see, any number of circumstances can lead to a surprise in your electric bill — all the more reason to pay attention to your power consumption on a daily or weekly basis. If things suddenly go awry, you now have the knowledge to assess your power demand and consumption, as well as the data to compare your abnormally high usage to your average, or base, usage. Unplugging appliances or turning off breakers while watching how fast the electric meter spins can help point the way to the problem appliance. Sub-metering can identify potential problems with most household items. If you just can't find the problem, you can call your electric company or state energy office and ask for a professional energy audit, or perhaps for an electrician to look things over.

Daily Power Consumption

Now that you are thinking in terms of power consumption rather than the cost of your electric bill, let's take a detailed look at that bill. Daily power consumption is a useful figure to know because there may not always be the same number of days between meter reads. Depending on when the meter reader comes around, one month you may be billed for 25 days of power, while the next period might be 35 days. Some power companies estimate bills every other month or when severe weather may prevent an actual site visit. Kilowatt-hours per day can give you a better picture of reality and, if you read your own meter, kWh per day is what you'll want to know in order to determine how your changing habits and appliance usage affect your bill.

Find your last few electric bills and take some time to look at all the numbers. There are probably lots of them. You are looking for the dates of the last two meter readings (*not* the billing date); and the total number of kilowatt-hours used between those dates.

Some utilities have a tiered billing system, meaning that the power you use under a certain threshold is billed at a lower rate than power used over that threshold. So your bill may show that 150 kWh was billed at five cents per kWh and 654 kWh was billed at nine cents per kWh. You have used a total of 804 kWh (150 + 654) during the read period. Be sure to include all the power used on the same meter, during the same read period for this analysis.

Math Box: Kilowatt-Hours Per Day

Once you've determined the number of days during the read period, you can figure your daily power consumption. In this example, you've used 804 kWh in a 31-day month.

$$804 \text{ kWh} \div 31 \text{ days} = 25.9 \text{ kWh per day}$$

Examine a whole year this way and look for any patterns that may emerge.

Table 2.1: Sample Billing History.

Read date	No. days	kWh/month	kWh/day	Comments
January 15	30	1950	65	furnace blower, electric heat, lots of lights
February 12	28	1274	46	more furnace use, less electric heat
March 9	25	1045	42	same as February
April 15	37	1150	31	close to base-load, still a little heat
May 14	29	785	27	base-load use no heat, no air conditioning
June 15	32	1505	47	opened the pool, June 1st, air conditioning
July 19	34	1231	36	two-week vacation, left pool pump on
August 15	27	1810	67	pool, air conditioning, dehumidifier
September 16	32	1152	36	less of all the above
October 14	28	804	29	base-load
November 14	31	1220	39	start of heating season
December 15	31	1739	56	same as January, less electric heat

Sample Billing History

Let's examine the electrical use of our fictitious family, Ken and Connie Sumer. Figure 2.7 shows a year's worth of usage history showing monthly and daily power consumption. Note the seasonal pattern of higher use in the summer and winter and lower use in the spring and fall. In this scenario, spring and fall power usage represents the *base-load*. Electrical base-load usage represents those things that you do in your home fairly consistently throughout the year. Refrigeration, lighting, water use, clothes washes, cooking, and other routinely operated appliances are considered base-loads. Base-load is differentiated from seasonally variable loads such as heating, air conditioning, and swimming pools.

Looking down the list of numbers, we see a base-load of around 28 kWh per day or 840 kWh per month. If their summer vacation lasted for the whole month, we could see what the house itself uses in a month (all the appliances left on but unused). But their two-week break does offer a clue to consumption habits. The one-horsepower pool pump is left on 24 hours a day and uses 730 kWh every month (1 kW × 730 hours per month) or about 24 kWh per day. Subtracting 24 from the actual July usage of 36 kWh per day, the resulting 12 kWh per day is by far the lowest monthly reading — even lower than the base-load months. This tells us that occupant behavior contributes quite a lot to the home's power consumption.

I would advise the Sumers to use a timer on the pool pump because it probably doesn't need to run 24 hours a day to keep the pool clean. Start with eight hours a day and adjust up or down from there. The dehumidifier is a good candidate for sub-metering, as it's difficult to say exactly how hard it's working (i.e. how often it cycles on and off is directly related to how much moisture it is removing from the air).

Knowing these numbers can help tease out the usage of the air conditioner. For example, the base-load is 840 kWh per month, the pool pump uses 730 kWh per month, and we'll estimate the dehumidifier at 75 kWh per month, for a total of 1645 kWh per month. In August, they consumed 1810 kWh, so it is likely that the air conditioner used around 165 kWh that month. Turn up the air conditioner thermostat as high as you can stand it, and make sure that it's not doing battle with the heating system thermostat. By this I mean that if the heating thermostat is turned up higher than the air conditioner thermostat, both heat and AC will be running simultaneously.

As you can see from the winter months, the Sumers have a real problem with electric heat use. Electric heat may be confined to only one or two back rooms, or may be used to take the chill off a cool morning, but it still consumes lots of power. A cost-effective solution might be to extend some furnace ductwork to those areas. If that's impossible, maybe a small, sealed-combustion gas or kerosene heater is the answer. Either choice would save some money. Read more about heating choices in Chapter 5.

Electrical Energy Audit

Performing an electrical energy audit in your home is not difficult. You will need all of the tools and skills you have learned about in this chapter, a little planning, and a couple of hours. Your goal is to unravel the kilowatt-hours used in your home, and if you do a thorough job, the total will be something close to what you are being billed for. When I perform a professional audit, I hope my estimates are within ten percent of actual consumption. You should be able to get closer because you can spend more time in your home looking around

Efficiency Before Renewables

Ken and Connie Sumer wanted to go off the grid because they were tired of paying high electric bills. "We really want to go solar," they said. "The electric company keeps raising the rates!"

I quickly deflated their balloon. "Not anytime soon," I told them. "With bills like yours, the sun would dim for all the power you would ask it to deliver!" But now, after their energy audit, they can tell their cat box from the water heater, so there is hope. They need to continue with a more thorough review of their efficiency options and put their house on a strict energy diet.

"What is needed in your home," I explained, "is a major investment in efficient products. Those big power users — the electric range, water heater, and clothes dryer — need to go. You can replace all these items with gas burning appliances, and consider hanging your clothes out to dry and installing a solar water heater. Next, buy a new ENERGY STAR-labeled clothes washer, dishwasher, and refrigerator. Then, replace all of your incandescent light bulbs with new energy efficient compact fluorescent bulbs, put switched power strips on the entertainment equipment, adjust your habits so that you automatically turn things off when they are not in use, and only wash full loads of laundry and dishes. Call me when your electric usage falls to less than seven kilowatt-hours per day and we'll talk about a solar power system." Once usage falls this low, it may not be cost-effective to go solar because the electric bills will be quite low.

I suspect the Sumers will also need the services of a family counselor to accept these changes in their lifestyle.

and metering things than I can. But don't be alarmed if you can't add up every last kilowatt-hour — the really important thing is to identify those items that are big users, and those that you can actually do something about. The end result of the audit is threefold:

- Become aware of what appliances you have and how you use them.
- Assess how much power each appliance consumes.
- Decide what actions to take to reduce electric consumption — either by eliminating the item, changing your habits, or investing in a more efficient appliance.

To prepare for your energy audit, gather a year's worth of billing history (twelve monthly bills) from the power company. If you don't save your bills, call your power company and ask for a printout of your past year's usage broken out by the month. Don't ask for dollars, we only care about kilowatt-hours. Using the sample billing history above as an example, make four columns on a piece of paper. In the first column, record the read date, in the second column figure out the number of days in the read period, in the third put monthly kWh, and in the fourth column divide kilowatt-hours per month by the number of days in the read period (from column two) to arrive at actual kilowatt-hours per day. When you are finished, you will probably see some seasonal patterns in your usage.

The next step is to make a detailed list of all the appliances in your home, and note how long each one is on every day. Use the "Appliance Use Chart" in Appendix C as a guide to help you keep track. Look around the whole house, and don't miss a thing! Remember, not everything has an obvious power plug. Things like well pumps, central vacuums, central air conditioners, and heating equipment may be connected directly to the circuit-breaker box. Don't forget the garage, barn, attic, basement or crawlspace, and outside outlets.

Once you've completed your list, the next step is to determine the monthly power consumption of each appliance in kilowatt-hours. Do this by first getting the wattage from the appliance identification tag, by using a meter, or by looking it up on the "Appliance Use Chart" in Appendix C. Then, multiply the wattage of the appliance by its monthly operating time — this gives you the result in watt-hours. Divide watt-hours by 1,000 to arrive at kWh per month, and finally you can divide by the number of days in the month to arrive at the appliance's daily contribution to your power consumption.

Now that you have everything sorted out, you can further separate each appliance into either base-load or seasonal usage. Any seasonal loads such as heat, air conditioning, swimming pools and the like will contribute to seasonal variations in your electric bill. In general, the base-load should add up to the kWh figure you see on the bills during the spring and fall. This is the time when winter and summer incremental loads will not greatly affect your power consumption. Adding seasonal loads to the base-load should approximate your power consumption for those months. You may also be able to see in your billing history the times you were on vacation. You might see when the relatives visited around the holidays, or when the kids came home from college in the summer — consider them a seasonal load!

If you have electric hot water, you will need to determine the water heater's power consumption (read the chapter on hot water). You may be able to find the water heater's consumption by figuring everything else out first. The hot water heater probably uses something close to the amount of power that's missing from your base-load when compared to your power bills. I often tease certain usage out of a billing history this way, especially if usage or occupancy is inconsistent, or if the appliance cannot be separately metered. Hot water heaters should be considered a base-load item — unless you know you only use it seasonally. If you must have a hot water number to get you started with your audit, use 1,000 kWh per year per person plus 500 kWh per year lost through the jacket of the water heater. Be aware though, that this is a very general average. There are many variables affecting hot water consumption.

Electrical Diet

The following list offers generalized ways to save electricity *and* money. Savings ideas for specific appliances are listed in Chapter 3.

- Know what you have.
- Identify all circuits in your home.
- Know what is on, when, and why.
- Call your power company and ask if they provide an energy audit service. Many have a *demand-side-management* (otherwise known as DSM, or simply "efficiency") program that can help reduce your electric use.
- Eliminate phantom loads with switched power strips.
- Buy only the most efficient ENERGY STAR-labeled appliances.

- Use only fluorescent lights.
- One person, one light.
- Avoid electric resistance heat.
- Identify all motors and the times they are running. Ask yourself, "Does this need to be on now?"
- If you don't absolutely need it, turn it off and unplug it.
- Turn it lower, put it on a timer, use it less.
- Maintain equipment.
- Coordinate needs such as laundry with the whole family.
- Switch to a cheaper fuel source.
- Consider non-electric ways of doing things. See the Lehman Hardware catalog: 1(888) 438-5346 or <www.lehmans.com>

Home Power Safety

Your power company owns everything up to and including the electric meter, and you own (and are responsible for) anything on the house-side of the meter. The power lines travel overhead or underground from the meter to the house and enter the house at what is called the "service entrance." From here the power lines travel into the primary electrical safety device in your house — the circuit breaker box, or in an older home, the fuse box.

The breaker box has a main breaker, which can turn off the power to the entire house with the flip of a single switch. Many branch circuits distribute power to different parts of the house. Each branch circuit is protected by a circuit breaker or fuse. Circuit breakers and fuses are rated in amps, and are designed to stop the flow of current if the circuit they provide power to exceeds their amp rating. The fuse or breaker is sized to prevent the wires from overheating. Never use a larger fuse or breaker than is recommended by local and national electric codes.

When doing your own home energy audit, take a look at the breaker box. Are all the circuits identified? If not, it may be worthwhile to identify where each branch circuit goes in the house. This will help you determine what equipment is connected to the house wiring. I often perform energy audits in older homes with lots of history. Rooms, appliances, and circuits have been added and removed and the breaker box labeling may get overlooked with each renovation. If nothing else, identify the 240-volt breakers (the big ones) as they will lead to equipment that can be potentially big power users.

Good Grounds

Your home's electrical system has a built-in grounding or safety system. It is called a "ground" because the power company actually uses the earth as a reference point from which to measure voltage generated at its power plants. The earth is electrically neutral and does not actually carry any electricity from the power plant to your house, but it is easier to understand grounding if you imagine that it does. The earth is used as a collection point into which errant electrons can be safely discharged (just as lightning dissipates when it strikes the ground). This is why it's important to have your electrical system properly grounded by means of a copper rod that is driven or buried eight or more feet into the ground near where the power goes into the house. This grounding rod uses the same reference point as the power plants do — the earth. If there is a wiring problem in the house electrical system, the short-circuit current will be carried safely to ground, tripping the breaker or blowing the fuse as it goes. If the grounding system in your home is damaged or sub-standard, it can lead to a dangerous, even deadly situation. Instead of the current being carried safely to the ground, it could travel through some unlucky person who happens to be handling an electric appliance at the time.

Possible grounding problems can include:

- Loose, missing, or inadequate grounding rods
- Loose connections in the meter socket or breaker box
- Oxidation or corrosion on the meter socket or breaker box
- Improper wiring in electrical outlets
- Faulty equipment

If you are unsure about the grounds in your home electrical system, you can buy a power line condition tester at most hardware stores. This simple tester plugs into a power outlet and indicates if a potential problem exists. If in doubt, consult a licensed electrician.

Ground-fault circuit interrupter (GFCI) outlets or breakers have a high sensitivity to electrical malfunction. These are important — and in most places required — in places where risk of electric shock is high, including potentially wet locations such as kitchens, bathrooms, and the outdoors. A small amount of current will trip the breaker in the GFCI, cutting off power to the outlet long before the circuit breaker in the main breaker box even realizes there is a problem.

Stray Voltage

Poor grounding can cause a potentially serious problem called *stray voltage*. Stray voltage is a phenomenon where a tiny amount of electrical current can be measured between two points where you would not expect to find any electrical current. For example, if you feel a tingling sensation when you touch an appliance, you may be experiencing stray voltage. The likely cause is faulty wiring either in the house or in the piece of equipment that is plugged in. Stray voltage has been a concern on farms where it can cause cows to behave strangely, have a noticeable reduction in milk production, or perhaps experience a higher incidence of mastitis. In extreme cases, it can kill instantly and without warning. Stray voltage can be due to:

- Worn wire insulation
- Loose wiring connections
- Faulty grounding
- Faulty equipment
- Electrical shorts
- Unbalanced power loads
- Physical damage to electric lines or appliances
- Underground lines nicked by rocks or excavation equipment
- Animals chewing on wires
- Internal damage to motor windings
- Poorly grounded fixtures in metal electric boxes
- Corrosion
- And plenty of other oddball causes that can be difficult to find.

Personal Safety

When I was fourteen years old, I watched my mother have a near-death experience while doing a load of dishes. This is *not* how anyone should leave the world! She had plugged in the portable dishwasher, then grabbed the machine to pull it closer to the sink while at the same time reaching for the water faucet. ZAP! She screamed, then collapsed limp on the floor. She came to about fifteen seconds later. After returning from the hospital, she made a call to the electrician who rewired the house. He was amazed that she was still alive. That incident was more than stray voltage. Her shock was due to antiquated wiring with improper grounding. Faulty wiring in the dishwasher had caused the entire unit to become energized with electricity. When my mother reached for the grounded water faucet (the copper water pipe was buried, and therefore was electrically grounded), she became part of the electrical circuit. Had the wiring been up to code, there would have been a ground fault circuit interrupter that would have tripped first, instantly cutting power to the circuit.

My mother was lucky. Usually you only get one chance to learn such a lesson, and that lesson, sadly, is usually only for the survivors. Please take this warning to heart and have any questionable electrical problems inspected and resolved.

I once did an energy audit at a house where the owner felt a tingle while working on a ladder leaning on the aluminum-sided house. He thought it was interesting, but never did anything about it. There was nothing obviously wrong, but I can tell you that when your aluminum siding gives you a shock, it's time to investigate. I called the power company to report this and they came out to investigate. Before I left, I made the owner promise to call his electrician as well.

How the Sumers Add Up the Power

Connie Sumer cooks waffles for the family every Sunday morning. There are only four of them in the family, so you wouldn't think it would take very long, but she's not a very good cook — she burns a few. It takes about an hour to cook enough for the family. Good thing they like their waffles cold. The waffle iron sucks up power at the rate of 1,000 watts, or one kilowatt. After one hour, the waffle iron has used one kilowatt-hour of power, or about 8.2 cents worth of electricity.

Ken Sumer has a reading problem — reading puts him to sleep. He has a 100-watt reading lamp by the side of his bed. He turns it on at about nine o'clock every night, reads a page or two, and before long he's in dreamland. His alarm goes off at 6 a.m. but he doesn't seem to realize he's left the light on all night. Connie usually remembers to turn it off an hour later.

The light has been on for ten hours. 100 watts x 10 hours = 1,000 watt-hours, or one kWh, again about 8.2 cents worth of electricity. These few pennies add up to a wasteful habit that costs about $30 per year. His kids learn from his mistakes though, and that compounds the problem. They leave the lights on continuously. Actually, kids don't learn *from* their parent's mistakes, they *learn* their parent's mistakes. Personal experience is far more important than the best-intentioned parental admonitions, so this pattern of waste repeats itself throughout the house, and throughout history.

Appliance Energy Use

Power Use of Household Appliances

THIS CHAPTER LISTS THE MOST COMMON household electrical appliances, along with some comments about their energy usage, and ideas on how to reduce their contribution to your energy bills.

The "Appliance Use Chart" in Appendix C goes on to list over 100 household appliances along with their average power usage. It will help you to:

- Identify the electrical appliances you have.
- Quantify the power consumption of each appliance.
- Determine the operating cost of each appliance.

Common Electrical Appliances

Air Cleaner: A small, plug-in, household-size air cleaner uses approximately 40 watts on low, 60 on medium, and 120 on high speed. A high quality vacuum cleaner with a good filtering system may reduce or eliminate the need for an air cleaner. Smokers should have a place outside to keep second-hand smoke out of the house.

Air Conditioning: Keep the filter clean. Reducing humidity can offer increased comfort at higher temperatures. Using an air conditioner in conjunction with a ceiling fan will offer increased comfort levels at higher temperatures.

Answering Machine: A phantom load, always consuming power, from five to ten watts. Look at the "wall cube" adapter that plugs into the power outlet to find the wattage.

Aquarium, Filter Pump: Various sizes, 5 to 25 watts. Ten watts is common for a 20-gallon aquarium.

Aquarium, Heater: Various sizes from 50 to 300 watts. 75 watts is common for a 20-gallon aquarium. Keep the aquarium in a warm room.

Aquarium, Light: Various sizes — usually a 15-watt fluorescent bulb. These lights can be used for long periods, so if the light is not fluorescent, switch it over!

Battery Charger: Varies. The cheaper hardware-store variety is very inefficient (about 60 percent). A 6-amp charger might draw 125 watts from the wall socket, but only deliver 75 watts to the battery. Look for more efficient, two-stage electronic chargers.

Blanket, Electric: Various sizes. Check the tag. These will cycle on and off depending on the thermostat setting. Don't forget to turn it off in the morning! A timer will help if you are forgetful.

Blender: Average draw is about 400 watts, with a small variation based on the speed and how hard it is working.

Boom Box: Varies from 5 to 50 watts. A good choice for the off-grid house, they use far less power than a full-blown stereo for times when you don't need to rock the house.

Bug Zapper: These things are best at attracting more bugs and annoying the neighbors. Unplug it. Uses about 40 watts.

Clothes Dryer, Electric: A potentially high use item, the main power draw in an electric dryer is the 5,000-watt heating element. The thermostat will cycle the element on and off so that the clothes do not burn. This cycle factor may allow the heating element to be "on" about 75 percent of the time. If your clothes take an hour to dry, the heating element will consume about 3.75 kWh per load, and an additional 0.3 kWh per load for the drum motor. Some new dryers have moisture sensors that turn the unit off automatically when the clothes are dry. Depending on local fuel prices, it may be worth while to switch to a gas dryer. Use a front-loading, ENERGY STAR-labeled clothes washer that will remove more water from the clothes in the final spin, reducing dryer run-time.

Clothes Dryer, Gas: The only electrical consumption here is the motor, using about one quarter to one half kWh per load, depending on the length of the cycle. It is important that the gas dryer be properly vented so that combustion by-products don't enter the home. New gas dryers have electronic ignition so there is no wasteful pilot light.

Clothes Dryer Venting: Would you pour two or three gallons of water on your basement floor? Dryers need to be vented to the outdoors. Dryer ducting (especially the flexible type) can easily clog with lint and water, effectively stopping air movement and ensuring wet clothes and high electric bills. Keep ducting short with minimal turns that aren't too tight, avoid dips or valleys, and try to use smooth-wall rigid ducting. Flexible ductwork may be easy to install, but its corrugations slow the air movement down and restrict flow, and it's easy to crush. Clean the vent pipe once a year or as needed. Use a tight-sealing vent hood so that cold air doesn't enter the house through the dryer, and periodically look at the vent from the outside to be sure that air is blowing out of it.

If you don't connect the vent and allow all that moisture to stay in the house, you may develop indoor air quality problems along with structural damage caused by the moisture. If you want to capture some of the moisture from the dryer because your house is too dry, you need to find out why your house is so dry by reading Chapter 6. The worst case is that you have a dryer vented to the basement, and then operate a dehumidifier to deal with the excess moisture.

Clothes Dryer Diet

- Dry full loads, but don't overload the dryer as it will take more energy to dry the clothes.
- Don't over-dry. Some new dryers have moisture sensors that automatically turn the dryer off when clothes are dry.
- Size your washer and dryer for equivalent load sizes.
- Wash and dry similar types of clothing together. Different fabrics dry at different rates.
- Clean the lint trap before every load.
- Be sure the dryer is vented to the outside to avoid moisture and lint build-up in the house.
- Be sure the outlet vent ducting is free of tight turns, or elbows. Lint can build up at elbows, slowing airflow out of the machine, increasing drying time, and creating a potential fire hazard.
- Rigid venting is better than corrugated flex vent at keeping air moving and avoiding blockages.
- Avoid kinking or crushing the vent material.
- Don't exceed 25 feet of vent length (or per manufacturer's instructions).
- A front-loading washer spins clothes out better, reducing drying time.
- Run loads in succession to capture residual heat of previous load.
- Use the cool-down cycle to complete drying.
- If you like how your towels feel after coming out of the dryer, try using it for only ten minutes or so and then hang dry.
- If your clothes tend to take longer to dry than they used to, perhaps the thermostat or heating element has gone bad. Are the clothes hot but not dry? Check the venting system.
- Never vent a dryer into a crawlspace or attic.

Off-Grid Tip: Renewable Clothes Dryer

The best clothes dryer is one powered by the sun and wind. It's also the cheapest. A $10 clothesline will dry your clothes for free, and clothes will last longer air drying on a line than in a machine. Where do you think all that lint in the filter screen comes from?

Fig. 3.1: This dryer vent has already started to burn through.

Fig. 3.2: The inside of the dryer vent in Figure 3.1, showing heavy lint buildup.

Dryer Fires

The US Consumer Product Safety Commission estimates that in 1998, clothes dryers were associated with 15,600 fires, which resulted in 20 deaths and 370 injuries. Fires can occur when lint builds up in the dryer or in the exhaust duct. Lint can block the flow of air, cause excessive heat build-up, and result in a fire in some dryers.

Plastic or foil duct material can burn, and lint is highly combustible. Only rigid metal venting should be used. Metal venting also resists crushing better than plastic and foil, Reduced airflow and the resulting lint build-up reduce dryer efficiency and create conditions ripe for a fire. Reduced airflow can also cause overheating and wear out the clothes and the dryer faster. Many state and local municipalities have placed requirements on new and remodeling projects to include all-metal dryer venting.

Figure 3.1 shows a dryer vent that started to burn and Figure 3.2 shows the inside of that vent.

Clothes Washer: Top-loading washers use from 30 to 60 gallons of water and 300 to 500 watt-hours per load (not including water heating). Up to 90 percent of the energy needed to wash clothes is attributed to heating water, so using cold water is the biggest energy saving action you can take when washing clothes. There are many good cold water detergents on the market. Experiment!

My horizontal axis (front-loading) washer uses about 200 watt-hours per load for the longest possible load. The water well pump requires an additional 33 watt-hours to pump the 25 gallons (with extra rinse) needed by the machine. If you have municipal water, you'll save on water and sewer costs. The front loader's action is gentler, reducing wear and tear on clothes, and it spins much more water out of the clothes, allowing for shorter drying time.

Clothes washers are rated for efficiency using the Modified Energy Factor (MEF), a figure that considers washer capacity, electrical energy used, water heating energy required, and how dry the clothes are when they come out of the washer. The higher the MEF, the more efficient the washer is. When buying new, look for a Modified Energy Factor of 1.42 or higher.

Coffee Maker: A popular automatic coffee machine consumes about 100 watt-hours to brew six cups. When on, a coffee maker can draw 800–1,100 watts and cycle on and off to keep the coffee warm. This is a potentially big electric user, so turn it off when you're done.

Computers: Computer energy consumption varies from 10 to 40 watts for a laptop, and 90 to 150 watts for a desktop model. If your computer salesperson tells you it's better to keep the computer on all the time, ask if it would be better

---

Clothes Washer Diet

- Wash full loads only (but don't overload) to save water, time, and energy.
- Weigh a load of clothes once to get an idea of what 15 pounds (or whatever the rated weight for your machine) looks and feels like. When buying, size your washer and dryer for equivalent load sizes.
- Use cold water.
- Adjust water level to the lowest practical setting.
- Use the shortest cycle needed.
- Avoid using too much detergent to eliminate the need for an extra rinse.
- Pre-soak especially dirty clothes.
- Use a front-loading washer to reduce water use and drying time.

Off-Grid Tip

I use an ENERGY STAR-labeled laptop computer in my solar-powered home office that uses only about 20 watts and goes to sleep (using less than five watts) after ten minutes. A laptop is the most efficient choice, though generally more expensive to buy than desktop computers. The additional power consumption of a desktop model can strain your solar-power budget. In order to power the desktop computer from my solar electric system, I would need to buy an additional 170 watts (about $1,000 worth) of solar electric panels. Table 3.1 shows the savings of using a laptop six hours a day instead of a desktop model.

for him or her to pay your electric bill. There really is no good reason to keep the computer on when it's not in use. Today's modern electronics are not as prone to on-off cycling wear and tear. If you keep your computer on to answer your faxes, you would do well to invest in a lower-power fax machine. If you're away from the computer for more than an hour, turn it off. Screen savers do not reduce electricity use. Sleep settings help, varying the power draw from not much less than the rated power to a quarter of that, depending on the model.

Printers, copiers, scanners, and other computer peripherals are all phantom loads. Plug the computer and peripherals into a switched power strip so that you can turn everything off easily and avoid any phantom power consumption.

Crock Pot: Draws around 300 watts over a long period of time. These are in the expensive category of electric resistance heaters, but can still use less power than an electric oven (see Cooking Diet).

Dehumidifier: Before using a dehumidifier, be sure you need one. It should be a last resort in dealing with

Table 3.1: Laptop vs Desktop Computer Savings

Use laptop instead of desktop computer		
	kWh use	Power cost
Desktop	219	$21.90
Laptop	44	$ 4.38
Savings	175	$17.52
Savings based on 6 hours use per day, $.10/kWh		

moisture problems. Try to eliminate the source of the moisture problem. Have you installed gutters and sloped the ground away from your house to drain water away from the foundation? Does the problem occur throughout the house or just in certain areas? Showers, plumbing leaks, unvented dryers, and dirt floors can contribute to high humidity in your home. Human activity

Dehumidifier Diet

- Remove moisture at its source and prevent it from entering your home.
- Use a hygrometer to avoid over-drying.
- Avoid using dehumidifiers below 60°F.
- Refer to Table 3.2 for help in proper dehumidifier sizing.

creates moisture that should be removed at the source (showers and cooking). Perhaps an exhaust fan is all that's needed to remove moist air from a damp room. This can be accomplished in smaller homes by running the bathroom exhaust fan. For larger homes, an air-to-air heat exchanger would be an efficient way to improve indoor air quality and deal with moisture problems. You can read more about these issues in Chapter 6.

If you do need a dehumidifier, buy the correct size. Dehumidifiers are sized by the amount of water the appliance removes from the air in pints per 24

Table 3.2: Dehumidifier Selection Guide.

Values in table indicate dehumidification required in pints per 24 hours, based on the area of the space to be dehumidified and the conditions that would exist in that space when a dehumidifier is not in use.					
Condition of the living space before dehumidifying during warm & humid outdoor conditions.	Area in square feet				
	500	1000	1500	2000	2500
Moderately damp — space feels damp and has musty odor only in humid weather.	10	14	18	22	26
Very damp — space always feels damp and has musty odor. Damp spots show on walls and floor.	12	17	22	27	32
Wet — space feels and smells wet. Walls or floor sweat, or seepage is present.	14	20	26	32	38
Extremely wet — laundry drying, wet floor, high load conditions.	16	23	30	37	44
Source: Association of Home Appliance Manufacturers www.aham.org					

Dishwasher Diet

- Wash only full loads.
- Avoid using the temperature boost setting — water heating can account for up to 80 percent of the energy required by a dishwasher.
- Keep your water heater temperature as low as possible and let the dishwasher heat what it needs.
- Try different settings and detergents to see which gives you the best performance (my dishes come out cleaner by filling the soap dispenser only two thirds rather than completely full).
- Air dry dishes — use the "no-heat dry" setting or allow dishes to air dry by opening the door after the wash cycle is complete.
- Don't rinse dishes before loading into the dishwasher — just scrape them off.
- Use the shortest possible cycle.
- Check the filter to be sure it is clear of food particles.

hours. Efficiency ratings are described as how much water can be removed for each kWh of power used. These ratings range from 2.7 pints per kWh (less efficient) to 5.7 pints per kWh (more efficient). To help you decide how much drying power you need, see the dehumidifier sizing chart, Table 3.2.

A dehumidifier's operation is similar to that of an air conditioner, and they can use nearly as much power. If you must use one, try not to overuse it. Comfortable relative humidity in a home is around 35–55 percent, and up to 70 percent is tolerable for long-term paper storage. Invest in a hygrometer to keep track of relative humidity so that you can adjust the dehumidifier's controls accordingly. Dehumidifiers use condensing coils to remove moisture. If the space is too cold (below 60°F), reaching the condensation point is more difficult and may cause icing of the coils, greatly reducing the dehumidifier's efficiency.

Dishwasher: Older dishwashers use 12 or more gallons of water, while those built after 1994 use between seven and ten gallons. My Asko dishwasher uses under five gallons of water per wash. Most of the energy used by a dishwasher is due to heating water, but the power consumption will vary with the control settings. Some have the option to raise the water temperature higher. Without using the temperature boost or heat dry cycle, the Asko uses 0.5kWh per normal cycle. With the temperature boost on, it will use 1.3 kWh per load, and the heat-dry cycle uses an additional 0.4 kWh. In this case, keeping the temperature boost and heat-dry cycles off saves 312 kWh per year if I do five loads a week.

Table 3.3: Dishwasher Savings

Dishwasher savings potential			
Full heat settings (kWh use)	No water temp boost, no heat dry (kWh use)	Energy savings (kWh)	Annual cost savings
390	130	260	$26.00
Savings based on 5 loads/week, $.10/kWh			

Table 3.3 is a savings table that shows the potential savings of turning off the heat-dry setting on the dishwasher.

Dishes: By Hand or by Machine?

Does it use more water and energy to wash dishes by hand or in a machine? Finally, there is a definitive answer. A study conducted by the University of Bonn, Germany, reported that volunteers washing dirty dishes in a sink used an average of 27 gallons of water and 2.5 kWh of water-heating energy to wash a complete 12-place dinner setting. An automatic dishwasher handling the same number of equally dirty dishes used only 4 gallons of water and about 1.5 kWh of total electrical energy. After the volunteers were finished with their task, about half the dishes were judged to be "really dirty" or at least not acceptable to be placed on a dinner table, while the machine dishwashers offered consistently cleaner dishes.

Fan, Bath: Look for an energy-efficient model using less than 40 watts with a "sone," or sound intensity, rating of less than 1.5 sones. Be sure it is vented to the outdoors, not into the attic where it can cause moisture, mold, or rot problems by introducing moist air from the house. Using rigid ducting will increase the airflow through the fan. Flexible ductwork may be easy to install, but its corrugations slow the air movement and restrict flow, while sagging vents can trap mold-growing moisture. Make sure the vent joints are properly sealed with foil tape, and keep elbows to a minimum.

Run the fan during and at least 15 minutes after showers to remove moisture from the room.

Fan, Attic: One way to cool your house in the summer is to use a fan that exhausts hot air from the attic and pulls cooler, outside air into the attic. This setup only works if there is enough air available from outside the attic — meaning outside the *house* — to make up for the air being removed by the fan. What you want to avoid is pulling conditioned air from the living space below into the attic, wasting energy and possibly bringing potentially damaging moisture into the attic. The attic should be well insulated and completely air-sealed from the living space below.

Using a whole-house exhaust fan for ventilation during warmer weather can be accomplished by using a fan installed in the top-floor ceiling that pulls air from the living area and exhausts it into the attic. In this case, it is important to ensure that there is enough free-vent area between the attic and the outdoors to match the air flowing through the fan. It is equally important to be sure that any air leaks between the attic and the house are thoroughly sealed, and that the exhaust fan is covered with insulation and seals tightly when not in use. This will prevent heat loss from the house during winter, and potentially damaging moisture problems in the attic. Tamarack Technologies makes one such whole-house fan.

You may want to consider adding insulation to the attic, which will keep excess heat out of the living area and reduce your heating and cooling loads. Solar-powered, temperature-controlled attic fans are available that will operate automatically when the sun is out and the attic is hot.

Fan, Ceiling: Use a reversible fan and switch it so it blows downward in the winter, bringing the heat down to where people are. In the summer, reverse the direction to keep the air moving. Turn off the fan when you're not in the room — they only work when someone is there to enjoy the breeze!

Fan, Window: On average, a three-speed box style window fan will use 60 watts on low speed, 100 watts on medium, and 200 watts on high. Many people run fans at night for "white noise" to block out extraneous sounds and help them sleep better. It's probably just as easy to get into the habit of sleeping without the fan as it was to get used to sleeping with it. Try earplugs, or if you really need white noise, try tuning a small radio to the static in between stations and put it across the room. It will save you a noticeable amount of power and money.

Fan, Range Hood: These are recommended to remove moisture, heat, and odors from the kitchen. Beware the high-powered exhaust fan as it may back-draft the chimney used for the heating system or water heater, pulling exhaust fumes into the house. If it's a big enough fan, you may need "make-up" air from a dedicated duct or nearby open window.

Fax Machine: A phantom load. If you're not expecting faxes, put it on a power strip and turn it off when not in use.

Garage Door Opener: The typical 0.5HP motor used ten minutes a day consumes about 100 kWh per year. There is an additional phantom load of around four watts for the remote-control receiver electronics, adding up to 35 kWh per year.

Hair Dryer: A big user in the resistance heat category. Maybe it's time to try the natural look. My wife's hairdresser gets a big kick out of the fact that she doesn't use a hair dryer. We both are amazed that she is the hairdresser's only client who doesn't regularly use a blow dryer!

Heat Lamp: You may not like this, but if you need heat, get it from your heating system. Heat lamps are high wattage incandescent bulbs ranging from 200 to 500 watts.

Heat Tape: A last resort to keep pipes from freezing. Look for the root cause of the problem, such as a cold air draft blowing on the pipe. Look closely around the pipe for clues. Use caulk or expanding foam to seal holes that may exist in the basement wall or perimeter band. Insulate the perimeter band joist cavities, as well as the pipes.

Heater, Engine Block: These are not all that necessary anymore due to low temperature fuel mixes and low viscosity engine oil. My diesel car and diesel generator have no trouble starting down to 25° below. I am diligent about using the proper grade of oil for cold weather, which helps greatly for low temperature starting. If you really need a block heater, put it on a timer to turn on 30 to 60 minutes before you need the vehicle.

Heater, Electric Baseboard: The worst offender for electricity abuse. Electric heat can turn your dollars to dust faster than you can count them. Baseboard heat demands 250 watts of power per foot. An average size home might need 50 to 100 feet, depending on the climate and size of the home.

Heater, Portable: Those little cube-style electric heaters average about 1500 watts. After an hour, it has used 1.5 kWh. Those portable electric, oil-filled radiator-style heaters are no exception; 1500 watts is 1500 watts, despite what the advertising says. The advantage these heaters have is "thermal mass," meaning the material inside can "store" heat, much like a rock outside stays hot for a few hours after the sun sets, then radiates the heat to you. These heaters may save a bit because the radiant heat helps you feel warmer at a lower thermostat setting.

Heating System, Hot Water Boiler: Varies depending on size and your climate. A boiler circulator pump uses about 100 watts. A well-insulated and air-tight house, with a properly sized energy-efficient heating system, coupled with a programmable thermostat will help keep your heating costs low.

Heating System, Furnace: Varies depending on size and your climate. A furnace-blower motor can use 250 to 1,000 watts, depending on the size. A rule of thumb for furnace-fan power consumption is that you can expect to use approximately one kWh for every therm (Ccf) of natural gas, gallon of oil, or gallon of propane. Again, a well-insulated and air-sealed house with a properly sized, energy-efficient heating system, coupled with a programmable thermostat will help keep your heating costs low.

Hot Tub: A well-insulated outdoor hot tub can use from 3 to 12 (or more) kWh per day depending on the climate, size, and temperature. If insulation is missing from the bottom or sides, you can try spraying on a two-part urethane insulation. These "Froth-Packs" can be found at good hardware stores or from efficiency product suppliers such as The Energy Federation <www.efi.org>. Most hot tubs are electrically heated, but they can be retrofitted to operate less expensively off a boiler heating system. Contact a good plumber or heating contractor.

Humidifier: Why is the air inside your house too dry? Human activity produces moisture. If your house is too dry, it may be due to excessive air moving through the house, carrying all that moisture outside. Try to eliminate the need for humidification by decreasing air migration into and out of the house. If you need to run a humidifier in the winter, be sure to keep an eye on humidity levels with a hygrometer so that the relative humidity does not rise over 40 percent. See also Chapter 6.

Lighting: OK, maybe you tried those efficient bulbs in the past and you gave them away. Let me reassure you that efficient lighting products have come a long way in the past ten years and I would encourage you to try them again. Lights are one of the easiest things in your home to make energy efficient by switching to low wattage compact fluorescent lamps (CFLs). There are many sizes and styles of CFLs on the market today using one-quarter to one-third the power with equivalent light output, and lasting six to ten times longer than an incandescent light. Those that have electronic (not magnetic) ballasts generally offer a better light quality, and flicker-free start-up and operation. Ask your electric company if they have a rebate program for CFLs. If the lights are in low-use locations such as closets, or in places where they tend to be turned on and off a lot, consider using a low-wattage incandescent bulb instead of a fluorescent bulb, as fluorescent lights may fail prematurely if used in these locations. When choosing a CFL, think about the incandescent wattage you normally use, and then divide by three. That is the fluorescent wattage you should use to replace it.

Lighting Diet

- One person, one light.
- If it's on for more than two hours a day, replace it with a CFL.
- Out of the room for more than 15 minutes? Turn off the light!
- Use day lighting wherever possible.
- Use light-colored lampshades.
- Keep bulbs and shades clean — dirt absorbs light, reducing output.
- Avoid halogen torchiere lighting. These lamps use from 250 to 600 watts and are a fire hazard. You can actually cook on top of them! Look for energy efficient torchieres using dimmable CFLs.
- Put lights where you need them. There are many kitchens with recessed lights shining wasted light onto the top of cabinets! Use low wattage, under-cabinet lights in the kitchen.
- Use overhead task lighting to concentrate light where you need it, allowing you to turn off background lights.
- Look into "Light Tubes" tubular skylights that bring light through the roof and attic, around corners and into your living area. Some brand names are Sun Tunnel, Sola-Tube and Natural Light.
- Fluorescent lighting runs cooler than incandescent, offering greater summer time comfort.
- To learn about efficient outdoor lighting and light pollution, look into the International Dark Sky Association at <www.darksky.org>.

Lighting Action

ENERGY STAR has issued a call to action:

"Make your next light an ENERGY STAR. If every US household makes their next light an ENERGY STAR, the reduction in air pollution would be equivalent to removing 1.2 million cars from the road for one year. This would amount to 8.5 billion kWh in energy savings. That's enough to power over 808,000 homes for one year yielding $840 million in savings on power bills nationally."

Traditional incandescent light bulbs are based on a design that's over 120 years old! Would you buy anything else with such antiquated technology? (Well, yes, your car's engine is about as old, and so is its starter battery, but that's another subject). Incandescent lights are only about ten percent efficient at turning electricity into light; the rest is wasted as heat. This puts them in the electric resistance heat category.

The next wave in lighting technology is the Light Emitting Diode (LED). LEDs are those little red or green lights you see on most appliances these days. They are extremely efficient and very long lasting. LED lights are being used in some traffic signals where they not only save energy, they greatly reduce maintenance costs. The city of Syracuse installed LED traffic lights at 299 intersections, saving $225,000 in energy costs each year. The city of Chicago estimates that it could save $4.4 million a year by replacing all of its traffic lights with LEDs. White light LEDs have not yet been found to be very efficient, and this is an area of current research. Some manufacturers are putting an array of whitish-blue LEDs in a standard bulb housing that will last about 100,000 hours, and use about 4% of the power of an incandescent light, but the color rendition may not be appropriate for all locations.

Fluorescent Lights: Mercury Content, Disposal and Cleanup

A coal power plant will emit ten milligrams (mg) of mercury to produce the electricity to light an incandescent bulb over five years, but only 2.4 mg of mercury to run a compact fluorescent (CFL) bulb for the same time. A typical CFL contains about 4 mg of mercury, while a watch battery can contain between 5 and 20 mg.

Anything that contains mercury should be treated as hazardous waste. Check with your local waste collection facility for proper disposal locations. If fluorescent lights break, do not vacuum! Using rubber gloves, pick up the big pieces and put them into a plastic bag. Use wide tape to pick up smaller pieces, wash the floor, and put all cleaning materials in the plastic bag. Bring the bag to your local household hazardous waste collection facility as you do your dead mercury-containing batteries.

If you have trouble getting the kids (or your parents or your spouse) to turn off the lights, you might need to take some more serious action:

- Occupancy sensors will sense motion (or lack of it) and turn the light on or off accordingly.
- For outdoor lights, use motion and/or light sensors so the light is on only when you need it.
- Try fines — my parents would fine us kids 25 cents every time they saw one of our lights on and we weren't using it. That was a big chunk of our allowance money back then.

Table 3.4 is a savings table that shows the potential annual savings from switching all your lights from incandescent to fluorescent.

Microwave: Uses a lot of power (up to 1,000 or more watts) while operating, but overall a very efficient way to cook, using from 11 to 50 percent of the energy of conventional ovens. Keeping the inside of the oven clean increases efficiency. See Table 3.5 for a comparison of cooking energy costs.

Table 3.4: Lighting Savings.

Annual lighting use and savings			
Incandescent kWh	CFL kWh	kWh savings	Energy savings
1,000	333	667	$67
Savings based on $.10/kWh			

Motors and Pumps: In general, motors of average efficiency will use about 1,000 watts for every rated horsepower. The actual power demand depends on the motor's size, efficiency, and how hard the pump is working. Surge current is a big issue in motors, using from two to ten times more power to turn on as compared to the amount of power they use to run continuously. So if you have a furnace that "short cycles," or a well pump with a bad pressure tank, the motors in the equipment will cycle on and off more frequently, dramatically increasing their power consumption.

Range top, Oven, and Broiler: If you have a gas range, keep the burners clean to ensure maximum efficiency and reduce carbon monoxide production. A blue flame indicates good combustion. If you see much yellow in the flame, call for service. It is difficult to find a new gas range without electronic ignition and "glow bars" in the oven requiring electric power.

Table 3.5: Cooking Energy Cost Comparison.

Appliance	Temp. °F	Time	$/unit	Unit	Btus used	Energy units used	Cost	Pounds CO_2
Electric oven	350	1 hour	$0.10	kWh	6,824	2.00	$0.20	2.7
Gas oven (nat'l)	350	1 hour	$1.00	therm	11,200	0.11	$0.11	1.4
Gas oven (LPG)	350	1hour	$1.40	gallon	11,200	0.12	$0.17	1.6
Frying pan	420	1 hour	$0.10	kWh	3,071	0.90	$0.09	1.2
Toaster oven	425	50 min	$0.10	kWh	3,241	0.95	$0.10	1.3
Crockpot	200	7 hours	$0.10	kWh	2,388	0.70	$0.07	0.9
Microwave oven	'high'	15 min	$0.10	kWh	1,228	0.36	$0.04	0.5
Adapted from Consumer Guide to Home Energy Savings								

Math Box: How Much Will a Single CFL Save Over its Lifetime?

If you replace a 100-watt incandescent bulb operating four hours a day with a 25-watt CFL, it will reduce demand by:

$$100 - 25 = 75 \text{ watts}$$

At four hours per day, it will reduce annual consumption by:

$$75 \times 4 \times 365 \div 1{,}000 = 109.5 \text{ kWh per year}$$

If you pay 10 cents per kWh, the bulb will save you:

$$109.5 \times 0.10 = \$10.95 \text{ per year in electricity costs.}$$

If the bulb costs you $10, it pays for itself in less than one year. If the CFL lasts for 10,000 hours, a burn time of four hours a day means that the bulb will last 6.8 years. An incandescent bulb's lifetime is only about 1,000 hours, or about 250 days at four hours per day. The lifetime energy savings of this 25-watt CFL is:

$$\$10.95 \text{ per year} \times 6.8 \text{ years} = \$74$$

What about the cost of the bulbs? You would need to buy ten incandescent bulbs at a total cost of about $6, in place of the single $10 CFL. Over 6.8 years, the CFL will save you a total of:

$$\text{(total energy cost savings)} - \text{(the difference in bulb costs)}$$
$$\text{OR:}$$
$$\$74 - (\$10 - \$6) = \$70$$

Cooking Diet

- Use the right size pot on the stove burner. A six-inch pot on an eight-inch burner wastes over 40% of the heat produced by the burner.
- Use flat bottom pans for better heat transfer.
- Cover pots and pans to keep heat in.
- Double up — steam vegetables over the pasta water.
- Check the oven door gasket.
- Keep burners clean.
- Keep range top reflectors clean.
- Inspect the oven wall insulation, especially if it has been in storage for a while.
- Minimize pre-heating time. Most ovens take only ten minutes or so to heat up.
- Use a meat thermometer to avoid overcooking.
- Water will not get any hotter after it's boiled — turn boiling water off!
- Allow sufficient air circulation inside the oven — avoid using foil on the racks, don't overfill the oven, stagger multiple pans.
- Avoid opening the oven door while it's on.
- If you keep an electric coffee maker on all day, try an insulated carafe instead
- Food continues to cook after the heat is turned off and the food is removed from the oven. Turn off the oven a few minutes early and use residual heat to finish the job.
- Use the range hood exhaust fan to remove excess moisture produced by cooking.
- Use a crock pot for soups or stews that need long simmering times.
- Pressure cookers reduce cooking times.
- Use a microwave oven to reduce overall cooking energy consumption.
- Avoid using foil around burners as it can block air flow and reduce efficiency.
- See Table 3.5 for a list of common cooking methods and their energy costs.

Refrigerators and Freezers: A new refrigerator or freezer can use as little as one-half the energy of a ten-year-old model. See the refrigerator section of the "Appliance Use Chart" in Appendix C to get an idea of savings potential based on type and age.

According to the Alliance to Save Energy, refrigerators in the US alone use the equivalent of the output of more than 20 large nuclear power plants. If all the nation's households used the most efficient refrigerators, electricity savings would eliminate the need for about ten large power plants.

I've heard it a hundred times: "I got a great deal on that fridge. Free!" Are you the proud owner of a free refrigerator or freezer from your brother-in-law? Well the old saying, "free ain't cheap" applies perfectly here. If you have an old refrigerator it's probably costing you more than it should to keep your food cold. The Sumers' fridge was old enough to replace anyway, but I metered it just for kicks. I estimated its use at about 2,000 kWh per year (I always add 500 kWh per year to my best estimate for those lovely colors from the 1970s: olive green, burnt orange, or chocolate brown). The metering proved a good idea — the fridge used just over 3,000 kWh per year! The likely cause of this was age, leaky door gaskets, and a self-defrost heating coil that

Cooking Efficiency

Research by the Electric Power Research Institute (EPRI) reports very high efficiency from new magnetic induction ranges using high frequency AC magnetic fields to induce heat in the bottom of iron-based cookware. Because the energy is transferred directly to the cookware, the range top's ceramic heating element stays cool. This heat transfer method has an efficiency of 92 percent (losing only eight percent of its energy as waste heat) compared to 72 percent for a standard electric range and 47 percent for a residential gas range, and only 30 percent for a commercial gas range.

appeared to be stuck on. I suspected this because my watt meter indicated the fridge used more power than I would have expected. While your fridge or freezer is running, you can expect it to use between 200 and 400 watts. High efficiency compressors and better insulation reduce both power demand and run time.

If you happen to have an old (1950s or earlier) manual defrost fridge or freezer (the ones that look like an old Buick), you may want to think twice before replacing it. Those nice thick walls are well insulated and they were built to last. Definitely meter this old gem before replacing it.

Refrigerators, Gas: Refrigerators are available that will run on liquid petroleum (LP) gas, natural gas, or kerosene. These are typically found in off-grid homes or camps where there is no electricity or where electricity is at a premium. Most are not very big — nine cubic feet is the average size. See the analysis comparing gas to electric refrigerators in the accompanying sidebar.

Satellite Dish (including receiver): A phantom load (20 to 40 watts) and a perfect candidate for putting on a switched power strip.

Swimming Pool Filter Pump: See motors. Put it on a timer and find the optimum time needed for proper cleaning. Choose a timer rated for the size of the motor.

Buying a New Refrigerator

How do you know when it's time to replace your refrigerator?

The answer, as usual, is that "it depends." It depends on the difference between operating costs of the old one and a new one. A refrigerator is a major electric user in your home with a high up-front purchase cost, a long lifetime (15 years or more), and the potential to cost you far more in operating expense than purchase price. Therefore, you don't want to buy one if you don't need to, but if you do need a new refrigerator, you want to get a model that will not be a long-term burden on your electric bill.

The only way to be sure of how much power your fridge or freezer consumes is to meter it. A week is a good length of time to meter the fridge to get the best data, though after a day you will have a good idea of what it uses. I have metered refrigerators for only two hours with a digital meter and was able to accurately estimate their annual consumption to within ten percent. I would not recommend this short a time though, as the defrost cycle can come on at any time, throwing off your calculations.

Depending on the size and type, a new energy-efficient fridge will use from less than 1 to 1.5 kWh per day. Look for the new size and style that you need, avoid energy-guzzling options such as cold water taps and automatic ice makers. When you have a model in mind, subtract its annual kWh consumption (from the yellow Energy Guide tag) from your current refrigerator's consumption and multiply that figure by your cost per kWh. This is your annual energy cost savings. If you don't have access to a watt-hour meter, the Appliance Use Chart compares refrigerator and freezer usage by size and age.

Here's an example of how much a new refrigerator can save:

Your old, olive green fridge from the 70s uses 2,000 kWh per year. The new ENERGY STAR model uses only 500 kWh per year.

2,000 − 500 = 1,500 kWh per year saved.
1500 kWh × $0.10 per kWh (use your own power cost here)
= $150 per year savings.

Your new fridge costs $700, which gives you a 4.7-year simple payback ($700 ÷ $150), or a first year, tax-free return on your investment of 21.4 percent ($150 ÷ $700). With these numbers at your disposal, you can decide if it's worthwhile to repair or replace an old or broken refrigerator or freezer.

Television: A phantom load of up to 12 watts. If you leave it on for background noise, try the radio instead; it will use much less power. Use a switched power strip to eliminate its phantom power draw.

VCR: Another phantom load of up to 13 watts. Put it on your entertainment center's switched power strip.

Water Cooler/Heater: These are convenient, but may use more than the convenience is worth. Put a pitcher of cold water in your fridge and use the stove or microwave to heat water as you need it.

Water Heater: A water heater is probably the second largest energy user in your home (after the heating system). Read Chapter 4 on water heaters for ways to trim hot water costs.

Waterbeds: Waterbeds have heaters ranging from 150 to 375 watts. An unmade king-size bed can use up to 1,800 kWh per year, a queen up to 1,200. Be sure that your waterbed is covered and insulated so that it is not heating your bedroom.

Waterbed Diet

• Avoid heating the room with your waterbed! Keep the bed covered and the room heated.
• Keep waterbeds made. The blankets will provide insulation.
• Keep the mattress away from exterior walls to prevent heat conduction through the walls.
• Keep the temperature as low as possible.
• Consider a quilted, insulating slip cover, a second mattress or a foam insulating pad that may allow you to turn the heater down or off.
• Look for the "soft-side" style with more built-in insulation.

Refrigerator and Freezer Diet

- Check the gasket by closing the door on a piece of paper. You should feel some resistance when the paper is pulled from the door.
- Clean the condenser coils behind or under the fridge. The black coils of metal tubing you see in back of (or under) your fridge are used to transfer the heat from inside the fridge, to outside of it. Any dust accumulation around the coils will act as insulation and the fridge will work harder. Unplug the fridge every few months and vacuum the coils and around the fridge.
- Provide three inches or more of space on all sides of the fridge to allow air to move and heat to escape from the cooling unit.
- Locate the refrigerator out of direct sunlight.
- Let air circulate between items in the fridge.
- Turn off the "anti-sweat" feature. A switch inside the fridge labelled "power saver" or "winter/summer" turns on a heating element inside the fridge to prevent condensation from forming on the outside of the unit during humid summer months. If the condensation bothers you, save energy and wipe it off.
- Don't put the fridge next to heat generators such as the stove or dishwasher.
- Let hot food cool before putting it in the fridge.
- Take out everything you need at the same time. Do the same with putting things back.
- Close the door! ·
- Defrost the freezer before ice becomes a quarter inch thick.
- Keep the proper temperature. Refrigerators should be kept at 36° to 40°F and freezers at 0° to 5°. To check the temperature, try using the outdoor probe of an indoor/outdoor thermometer.
- Keep it full! Fridge or freezer, it will use less power if you keep it full. It is easier to keep jugs of water or ice cold than it is to keep air cold.

This is due to the *thermal mass* of a material. The denser a material is, the longer it takes to absorb and release heat or cold. Opening the door of an empty fridge allows most of the cold air to escape and be replaced by warm air. The fridge then comes on to cool off the air inside. If the fridge is full and you open the door, it will take a long time for the food items inside to lose their cool. They have more thermal mass than air and hold the cold much as a rock outside stays hot long after the sun sets. A full fridge or freezer keeps food colder longer in the event of a power failure.

- Humidity makes the fridge work harder: cover foods to keep moisture in and wipe containers dry before putting them in the fridge.
- Mark items for fast identification.
- Size the fridge and freezer appropriately for your needs. Too big wastes energy and food.
- Defrost frozen foods in fridge, not the microwave.
- Remove the two 60-watt bulbs (which are really electric heaters) from the inside of the refrigerator, and put in a single 15-watt bulb. Although they will work, refrigerators are not a great place for compact fluorescent bulbs due to the cold.
- It's more efficient to make ice in ice trays than to have an in-door icemaker.
- Manual defrost models use less power than auto defrost.
- Chest freezers typically use less power than upright freezers.
- In general, top-mounted freezers use less power than side-by-side models.
- Avoid options such as automatic icemakers, cold water, and specialized compartment warmers.
- Consolidate! Try to use only one refrigerator/freezer unit.

Electric vs. Gas Refrigeration Costs

Is a gas refrigerator the right choice for you? It depends on what your needs are. The short answer is that they are worthwhile where electric costs are at a premium. Let's look at the numbers.

A popular gas fridge uses about two gallons of propane gas per week. We know (from Table 1.2 in Chapter 1) that there are 91,690 Btu in a gallon of LP gas.

• In one week the fridge uses 183,380 Btus.

• In one day, it consumes 26,197 Btus.

Now let's translate this into equivalent kWh. First, we'll need to convert kWh to our common energy denominator, the Btu.

• We know that there are 3,413 Btus in a kWh.

26,197 Btu per day ÷ 3,413 Btu per kWh = 7.67 kWh per day.

Over the course of a year, this gas fridge uses the equivalent of 2,800 kWh. That's five times more than a new fridge twice the size. In reality though, this is an unfair comparison because if you were to run this fridge on electricity, it might only use about 1,500 kWh per year (or 14,026 Btus per day). The reason is that the conversion of LP gas to usable cooling energy by the fridge is not a very efficient process. Much energy is lost as heat.

A gas refrigerator might be the right choice if your electric cost is more than twice your gas cost per equivalent Btu, or where you have no electricity and can easily transport gas bottles to the site.

What would it cost to operate the gas fridge over the course of a year?

2 gallons LPG per week × 52 weeks per year = 104 gallons LP gas per year.

If you pay $1.50 per gallon of LPG, that's $156 per year. To run this fridge on electricity at $0.10 per kWh would cost $150 per year. A toss-up.

However, were you to buy an energy-efficient 19-cubic-foot electric refrigerator using 500 kWh per year, you'd pay only $50 per year in electricity cost.

If you want to go off-grid, then you need to weigh the costs of supplying propane to fuel the fridge for ten or fifteen years, and the possibility of buying extra generating and storage capacity to meet the electrical needs of the refrigerator. Often, choosing a new, highly efficient electric refrigerator and buying more solar panels is the most cost-effective solution.

Well Pump: See motors. Make sure your well pump isn't stuck on due to a faulty pressure tank or switch, underground or in-home water leaks, faulty foot valve (check valve at the bottom of the well), or a dry well. Water-saving efforts will reduce pump run-time. Water softeners will increase pump run-time during the backwash cycle.

Power consumption of a well pump for an average family can range from 100 to 400 kWh per year or more, depending on the size of the pump, size of the household, and water use habits.

Appliance Recycling

The Association of Home Appliance Manufacturer's (AHAM) data shows that US manufacturers ship nearly 54 million major home appliances every year. When you buy a new appliance, what should you do with the old one? Recycle it! Recycled steel can be used to make new appliances with significant environmental benefits.

The Appliance Recycling Information Center (ARIC) maintains a website (<www.aham.org/aric/aric.cfm>) and phone hotline (1-800-YES-1-CAN) to answer consumer's questions about appliance recycling. ARIC reports that "discarded appliances are second only to old automobiles as a source of recycled metals, particularly steel. It takes four times more energy to manufacture steel from virgin ore as it does to make the same steel from recycled scrap. Steel is the most abundant recyclable component in appliances, but not the only one. Major home appliances, or 'white goods,' also contain other metals like aluminum and copper, as well as recyclable plastics and CFC refrigerants."

The US Environmental Protection Agency has identified six major benefits of using scrap instead of virgin materials in making new steel:

- 97 percent reduction in mining wastes
- 90 percent savings in virgin materials use
- 86 percent reduction in air pollution
- 76 percent reduction in water pollution
- 74 percent savings in energy
- 40 percent reduction in water use

Proper recycling procedures also encourage proper disposal of harmful substances used in appliances, such as mercury, CFCs and PCBs.

CHAPTER 4

Hot Water

Introduction

HAVE YOU THOUGHT ABOUT YOUR DOMESTIC SUPPLY?" If your plumber asks questions like this, he's not asking about gross national product but more specifically about the rules of supply and demand of hot water. Domestic Hot Water (DHW as it's known in the trade) means the hot water used by people living in a home for bathing, dishwashing, clothes washing, and the like. It's the water that comes out of your faucet, and if a plumber used those simple words, his job would seem less mysterious and you might not be willing to pay him quite so much.

You probably have a water heater. Maybe you even know where it is. But when was the last time you actually thought about this under-appreciated servant? What makes the water hot? What is the fuel source? How can you tell if it's working properly? Is it safe? What can you do to cut down on water heating costs? What can you do to make the water heater last longer? How do you choose a good one? This chapter will answer these questions by exploring and assessing your water heater and your water-using habits.

Your water heater is probably the second biggest energy user in your home, just after space heating. So it is worthwhile to get close and personal, because if you ignore your water heater, it *will* go away — and then it will cost you. When you're done with this chapter, steel yourself to descend into your basement; gather a broom to clear the cob-webs and a garbage bag. Aim for the water heater and don't stray from your goal of clearing a path up to it and all the way around it. After you've dealt with the recycling, cleaned out the cat box, found that screwdriver you needed a few weeks ago and finally cleared the path, you'll feel good about the accomplishment, I promise. You might even be safer for it. Paying a little attention to your water heater once in a while goes a long way.

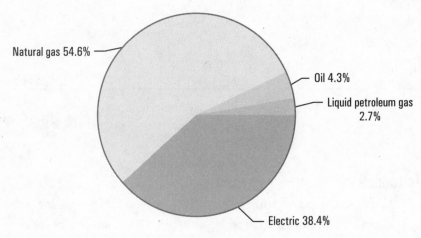

Natural gas 54.6%

Oil 4.3%

Liquid petroleum gas 2.7%

Electric 38.4%

Fig. 4.1: Hot water fuel types.

Awareness: The Big Picture

The United States Geological Survey (USGS) estimated that in 1995, the United States used about 398 billion gallons of water every day. That's about 1,500 gallons for each person, but includes industrial uses as well. Residential water use is about 60 gallons per person per day, while the average person uses about 17 gallons of hot water every day. According to the US Department of Energy's Energy Information Administration (EIA), the average American household used about 16 million British Thermal Units (Btus) for DHW annually. Residential water heaters consumed 1.7 quadrillion Btus of energy (quads), or about 21 percent of an average home's total energy use.

As a nation, our actual wateroheating energy use per household has remained fairly consistent over the last 50 years. Figure 4.1 shows the percentage of DHW fuel types used by the one hundred and seven million US households in the US in 2001.

Reducing water consumption has a cumulative savings effect. Perhaps you pay for municipal water and sewage by the gallon or cubic foot (there are 7.48 gallons in a cubic foot of water). If you have a private source of water and sewer, pump run-time is reduced, saving electricity and increasing pump life, while taking some of the load off your septic system. And of course there are energy and dollar savings associated with reducing hot water usage.

Types of Water Heaters

There are several different kinds of water heaters. The differences are in the type of fuel they use and how they transfer heat from that energy source to the water. It is a good idea to plan for maintenance when a new water heater is being installed. Make it easy to drain and flush the tank; repair or replace heating elements, burners, heat exchangers, thermostats, and the temperature and pressure relief valve; inspect and replace the anode rod; and leave enough space around the unit to add an insulation blanket. Each of these items are discussed in detail later in this chapter. Following are descriptions of five different kinds of water heaters.

Direct-Fired Tank-Style Water Heaters

Direct-fired tank storage is the most common type of water heater. A volume of water is kept hot by direct-heat input from electricity, gas, or oil. Cold water enters the water heater through a *dip tube* that brings the cold water down to the bottom of the tank, and hot water flows out the top of the tank. Bringing cold water to the bottom of the tank puts stratification, or temperature layering, to use as hot water rises to the top. A thermostat controls the on/off cycling of the fuel source to maintain a constant water temperature.

Electric Water Heaters

Direct-fired electric water heaters for homes typically use one or two 240-volt resistive heating elements that draw about 4,500 watts each. Heat from a resistive heating element is generated in much the same way that heat and light are produced in an incandescent light bulb. When electricity is applied to the heating element, the resistance to the flow of current in the element produces heat. The heat generated is transferred directly to the water. If removed from water, the electric heating element will glow bright red and quickly burn itself out from overheating. The water acts as a heat-sink to keep the element from destroying itself.

In larger water heaters (over 30 gallons), you will find two of these heating elements, one on the top and one on the bottom. They are each controlled by a separate thermostat that turns the heating element on and off based on the temperature of the water in the tank. The thermostats are located behind the access panel(s) on the side of the water heater, and are easily accessed with only a screwdriver. When adjusting the temperature of an electric water heater, be sure to turn off the power supply. The wires connected to the thermostat are "live" with voltage! Read the section later in this chapter on adjusting thermostats.

As you use hot water, cold water comes into the tank at the bottom and is heated by the lower element. As cooler water makes its way toward the top of the tank, the upper element comes on. Even though there are two heating elements in an electric water heater, only one is activated at a time, alternating between top and bottom. This allows the water to be evenly heated without the need for greater electrical service to the water heater.

An electric water heater's conversion of electricity into heat, and the heat's transfer to the water, are nearly 100 percent efficient. This is because there are no intermediate conversions or transfers of energy between the fuel source and the water being heated, as with fossil fuel water heaters. With a gas or oil water heater, a portion of the heat generated by the flame goes out the flue, and additional energy is lost in heat transfer between the flame and the water. An electric water heater has none of these inefficiencies, but due to the high cost of electricity it may still cost more to heat water with electricity. If you decide that an electric water heater is the right choice for you, choose a model with good insulation, such as the Marathon brand with an advertised insulation value of R-22. Figure 4.2 shows a cutaway view of both a gas and electric water heater and their components.

HowStuffWorks.com

- **❶ Electric**
- **❷ Gas**
- **Ⓐ Cold**
- **Ⓑ Hot out**
- **Ⓒ Shutoff valve**
- **Ⓓ Temperature /pressure relief valve**
- **Ⓔ Insulation**
- **Ⓕ Outer case**
- **Ⓖ Anode rod**
- **Ⓗ Thermostat**
- **Ⓘ Electric heating elements**
- **Ⓙ Drain valve**
- **Ⓚ Burner control**
- **Ⓛ Dip tube**
- **Ⓜ Overflow**
- **Ⓝ Steel tank**
- **Ⓞ Burner**

Fig. 4.2: Cutaway view of gas and electric water heaters.

Gas Water Heaters

In a direct-fired gas water heater, the heat source is a flame burning on the bottom of the water heater. On the lower side of the water heater is a plate covering the pilot light. This plate can be removed to view the burner. There are many orifices in a gas burner, and each orifice sports a small flame. A good-looking gas flame is blue, with just a little orange at the top of the flame. The flame as a whole should look even all around the burner. If there are any dead spots on the burner where there is no flame, or if you see lots of orange flame, it's time for a service call.

As a result of combustion, the flue pipe slowly breaks down and rust flakes can accumulate at the bottom of the water heater, underneath the flame. Eventually, the flue pipe will rust through, and a leak will develop. Keep an eye on the level of rust through the burner view port, and make sure the rust doesn't impede the flame. Have your gas water heater professionally cleaned, tuned, and inspected for safety every two years.

If you are switching from an electric to a gas water heater, you can probably install a smaller capacity model because gas water heaters heat water faster. Efficiency ratings of gas water heaters range from 50 to 65 percent. Energy is lost in the transfer of heat from the flame to the water, and some heat is lost up the flue. A thorough discussion of water-heater efficiency ratings appears later in this chapter.

Oil Water Heaters

A direct-fired oil water heater is similar to a gas water heater. The difference is of course the fuel, which requires a different type of burner. The heat input from the burner is typically on the order of 80,000 Btus or more, making for very fast heat recovery, meaning you can take more showers without running out of hot water. Most of the information presented about gas water heaters applies to oil units, though there may not be an observation port to view the flame on an oil water heater, and a professional should inspect the oil burner once a year. Oil water heaters are quite a bit more expensive than gas or electric, but may be cheaper to operate depending on local fuel costs.

Indirect-Fired Tank Water Heater

If you use a hot water boiler to heat your home, your DHW can be integrated with your boiler by way of an indirect-fired (or simply "indirect") water heater. It is so named because the water is heated indirectly by the boiler through a heat exchanger. This system consists of a storage tank (usually 40 or 50 gallons) and a heat exchanger. The heat exchanger can be located either inside or outside of the storage tank. Its function is to transfer the heat from water circulating through the closed loop of heated boiler water to the water in the hot water storage tank that will eventually flow out of your tap or shower head. These fluids come in very close contact with each other, allowing the heat to transfer from the hot (boiler) side to the cooler (DHW) side, but the fluids are never allowed to mix. The indirect water heater operates as a separate heat zone, as if it were a separate room in the house, with its own circulator pump and thermostat — in this case called an *aquastat*. The boiler comes on when the water heater calls for heat, and it stays on long enough to heat up all the water in the storage tank.

The efficiency of an indirect water heater is related to boiler efficiency and how efficiently the heat exchanger transfers heat. While heat exchange efficiencies vary with fluid flow rate and temperature difference, a typical operating efficiency for indirect-fired DHW is about ten percent less than the rated boiler efficiency. Figure 4.3 shows an indirect water heater and the boiler which provides the heat. The oil boiler (on the right) heats the water, which

then circulates from the boiler to a heat exchanger that is internal to the water heater (on the left). The small gray box on the lower left side of the water heater houses the aquastat, which allows adjustment of the DHW temperature.

Fig. 4.3: Indirect-fired water heater off boiler.

Instantaneous Water Heaters

On-demand, tankless, or instantaneous water heaters (same thing, different names) heat water instantly when it is called for, and so there is no need for a storage tank. On-demand water heaters are activated by the flow of water. When you turn on a hot water faucet, a fuel valve opens, igniting the burner. Cold water enters one side of a coil of copper pipe, which then twists and turns through a heat exchanger that is engulfed in flame, and hot water exits the other side of the heat exchanger. Tankless water heaters can be integrated with a hot water boiler used for home heating, or they can be dedicated DHW heaters operating from any type of fuel. The main advantages to on-demand water heaters are:

- No storage tank full of water to keep warm
- Potentially high efficiency
- Little space required
- Endless flow of hot water
- Ability to set water temperature easily according to a specific need

Dedicated on-demand water heaters can be fueled by natural gas, LP gas, kerosene, or electricity. Some smaller units are located under a sink, offering instant hot water at a single tap rather than waiting for it to arrive from the distant primary water heater in the basement.

The efficiency of an on-demand water heater is based on the heat transfer efficiency of the heat exchanger or, in other words, how much heat is transferred from the flame to the water. On-demand water heaters are on the order of 70 to 90 percent efficient in this conversion. What they lack, compared to conventional water heaters, is a volume of hot water to *keep* hot, therefore reducing tank loss (the heat lost through the walls of a tank-style heater) and increasing overall efficiency. The more efficient on-demand units do not have a wasteful standing pilot light. Rather, they use electronic ignition, further reducing fuel consumption.

When an on-demand water heater is on, it is using *a lot* of fuel! A popular residential model, the Aquastar 125, burns gas at the rate of 125,000 Btus per hour. Compare this to a tank-style gas water heater consuming about 40,000 Btus per hour. This high-energy consumption is because the on-demand water heater has only a few moments to heat the water as it flows through the heat exchanger. A tank-style storage heater can heat the water more slowly, as it has a reserve of hot water to draw from. One of the advantages to on-demand water heaters is that they supply continuous hot water — you will never run out. But if you use it that way, with its high Btu flame, it may cost you more than using a storage-tank water heater and may not be the right choice for a large family with heavy water needs.

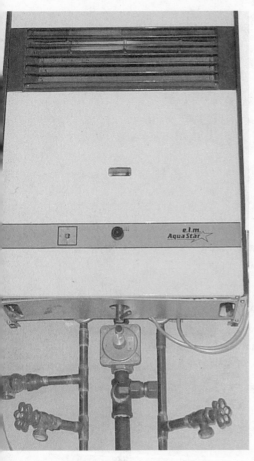

Fig. 4.4: Aquastar on-demand gas water heater. Note the drain valves on both hot and cold water pipes allowing the heat exchanger to be flushed.

On-demand water heaters do have some drawbacks. First, they require good water pressure at a minimum flow rate (usually about three quarters of a gallon per minute) in order to activate the burner. This means that you can't get a slow stream of warm water at the tap (which I like for doing dishes). Another minor inconvenience is that the length of piping through the heat exchanger is long enough that it reduces the pressure of the hot water at the tap. Also, the temperature at the tap is dependent upon the flow of water through the water heater; the slower the water flow, the more time it spends in the heat exchange area, and the hotter it gets. As the flow increases, the temperature decreases. This is normally not a problem if only one person uses hot water at a time, but if one is taking a shower, and another is doing dishes or laundry, the person in the shower may not be very happy with the temperature fluctuation. If you and your family can adjust to these situations, then an on-demand water heater may work for you, but it will require some getting used to. Some newer models offer higher flow rates and modulating burners (the flame adjusts with the flow of water) to maintain a constant temperature.

Figure 4.4 shows an older Aquastar on-demand gas water heater with drain and flush valves plumbed on each side of the heat exchanger for easy maintenance.

A different kind of on-demand water heater, called a *tankless coil*, is integrated with a hot water boiler. It is so named because it consists of a coil of finned copper pipe, and there is no tank of water to heat. Instead, the coil of copper pipe sits inside the boiler and is heated as water flows through the coil.

Figure 4.5 shows a boiler with a tankless coil. The water pipes traveling down and then back up the side of the boiler are attached to the heat exchange coil installed inside the boiler. The gray box on the top right side of the boiler houses the aquastat. Towards the bottom, you can see a mixing valve connecting between the hot and cold water pipes. You will read more about both of these devices soon.

The tankless coil can be one of the least efficient ways to heat water. One study showed as low as 12 percent efficiency under low-use and low-flow conditions. A boiler is most efficient after

Fig. 4.5: Tankless coil water heating loop inside a boiler.

it warms up, which may take ten minutes or more and least efficient when it turns on and off every few minutes, as may be the case with the use of a tankless coil. During winter months (when the boiler is being used regularly), a tankless coil may work well because the boiler is usually hot. During non-heating months, the boiler has to cycle on and off frequently just for water heating, wasting energy the way a car wastes gas in stop-and-go traffic.

Another disadvantage of all on-demand water heaters is the intense heat the coil is exposed to. This heat accelerates the precipitation of mineral particles out of the water and their deposit onto the inside of the coil. Think of this as a cholesterol build-up in your plumbing that eventually restricts the flow of water. Angioplasty surgery for plumbing consists of flushing the coil every year or so with a mild acid solution to dissolve calcium build-up. Be sure to ask your plumber to set up a valve and drain system on each side of the heat exchanger so that you can do this easily. Periodic flushing is also necessary with tank-style heaters, but not as often as with tankless DHW heaters. A filter or water softener can often alleviate this problem. It is best to check with professional plumbers or water treatment experts in your area for the best water treatment plan. Read more about dealing with sediment later in this chapter.

Solar Hot Water Systems

Solar thermal collectors are designed to collect as much of the sun's heat energy as possible and transfer this heat to a heat transfer fluid (usually an anti-freeze solution). The fluid circulates in a closed loop between the solar collectors and a heat exchanger that transfers the heat to the domestic hot water storage tank. Solar hot water systems are often used to pre-heat water before it enters a storage tank where it may be further heated by a secondary energy source if there is not enough sun to bring the water up to temperature. It is most common and cost-effective to design a solar-water heating system to provide about 70 percent of your average annual hot water needs. This means you'll get more than you need in the summer, and less in the winter.

A solar hot water heater consists of two main parts:

1. The *collectors*, mounted on the roof or the ground, absorb the sun's energy and transfer it to water or a heat exchange fluid (also called a "working fluid"). The collector is part of either an *active* or *passive* system. Active systems use electric pumps (these can be solar-electric powered) to move heated fluid, while passive systems use a naturally induced thermosiphon to transport heat between a hot solar collector and the cooler hot water storage tank. For this to work, the water storage tank must be higher than the solar collectors. The volume of hot water you need and how much sun you can expect will determine the square footage of collector area required. An average household might need two to four 16-square-foot collectors to supply most hot water needs. There are two types of collectors commonly used for residential solar hot water:

 • *Flat plate* collectors are the most widely used type of solar thermal collector. They are large, flat, insulated boxes with one or more glass covers. Inside are dark-colored metal plates that absorb solar heat. A liquid,

Can I Use a Water Heater to Heat my House?

Yes, but … a small, energy-efficient house can be heated with a water heater. A typical water heater provides about 40,000 Btus of heat energy. A heat loss calculation of the home can determine if a water heater will provide enough heat to meet your needs (read about heating in Chapter 5). There are a few very efficient combination water/space heaters made specifically for this application that have higher heat outputs.

The advantage is that you get your heat and hot water from a single, relatively inexpensive appliance. The disadvantage is that a water heater is not as efficient as a furnace or boiler. In most cases, you'll need a heat exchanger to keep the potable domestic hot water separate from the closed-loop of the heating system. Find a contractor who is familiar with plumbing such systems.

such as water or anti-freeze (used for heat transfer), flows through tubes and is warmed by heat from the plates.

- *Evacuated tube* collectors are made up of rows of parallel, transparent glass tubes. Each tube consists of a glass outer tube and an inner tube or absorber, covered with a selective coating that absorbs solar energy but inhibits radiation heat loss, through which the heat transfer fluid flows. During manufacture, the air is withdrawn from the space between the tubes to form a vacuum, which eliminates conductive and convective heat loss.

2. The *storage tank* holds the heated water. Fluid is heated in the collector and travels to the storage tank where it releases its heat to the hot water supply through a heat exchanger. The solar storage tank can be the same tank as the secondary heater, or a separate tank can be used allowing for greater storage volume. A larger storage tank stores more of the sun's energy, giving you more reserve capacity during times of lesser solar gain.

Solar Collector Ratings

Solar hot water collectors are rated for thermal output in terms of Btus per square foot per day. The Solar Rating and Certification Corporation (SRCC) is a nonprofit, independent, third-party organization formed by the solar industry, state energy officials, and consumer advocates to certify and rate solar water heaters. A certified solar water heater carries the SRCC OG-300 label, and the system performance is listed in a directory published on the SRCC website <www.solar-rating.org>. The Florida Solar Energy Center provides similar ratings that you can learn about on their website: <www.fsec.ucf.edu>

In addition to the collectors and storage tank, a solar water system requires *balance of system* components such as a pump and controls:

- Using a solar-powered pump is an elegant way to move the working fluid because when the sun shines, the water in the collector heats up. The brighter the sun, the hotter the water and the solar electric pump spins faster with brighter sun on the solar electric panel.
- An expansion tank relieves excess pressure build-up as water heats up and expands.
- Temperature and pressure gauges aid in monitoring system performance.
- A control box is often used to monitor collector and storage tank temperatures, and automatically turn pumps on or off as required for optimum system performance.

There are several types of solar water heaters categorized by their method of operation. The one that works best for you is determined by your climate, how much hot water you need, and of course your budget. Consulting local dealers is the best way to find out what will work best for your particular situation. A well installed and properly maintained solar water system can last up to 40 years and cost between $1,500 (if you do the work yourself) to $5,000 on average.

The return on your solar hot water investment depends on the type and cost of the system you choose, and the type and cost of fuel you currently use to heat your hot water. Electric water heater users often will realize considerably more savings than those with an oil or natural gas water heater. Of course, energy costs vary regionally, so you will need to determine savings based on your actual energy costs. Typically, a solar water heater is designed to provide about 70 percent of your annual hot water needs. This sizing scheme combines reasonable system costs with noticeable energy-cost savings. For example, if you have an electric water heater that uses 4,500-kilowatt-hours per year to heat water, and you pay $0.10 per kWh, the solar water heater would offset your water heating costs by $315 per year. If you spend $4,000 to achieve these savings, your simple payback is 12.7 years and the return on your investment is 7.8 percent.

Maintaining Your Water Heater

For maximum life and efficiency, you will want to periodically inspect your water heater and perform preventive maintenance on it. If the water temperature seems excessively hot or cold, or if you run out of hot water sooner than you used to, you may have a faulty thermostat or heating element. Try adjusting before replacing. This symptom may also indicate sediment build-up inside the water heater, which effectively reduces the volume of water it can hold, and reduces the heat-transfer efficiency.

Keeping an eye on your water heater and its performance can clue you in to any potential problems that may need to be addressed by a plumber. A few minutes a month can save you the cost of premature replacement of your water heater, or costly loss of efficiency. Here are some simple checks you can do on your own.

Water Heater Inspection

The first thing to make yourself aware of is the location of the power or fuel shutoff, and the cold water inlet shutoff valve. In case of trouble, you want to be able to turn off the water or power as quickly as possible.

During your monthly visual inspection of the water heater, look for rust on the water heater and wet spots on the heater or the floor nearby, indicating a leaking water heater or pipe connection. Don't be misled by dripping condensation — if it's warm and humid in the basement, cold pipes can collect condensation and drip water. Eliminate or reduce condensation by insulating the cold water pipes with foam pipe insulation. Put your hand on the tank. Does it feel warm? If it does, you may want to put an insulating jacket on it (see the section on "Water Heater Insulation"). There should not be any hot spots on the tank.

What does the plumbing look like? It should be clean with no green or white build-up, indicating a slow leak. Look at the temperature and pressure relief valve (TPRV, see below) — it should not be dripping or have any evidence of rust or corrosion. Do you hear anything? If you hear hissing or popping, it could indicate a leak or sediment build-up inside the tank. Be sure that electrical connections and thermostats are safely covered.

For fossil fuel water heaters, make sure the air intake is not blocked. Sniff around for gas or oil odors. Make sure the flue pipe is properly connected and look for rust spots, holes, or sags in the pipe — it should have a slight upward pitch and few elbows. Problems with venting should be taken care of immediately. Corrosive materials such as solvents that are stored in the basement can off-gas and these corrosive gases can be drawn into the combustion air inlet, degrading the burner and flue. Flammable liquids can vaporize and catch fire if they are too close to the water heater flame. Rust on top of or on the floor around the water heater may indicate a disintegrating flue pipe.

There may be a visual access port on the bottom of a gas or oil water heater. Get down on your hands and knees and take a peek inside if it's a gas heater. Do you see a pilot light? Is it a steady blue flame? If the water heater is on, you might see the entire heating flame — it should be a nice steady blue flame, with not too much orange. If it's not on, turn it on by turning up the thermostat – move away from the view port as you turn up the thermostat in case there is any "flame rollout" (indicating a need for professional service). The burner should light within a few seconds of turning up the thermostat. Make sure the flue pipe is in good shape all the way to where it leaves the house. If the flue goes up to the roof, binoculars may point out something obvious like a bird's nest on top. A service person or energy auditor can perform a combustion analysis and draft test to measure efficiency and to make sure that exhaust gases are being properly vented outdoors.

Some of my visits to basements have been truly shocking. I've seen rusted and disconnected flue pipes pumping toxic flue gases right into the house; lint and cobwebs blocking air flow to the combustion area; obvious pipe leaks; and stuck and leaking — even steaming — pressure relief valves. Open containers of paint thinner near the water heater are fires waiting to happen!

Do not ignore the utility room. Be observant around your water heater. Appliances are like living creatures; they need attention and observation from time to time. A little awareness early on can sidetrack big problems later, and help keep your water heating costs to a minimum.

Temperature and Pressure Relief Valve

All water heaters have a Temperature and Pressure Relief Valve (TPRV). The purpose of this safety valve is to blow off steam in the event of high temperature or pressure inside the water heater. The TPRV is located on the upper side, or on the top of the water heater, and usually has a silver handle on it for the sole purpose of annual testing. Be careful when checking this valve; the water coming out of it will be hot! Be sure the handle is free from obstructions that might prevent it from operating, and look for obvious signs of damage, rust, drips, or sediment deposits around it. If you see any of these signs, it is time to replace the valve. The valve *must* be able to operate or you have a potential rocket ship in your basement! To test the TPRV, hold a bucket under the valve outlet, and carefully lift the little silver handle. Hot water should flow out of it. If you can't move the handle, or if no water comes out, or if the water doesn't stop coming out, then it's time to replace the valve.

This valve should be checked once a year for proper operation. Plumb the outlet of the TPRV to a drain or direct it down to a bucket so the floor doesn't get wet if it should happen to do its job by venting off hot water. This also makes it much faster and easier to check the valve. Figure 4.6 shows a close-up of a TPRV with a cut-out in the insulating jacket to allow proper operation.

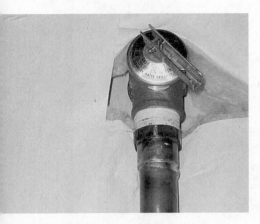

Fig. 4.6: Temperature and Pressure Relief Valve.

Temperature Check

It's easy to check the temperature of the water at a sink faucet using a candy thermometer. Put the thermometer into a glass, let the hot water fill up the glass, then take the temperature with the water still running into the glass. If you simply hold the thermometer under the stream of water it may read low due to aeration. Factory and plumber settings can vary from 115° to 150°F. An average shower temperature is 104°. A good temperature setting for energy efficiency is 110° to 120°. This temperature allows a comfortable shower and is about as hot as your hands can stand to wash dishes, and also prevents scalding accidents. This is especially important for younger and older skin. You middle-aged readers have thicker calluses.

You may feel that you need 140° or hotter water to kill germs on dishes. It is cheaper and more efficient to turn your water heater temperature down and use the dishwasher's temperature boost control to heat up the relatively small amount of water needed for that job. Hopefully you have a relatively new energy-efficient dishwasher using only five gallons of water instead of the average 10 to 15 gallons for older machines.

As for clothes washing, most of the energy used by a clothes washer is due to heating water. If you're still using hot water for this chore because you don't trust those new liquid detergents to work just as well in cold as in hot water, I say: "Yes, your mother *was* right, but times have changed. Experiment!" For allergy control, we have found a laundry detergent that kills dust mites in cold water made by Allersearch, and available by mail order from Allergy Control Products <www.allergycontrol.com>. New front-loading washers use less water and spin faster so the clothes are dryer when removed, reducing dryer run-times. Read more about washers and dryers in Chapters 2 and 3.

During times of heavy hot water use, the temperature inside the water heater will soon drop and if you're the last in line for the shower you'll be standing naked in the cold. If you consistently run out of hot water, and you're sure the water heater is in good operating condition, *and* you have implemented all the efficiency measures described in this chapter, you may not want to turn down the temperature. Lower temperature means a greater percentage of hot water in the mix to achieve the desired temperature at the tap. If you consistently run out of hot water, you may need to turn the temperature up (please understand how difficult it is for me to write these words). Try staggering the shower schedule before taking this drastic measure. Raising the water temperature will allow you to use less hot water in the mix to meet the same temperature needs at the tap, but you will pay an energy penalty. As you can see from Table 4.1, turning the hot water temperature down 10° can save about 13 percent of your hot water energy consumption. At $0.10 per kWh, you can save over $60 per year for about ten minutes of work.

In addition to saving energy and money, lower DHW temperatures are safer. Table 4.2 shows how quickly skin can be burned with hot water.

Table 4.1: Savings from 10° Setback of Hot Water Temperature.

Reduce water temperature by 10° F	
Type of fuel	Energy saved
Electricity	684 kWh
Natural gas	23 therms
LP gas	25 gallons
Oil	17 gallons

Adjusting Water Temperature

Each type of water heater has a temperature control, or thermostat. Thermostats provided on water heaters are not finely tuned instruments, so expect some variation between what you see at the thermostat, and what you get at the tap. How you adjust the temperature of your water heater depends on what kind it is. Check your owner's manual for instructions specific to your water heater.

Electric Water Heaters

To adjust the thermostat on an electric water heater, first disconnect the power at the circuit breaker. Failure to disconnect the power before working on a water heater can result in death! It is very easy to slip with a tool or finger and hit a live wire. Next remove the heating element access cover(s) located on the side of the water heater; there are usually two screws holding each cover on. Pull

Table 4.2: Water Scalding.

Water temperature °F	Time for 1st degree burn	Time for 2nd and 3rd degree burns
110	(normal shower temp)	
116	(pain threshold)	
116	35 minutes	45 minutes
122	1 minute	5 minutes
131	5 seconds	25 seconds
140	2 seconds	5 seconds
149	1 second	2 seconds
154	Instantaneous	1 second

Credit: The Engineering and Sciences Division of the US Consumer Product Safety Commission.

back the insulation that may be behind the access panel filling the space around the thermostat. You may also find a plastic shield covering the wiring with an access opening to adjust the thermostat. You should now be able to see the thermostat. It should look something like Figure 4.7, where the heating element is at the bottom of the picture, the temperature control in the middle, and the thermostat at the top. While you're there, look for leaks or rust around where the element disappears into the tank.

Use a flathead screwdriver to turn the dial to a lower temperature. Some thermostats have no temperatures printed on the thermostat, just the vague words "warm" and "hot." Or maybe it is not even adjustable at all, as some thermostats are pre-set to a single temperature. If there are two heating elements, set both the top and bottom thermostats to the same temperature. If you have a new thermostat installed, be sure the plumber sets the temperature where *you* want it — not the factory pre-set.

Gas Water Heaters

If you have a gas water heater, the thermostat is usually mounted outside on the bottom half of the unit and is fairly obvious, as shown in Figure 4.8. There is no need to turn off the gas to make the adjustment.

Legionnaires' Disease

Legionella pneumophilia are bacteria that can cause a potentially serious lung infection in humans known as legionnaire's disease. *Legionella* are quite common in natural and artificial aquatic environments — including water heaters and hot water pipes — usually at extremely low concentrations. Under certain situations, the bacteria can multiply to unsafe levels. *Legionella* bacteria can survive in water temperatures between 32° and 122°F, but thrive at temperatures common in household plumbing, including hot water heaters. This situation is compounded when water or water vapor is stagnant, or in the presence of sediment, scale, or microorganisms that can act as nutrients for the bacteria. The bacteria first need to be introduced into an environment that allows them to multiply. Then they need to be transported away from their source and transmitted by way of water vapor to a susceptible individual where the bacteria are inhaled in water vapor. Water droplets of less than five micrometers can be created by showerheads, aerators, and spray nozzles, and then be inhaled. A study by the American Society of Microbiology suggests that about 20 percent of legionnaires' cases can be traced to residential plumbing.

Most individuals exposed to *legionella* never get sick, but if you're concerned, the recommended practice to reduce exposure potential is to keep cold water at or below 68°F, and hot water at or above 120°F. *Legionella* can be controlled by "shocking" the system by turning the heat up to 140°F or higher, followed by flushing the hot water pipes by opening hot water taps and letting water run for half an hour. High dosage chlorine treatment of the water has also been shown to remove the bacteria. Because the bacteria will return, this procedure should be done every two or three months. For more information on legionnaires' disease, see <www.legionella.org>.

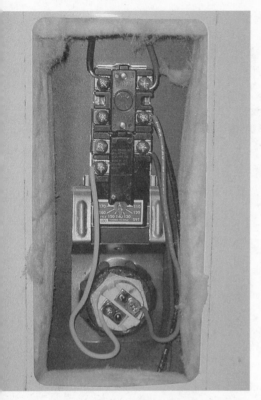

Fig. 4.7: Behind an electric water heater control cover. Assume that all wires are electrically live unless the circuit breaker is off.

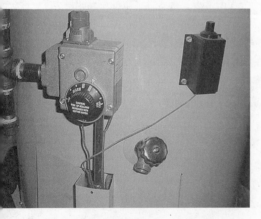

Fig. 4.8: Gas water heater thermostat. Note the red gas shutoff valve above the control.

Finding and Adjusting an Aquastat

Oil and indirect-fired water heaters use a not-so-obvious aquastat. Figure 4.3 shows a heating system with an indirect-fired water heater. The aquastat is the small gray box attached to the lower left of the water heater. An aquastat, like a thermostat, is a temperature-sensitive switch designed for water systems. It uses a probe that is in contact with the water to be monitored, and is connected to a switch that activates a hot water circulator. The temperature-adjustment dial is inside the aquastat housing. When the water cools off, the switch closes, and the heat source (a circulator pump on an indirect-fired water heater, or the burner on a direct-fired oil water heater or tankless coil) is activated.

To adjust the temperature, remove the control box cover (there are usually one or two screws holding the cover on) and you will see a well-camouflaged temperature dial inside. Look closely at the dial for temperature markings, and turn it to make the adjustment. Figure 4.9 shows a close-up of the inside of an aquastat with the temperature adjustment control.

Anode Rod

The mysterious anode rod lives and dies silently inside your water heater, sacrificing itself so that your water heater may live. It works to prevent rust inside the water heater by attracting the electro-chemical activity that would otherwise corrode the steel tank. Anode rods are about one-half inch in diameter, three or four feet long, and are usually made of aluminum, magnesium, or zinc. The rod is sometimes attached to the hot water output side of the water heater, but is often separate. It should be removed and inspected every few years — more often if you have hard water.

If you have a water softener, you may want to check the anode rod every year. With a water softener, hard minerals in the water are exchanged for salt, and this salt can consume an anode rod up to three times faster than calcium carbonate, the typical anode-consuming mineral in hard water. Once the anode rod is depleted, your water heater's days are numbered.

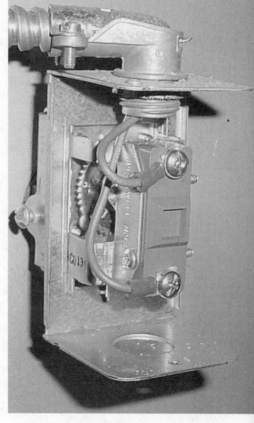

Fig. 4.9: Inside an Aquastat. Note the notched silver dial on the left to adjust temperature.

When installing a new water heater, ask your plumber to show you where the anode rod is and explain how to inspect it. Don't listen if you hear "Oh, don't bother with that, they last forever." Well, "forever" to your plumber means "until the end of the warranty period" at which time he can sell you a new water heater, earning him more than simply replacing an anode rod for you every few years.

Sediment

Unless a water filtration system is in place, rust, debris, and minerals enter the water heater along with water. These impurities will settle to the bottom of the tank or precipitate out of the water onto the electric heating elements, coating them and reducing their heat-transfer efficiency. In a gas or oil water heater, the debris settles onto the bottom of the tank, hardening with heat from the burner, and insulating the water from the heat source. This sediment needs to be removed and cleaned periodically by draining and flushing the system. Excessive sediment can cause overheating and breakdown of the tank itself and inhibit the beneficial activity of the anode rod. If you hear a boiling or popping sound in the water heater when it is heating, it may be due to sediment build-up. The noise is due to boiling water trapped under the sediment.

Drain a quart or two out of your water heater every year to remove sediment; there is no need to turn off the power or gas for this. If you open your drain valve and little or no water comes out, you're in trouble. That means that the sediment is blocking the drain. Before making any repairs or draining your water heater, be sure to turn off the power or shut off the gas or oil, or you risk expensive damage to the equipment and possibly yourself. If you have an electric water heater, you should be able to drain the tank, remove the lower heating element (which may also have a calcium frosting) and use the opening to chip away at the debris on the bottom of the tank with a long, skinny rod. On a gas heater you'll need to remove the drain valve. Be careful though, the tank itself may have weakened over the years, so try not to bang the sides or bottom of the tank too much. You can also get creative with a wet/dry vacuum cleaner by attaching a small hose to the existing hose and poke it though the thermostat opening to vacuum out the scale.

An article published in *Plumbing Systems and Design*, the official journal of the American Society of Plumbing Engineers states: "For every half-inch of sediment on the bottom of a gas fired water heater, it requires 70 percent more fuel to heat the water." Heat accelerates sediment accumulation. Niagara Mohawk Power Corporation reports that for every 20°F rise in temperature, the chemical reaction causing rust and corrosion inside your water heater doubles. More proof that energy efficiency pays in more ways than lower fuel bills.

Flushing your Water Heater

Every year or two, drain and flush the water heater to keep it clear of sediment. Keep an eye on what comes out the hose. Drain it into a five-gallon pail, and as the water comes out look for chunks or flakes of things you'd rather not see in your water. Don't wait too long to flush your water heater or you'll be discouraged by having to scrape out the "buckets full" I've heard homeowners tell me about. If it's an electric water heater, pull out the heating elements. Are they caked with debris or a white deposit? If so, you can flush the water heater with a mild acid solution to dissolve the calcium. Look for a descalant or de-liming product (such as "Mag-Erad" or "Un-Lime") at hardware stores. Alternatively, you can use straight white vinegar, or muriatic acid (mixed with ten parts water to one part acid).

I pour a quart or two of vinegar into the tank through the *union*, then add a gallon or two of water and let it sit for a few hours. A union is a threaded plumbing connection that allows you to easily disconnect the water supply pipes. Adding a union will only cost a few extra dollars when installing the water heater and is well worth the convenience. Be careful: too strong an acid solution can eat through the walls of the tank, especially if it is old or damaged. If your tank is more than 15 years old and you've never flushed it, or if there is evidence of rust or leaks anywhere on the tank, you can flush the tank, but do not use the acid solution.

Here's how to flush your water heater step by step:

- Turn off the power or fuel supply to the water heater.
- Turn off the cold water supply to the water heater.
- Attach a hose to the drain valve and open the valve to drain the tank.
- Open a hot water tap to allow air into the DHW tank or the water won't drain completely.
- Take note of the water condition as it comes out of the tank.
- Once the tank is empty, and with the drain valve still open, pulse the cold water by quickly turning the cold water inlet valve on and off. This will help loosen scale.
- Close the water supply valve and the drain valve.
- Loosen the plumbing union on the hot or cold pipe. If no union exists, you will need to have a plumber install one. If you have an electric water heater, you can pour the descaling solution through the hole that exists after you remove the heating element.

- Mix the flushing solution.
- Using a funnel, pour the mixture into the water heater by way of the open union and let it sit for as long as the instructions indicate.
- Pulse and drain again.
- Repeat this procedure until water runs clear.
- Close the drain, remove the hose, and open the cold water inlet valve to fill the water heater. Leave the hot water tap open until the air is cleared from the line and water flows.
- Also check the TPRV for proper operation by activating its lever.

Electrolysis Resulting From Dissimilar Metals

Big words, simple fix. Chemical reactions between steel connectors on the water heater will cause corrosion in the presence of the copper or brass used in plumbing these connections. The solution is to isolate these materials from each other by way of *dielectric unions* or plastic-lined steel nipples on the water heater. A dielectric material is one that does not conduct electricity but allows the transfer of magnetic force. Rubber, glass, and plastic are examples of dielectric materials. A dielectric material breaks the flow of electric current in a metallic path or circuit. Ask your plumber about dielectric unions before selecting or installing your next hot water heater.

Fig. 4.10: Mixing valve.

Mixing Valves

Mixing valves, also called tempering valves, can confuse the issue of water temperature. A mixing valve is a temperature-sensitive valve that allows some cold water to mix with the hot to keep a safe and steady temperature at the tap. It is possible that your water heater is set for 150°F or higher and you'd never know it because the mixing valve is doing its job, keeping water at the tap a steady 120°. If you have a mixing valve in your DHW system, take a look at the thermostat setting on the water heater and adjust it visually. Figure 4.10 shows a typical mixing valve, but they can be difficult to find. It could be located near the water heater, near a particular faucet, or anywhere in between. The knob on the top of the valve allows for temperature adjustment.

Water Heater Efficiency Measures

Proper maintenance helps your water heater last longer and operate as efficiently as it was designed to. We've already discussed maintenance as well as temperature adjustments. You can also help increase your water heater's efficiency and save money by keeping the heat inside the tank, and reducing your consumption of hot water.

Water Heater Insulation

When it comes to reducing heat loss, insulation is always a good idea, and more is better. "My water heater is inside where it's warm," you say. "Why do I need more insulation?" The water inside your water heater might be 120°F or higher. All that heat wants to escape (heat always moves from hot to cold) and heat up your 70° house. If you want the space where your water heater lives to be heated, don't rely on your water heater to do it. Your home's heating system is much more efficient and better equipped to do that job properly.

Fiberglass and foam are the two types of insulation most commonly found in water heaters. Fiberglass offers an insulating value of about R-3 per inch of thickness, and foam weighs in at R-6 per inch. An inch of foam is not uncommon in new, more efficient models, but two inches are better. To check the insulation type and thickness, pull off a thermostat

---

Water Heater Maintenance Schedule

Once a month:
• Clean around the water heater.
• Look for leaks ad/or wet spots on the floor or pipes.
• Check for sags or tears in the insulation jacket.
• Drain a gallon or two from the water heater.

Once a year:
• Check temperature.
• Test the TPRV.
• Drain and flush.
• Check the flame on gas water heaters.
• Check venting system integrity.

Every two to four years:
• Check the anode rod.

cover plate (turn off the power first!) and look inside. Pink or yellow fluffy stuff is fiberglass. The harder, but still pliable material is foam. Now measure the thickness or depth. If you can't get a tape measure in there, insert a thin wooden skewer and measure how deep it went. On a gas or oil water heater, you can poke your skewer in around the drain valve sleeve.

Adding an external insulating blanket will reduce heat loss through the skin of the tank (called *tank loss*), but the more insulation that's built in to the tank, the less cost-effective it will be to add more externally. You may feel that you don't need an external insulation jacket because your water heater doesn't feel warm to the touch. Here's a test: fold up some towels or clothes and put them on top of the water heater. After a day, put your hand under the clothes and see if it feels warm. You might be surprised.

If your water heater's factory-installed insulation is less than about R-15, it would be cost-effective to install an external insulating jacket. The most common after-market water heater insulating jacket is made of vinyl-faced fiberglass with an insulating value of around R-10. You can buy one at hardware stores, or make your own out of fiberglass batts or reflective bubble-wrap insulation. Table 4.3 presents the potential energy savings you can expect by installing an insulating jacket on a water heater set to 130°F with a factory insulation value of R-7. If you pay $0.10 per kWh, and the tank wrap costs $15, your return on investment is 220 percent!

When choosing a new water heater, look closely at the information tag on the unit. There are lots of numbers, which may or may not include the insulating value. If the R-value is not listed, ask the plumber or supplier to find out. If they want to make a sale, they'll do that much for you. Newer water heaters generally have better insulation installed by the manufacturer. Look for the yellow Energy Guide tag on the unit to compare the energy costs of similar models.

Use care when insulating a water heater. If you are wrapping a gas or oil water heater:

Table 4.3: Insulated Water Heater Savings.

Install R-10 insulating jacket on water heater	
Type of fuel	Energy saved
Electricity	331 kWh
Natural gas	11 therms
LP gas	12 gallons
Oil	8 gallons

Stand-By Loss

Stand-by loss is all the heat or energy lost by the water heater and its heating process. These losses are used to determine the water heater's overall efficiency rating. Stand-by loss can be broken down into:

1. Tank loss is energy lost through the skin of the tank. Tank losses are a function of the temperature difference between the hot water and the surrounding ambient temperature, the surface area of the water heater, and the insulation level of the water heater. Tank loss can be reduced by adding insulation around the water heater or turning down the temperature. Tank loss applies to all water heaters that store hot water in a tank.

2. Pilot lights are used to ignite the burner in a gas water heater. The pilot light is a small flame that is always on. Some of this heat is transferred to the water while some goes out the flue. More efficient gas water heaters use electronic ignition, eliminating the waste of a pilot light.

3. Heat transfer efficiency means how well the heat from the flame or heating element is transferred to the water. Heat transfer efficiency is more of an issue for fossil fuel water heaters than for electric units, and is called *recovery efficiency*. More on water heater efficiency ratings will appear later in this chapter.

- Do not cover the top as it may block the draft vent or be exposed to high temperature around the flue.
- Be sure that the air intake (at the bottom near where the pilot light and thermostat are located) is not restricted.
- Do not cover the thermostat.
- Do not allow insulation to come within two inches of the floor, which may prevent blockage of combustion air flow to the burner.

- Fasten the jacket firmly around the water heater.
- Inspect the condition of the jacket periodically for sags or loose tape that can lead to blockage of air intakes.

On all water heaters:

- Ensure the pressure relief valve is free to operate by cutting a hole in the insulating jacket around the valve, leaving an clear inch around the valve with no pieces of fiberglass to interfere with its operation. This is *extremely* important. Arrange the jacket and the pressure relief valve drain line so that water runs down the outside of the jacket into a bucket or drain.
- Cut a flap in the jacket to access thermostats.
- Don't cover up the instruction manual or warranty information usually located in a pocket taped to the side of the water heater.
- If the water heater is in a wet area, moisture can get trapped inside of the jacket, resulting in rust. Be sure the insulation does not get wet.

When NOT To Add Insulation

Some manufacturers state that installing an external insulating jacket will void the warranty. While a few have rescinded this warning, the issue is one of safety and liability — manufacturers do not want you to cover any labels or controls. If you are in doubt, contact the manufacturer. Some plumbers do not like tank wraps: they get in the way of service. One plumber told me that he was sure that external insulation was causing heating elements and thermostats to burn out from overheating. He was unable to explain to me why it would be any hotter inside a water heater set to 120°F with or without a tank wrap (because it's not, his idea was a myth). Keep the heat where it belongs: in the water.

Heat Traps

Hot water rises just as hot air does. Your living room is warmer at the ceiling than at the floor. The water in your water heater is hotter at the top. That heat wants to keep going, and that means up and out of the pipes, both cold and hot, with no consideration for your wishes or desires.

A *heat trap* can be used to stop this flow of heat. A heat trap is simply a valve that automatically closes when no water is flowing. It can be installed in the plumbing leading to and from the water heater. Some water heaters have built in heat traps. If yours doesn't, make sure your next one does.

You (or your plumber) can make a simple heat trap that is very similar to a drain trap, but installed on the pipes leading to and from the water heater. Instead of plumbing a straight pipe into and out of the water heater, this sideways "S"-shaped trap stops heat from rising out of the water heater by breaking the easy upward movement of heat. Heat rises up to it, but doesn't make the downward turn in the trap, so there it stops.

Heat traps offer an overall increase in water heater efficiency of about two percent. This may not sound like much, but over the 12- to 15-year life of the average water heater, it really adds up in energy-cost savings.

Timers

Some electric companies offer a credit on your bill if you allow your water heater to be put on a timer. The timer is set to turn off the water heater for a few hours during times of peak demand for the power company. Peak power demand in homes is usually in the morning when we get up, and again in the late afternoon when we come home from work and start using hot water. While this allows the utility to spread out a thinning power supply, timers are not an effective way to control hot-water energy consumption.

When you turn off the power to your water heater, it doesn't use energy. It will continue to lose heat through the jacket though, and if you use enough hot water, you will run out. When you turn the water heater back on, the water needs to come back up to temperature to supply hot water for your dishes and showers. You haven't saved anything.

A well-insulated tank will have minimal tank loss, but if you plan on being away for more than a week, it would be worthwhile to turn the water heater off. My gas water heater has R-10 factory insulation, plus an R-10 external insulating jacket. I can turn the water heater off and after being away for a week, the water is still hot enough for a shower.

Table 4.4: Flow Rate in Gallons per Minute.

Number of seconds to fill	Quart jug	Gallon jug
3	5.00	20.0
4	3.75	15.0
5	3.00	12.0
6	2.50	10.0
7	2.14	8.6
8	1.88	7.5
9	1.67	6.7
10	1.50	6.0
12	1.25	5.0
15	1.00	4.0
20	0.75	3.0
30	0.50	2.0
40	0.38	1.5
50	0.30	1.2
60	0.25	1.0

Showerheads and Flow Rate

Is it worthwhile to get a low-flow showerhead? That depends. First, you need to know what your shower flow rate is now. You'll need two things: a container of known quantity (I use a one-quart, wide-mouth canning jar), and a watch with a second hand.

Turn on the shower and adjust the water to where you normally set it when you take a shower. If you are using a one-gallon jug, just time how long it takes to fill the jug. If it takes 60 seconds, that's one gallon per minute (GPM). To calculate flow rate for a one-quart jar, see Table 4.4, or use the following math. To fill a one-quart jar, the formula for flow rate in GPM is:

$$\text{60 (seconds per minute)} \div 4 \text{ (quarts in a gallon)}$$
$$\div \text{ number of seconds required to fill the jar} = \text{GPM}$$

Example: if it takes five seconds to fill your one-quart jug, then:

$$60 \div 4 \div 5 = 3 \text{ GPM}$$

If your showerhead flow rate is more than 2.5 GPM, it's probably worthwhile to get a new one with a lower flow.

Connie Sumer argued against replacing her indoor waterfall with a low-flow showerhead. "How will I ever rinse my hair?" she complained. I pointed to my own mop and said "One-and-a-half gallons per minute. But I *do* take a ten-minute shower because I'm a glutton and life is short."

She seemed amused. I promised her that it wouldn't take any longer to rinse, and if she didn't like it, I'd take it right out — it only takes a few minutes to replace a shower head including wrapping the threads with Teflon tape to ensure leak-free operation. The new flow rate of two GPM seemed acceptable, and she liked the twist-flow option that varies the flow stream when you twist the showerhead.

Table 4.5 represents the potential annual energy savings of reducing shower flow rate by one GPM for a family of four, each taking five ten-minute showers every week, plus additional, average hot water use.

Table 4.5: Reduced Showerhead Flow Rate Savings.

Reduce shower flow rate by 1 GPM	
Type of fuel	Energy saved
Electricity	1,333 kWh
Natural gas	45 therms
LP gas	50 gallons
Oil	33 gallons

If you pay $0.10 per kWh, you'll save almost $130 a year. A $10 shower-head will give you a first year return on your investment of over 1,300 percent!

Does It Use Less Water to Take a Shower, or a Bath?

As usual, the answer is, "It depends." Specifically, it depends on three things:

• What is the shower flow rate?
• How many minutes are your showers?
• How many gallons does your bathtub hold?

Let's say you have a three GPM shower flow rate, you take seven-minute showers, your bathtub holds 30 gallons, and you like it full. You can determine your bathtub volume by measuring the faucet flow rate in GPM, then multiply that by the number of minutes it takes to fill up the tub. Assume the temperature is the same for both, though you may use a little more hot water for a bath to warm up the tub, and perhaps you add a little heat after soaking a while.

Your shower water use is calculated by multiplying the flow rate in GPM by the number of minutes you are in the shower.

3 GPM × 7 minutes = 21 gallons water used for your shower

In this case, your shower uses 9 gallons less water than a bath.

Drips

Careful scientific analysis by an expert (that would be me with a stopwatch and a 10-milliliter test tube), proves that there are five drips in a milliliter, 148 drips in an ounce, and 18,990 drips in a gallon. A faucet dripping at the rate of one drip per second will waste 4.5 gallons per day or 1,661 gallons per year. If you pay for water by the cubic foot (CF), that's 222 CF wasted every year (there are 7.48 gallons of water in a cubic foot). If that drip is a 130°F *hot* water drip, Table 4.6 shows the savings to repair the leak.

Insulate Water Pipes

The most common residential water pipe size pipes are ½ and ¾ inch. It takes 98 feet of ½-inch pipe or 43.5 feet of ¾-inch pipe to hold one gallon of water. If your water heater is 100 feet away from the shower (remember, we're talking about the actual length of the pipes), and you have ¾-inch plumbing, you have over two gallons of hot water that will cool on its way to your shower, causing you to turn up the heat. How much water (and time) do you waste standing around waiting for the water to get hot at the tap?

You don't stand around waiting? That's even worse! That means you're doing something else and will probably forget the water is running until several gallons of heat (read:money) have gone down the drain.

This scenario compounds itself if there are several people in your home, all using water periodically. The water in the pipes heat and cool over and over, and everyone stands around waiting or forgetting, turning two gallons into twenty.

Some hot water systems with very long runs between the water heater and the tap have re-circulation loops on them. This system keeps hot water circulating between the water heater and the tap — just waiting for someone to turn on the hot water faucet. This situation can save a few gallons of water and a few minutes of time, but will cause a great deal of heat loss through the pipes. If you have such a system, be sure all the pipes are insulated and consider

Table 4.6: Leaky Hot Water Faucet Repair Savings.

Eliminate hot water leak of 1 drip per second	
Type of fuel	Energy saved
Electricity	304 kWh
Natural gas	10 therms
LP gas	11 gallons
Oil	8 gallons

using a timer to turn off the pump during times of low hot water use.

Pipe insulation is very inexpensive, readily available from hardware stores, and easily installed. You will realize cost-effective energy savings, but you will also gain a few extra minutes by not waiting around for the shower to heat up. In fact, the primary benefit of pipe insulation is one of comfort. Insulate all the hot water pipes and the first few feet of cold water pipe leading into the water heater. The cold water pipe heats up because it is in contact with the hot water, and conducts that heat out of the tank. You may find it useful to insulate all the cold water pipes to reduce condensation. Table 4.7 presents potential savings associated with insulating 100 feet of ½-inch hot water pipes. The savings assumes that all the water in the pipes cools and is reheated twice per day.

Table 4.7: Insulated Hot Water Pipes Savings.

Insulate hot water pipes	
Type of fuel	Energy units
Electricity	136 kWh
Natural gas	4.6 therms
LP gas	5.1 gallons
Oil	3.4 gallons

Wastewater Heat Recovery

When you shower, the water temperature is somewhere around 104°F. The heat contained in the water is used only briefly before going down the drain. What if there was a way to capture that waste heat and re-use it? Waterfilm Energy makes a device called the Gravity Film heat eXchanger (GFX). It consists of a length of copper drain pipe wrapped with a long coil of ½-inch copper plumbing supply pipe. Cold water is fed into one end of the supply pipe. As warm water travels down the drain pipe, it warms the water in the supply coil, and this pre-heated water is routed to the water heater, thus reducing the energy demand of the water heater. The GFX can be used in new or existing homes. You can learn more about this product on the company website at <www.gfxtechnology.com>.

Hot Flushes

One of the most absurd things I've seen is hot water plumbed to the toilet bowl, literally flushing dollars down the drain! This is done to prevent condensation build-up on the outside of the tank, which can drip onto the floor. If you've never thought about it before, go look at (or feel) the toilet tank. Most places where I've noticed this, the owners had no idea they were flushing somewhere between two and seven gallons of hot water down the drain several times a day.

If condensation on your toilet tank presents a problem, install a toilet tank insulation kit consisting of rigid but flexible insulation on the inside of the toilet tank. They are available at plumbing supply stores for under $20.

How to Choose a New Water Heater

After you determine which type of water heater and fuel source you want, there are a few guidelines to help you sort through the remaining choices.

If your water heater just died and you need a new one now, then all you need to do is shop according to the yellow Energy Guide tags attached to all appliances, water heaters, and space heating equipment. Look at the numbers, look at the bar graph, and buy the one that uses the least energy or costs less to operate within the size range you are considering. Refer also to Chapter 7 on buying new appliances. The Gas Appliance Manufacturers Association (GAMA) maintains a website listing most water heaters available today and their efficiency ratings at <www.gamanet.org>. Water heaters are not yet labeled for the ENERGY STAR.

I view the warranty as a good indicator of the manufacturer's confidence in its product. Buy a unit with a long warranty, and don't pay for extended warranties. Learn to take care of general repairs yourself. Attention and timely preventive maintenance precludes the need for buying extended warranties, and a good installation allows for ease of maintenance. Let's look more closely at how water heaters are rated.

First Hour Rating

The maximum amount of hot water a water heater can supply in the first hour of operation, starting with a full, hot tank is called the "first hour rating." It is a combination of how much water is stored in the water heater and how quickly cold water can be heated to the desired temperature. The first hour rating is the first thing you need to consider so that you can properly size the water heater in terms of storage capacity. If you determine that you need 70 gallons of hot water during the hour of greatest hot water use, then you need a water heater with a first hour rating of 68 to 72 gallons. Under-sizing leads to a shortage of hot water, while over-sizing wastes energy. When selecting a water heater, choose the required first hour rating first, then look for the highest efficiency rating or *energy factor* in that range.

Energy Factor

Energy factor (EF) is a measure of the overall efficiency of a water heater. It is a ratio of the energy supplied in usable, heated water to the total fuel energy input to the water heater. The higher the number, the more efficient the water heater will be at this energy conversion, and at keeping the water inside the tank hot. Energy factor is expressed in hundredths of a point, 1.00 being 100 percent efficient. More efficient gas water heaters will have energy factors in the low to mid 60s, expressed as 0.60 or 0.65. An EF of 0.62 means the overall efficiency of the unit is 62 percent. More efficient electric water heaters will have EFs approaching 0.95, and a good oil water heater will have an EF of 0.62 to 0.68. The higher EF units generally have higher insulation values as well as heat traps. The reason that electric water heaters have higher energy factors (0.82 to 0.95) than gas or oil water heaters (0.48 to 0.65) is primarily because they have lower stand-by losses; that is, there is no pilot light waste or heat lost through the flue. Energy loss from an electric water heater is almost completely due to heat lost through the tank.

It is important to remember that EF is based on a very specific test specified by the US Department of Energy. Think of it as similar to the EPA test that rates automobile mileage — it's a good way to compare, but actual conditions in your home will vary. See the sidebar on the numbers behind the energy factor rating for more details.

Energy Factor — the Numbers Behind the Numbers

Most water heaters are rated by the Gas Appliance Manufacturers Association or GAMA. GAMA is a national trade association whose members manufacture over 90 percent of all the residential, commercial, and industrial gas appliances made in the United States, along with certain products using oil or electricity as their energy source. GAMA retains the services of a third-party testing lab to verify manufacturers' equipment efficiency ratings in accordance with federally mandated test procedures.

When GAMA tests water heaters for efficiency, every unit, regardless of fuel, is tested the same way. The energy factor rating compares the energy supplied in heated water to the total daily energy consumption of the water heater. The test assumes a daily hot water energy use (energy that provides usable hot water) of 41,045 Btus for gas and oil water heaters, and 12.03 kWh for electric. Any additional fuel required by the water heater to heat the water and keep it hot is considered a stand-by loss.

For example, under GAMA test conditions, a water heater with an EF of 0.58 has actually used:

41,045 (heat output in usable hot water) ÷ 0.58 (EF) = 70,767 Btus

70,767 Btus of fuel have been consumed to deliver 41,045 Btus of heated water.

While this test works well under the prescribed conditions, you are probably not average. If you actually use more hot water than was used for the test, the effective efficiency increases. This is because you are now using more hot water and losing proportionally less energy. The more hot water you use, the lower the percentage of stand-by losses. If your hot water heater burner is actually on 24 hours a day and just keeping up with the demand for hot water, it would be running at its peak efficiency. If you go on vacation for a month and leave the heater on, it is operating least efficiently, as none of the water is actually being used, but the heater is still consuming energy to keep the water hot to offset stand-by loss.

For more information, you can visit GAMA on the web at <www.gamanet.org> and download efficiency ratings of hundreds of space and water heating appliances.

Recovery Efficiency

Recovery efficiency represents how efficiently heat energy is transferred from the heat source to the water. This figure is generally used when speaking of gas or oil water heaters, as the recovery efficiency for all electric water heaters is 98 percent. Most gas and oil water heaters have recovery efficiencies between 75 and 82 percent. Higher numbers are better. Recovery efficiency is different from energy factor in that the energy factor test takes into account all losses of the water heater, *including* recovery efficiency.

Your Hot Water and Energy Consumption

So, exactly how much energy does your water heater use? The answer depends on many variables. A thorough analysis with plenty of math is really what's required. But if you really, really don't like math, and you don't want to hire a professional energy auditor, I can only offer you a very vague, ballpark estimate using some gross assumptions about your hot water use, water heater efficiency, and your water heater's environment:

- For electric water heaters, assume about 1,000 kWh per year per person, plus another 500 kWh per year for tank loss.
- If you have a natural gas water heater, assume about 34 therms for each person per year plus another 60 therms per year in tank loss.
- For an LP gas water heater, assume about 37 gallons per person per year plus 65 gallons per year in tank loss.
- For oil water heaters, assume about 25 gallons per person per year plus 43 gallons per year in tank loss.

Asking Questions

There I am in the driveway, and the dog runs up to greet me, whimpering in tortured anticipation as I sit in the car for a minute gathering up my stuff after it rattled onto the floor on the way up. Opening the car door, I stand up and the dog's wet nose lands squarely in my crotch. "Good dog," I say half-heartedly, and hope that it really is. Closing the car door, I kindly place my knee firmly under its jaw. I head for the side door with the dog on my heels, barking an announcement to its faithful master, who's inside with the TV blasting. Wondering if they remembered my appointment, I knock on the door, anticipating what's on the other side. The door opens, a curler-headed woman balances a baby on her hip, a cigarette hangs from her lips, the dog barks, the baby cries, the TV blares.

"Hi, I'm from the power company, Have I found the Sumers?"

"Oh yeah, yeah, right. I'm Connie. You're the energy guy, right? I forgot you were coming. Come on in, excuse the mess, I can't hardly keep this place clean anymore."

I step in and try to squeeze through the door so the dog doesn't make it in with me.

It's always challenging to view other people's living space as your job site. You see right past whatever mess there may be, and even if the place is immaculate, people are compelled to make excuses. I just want to get to work.

"So can I get some of those free light bulbs?"

"Well, first I need to educate you about your sinful, energy-guzzling habits," I say smiling, as I launch into the Q and A portion of "The Energy Audit." "So how old is that refrigerator?"

"Well, geez, we got that when we were still over on Plainfield. Yep, my daughter was four years old. But when we bought it, the salesman said it was one of them 'energy sufficient' ones."

Gulp. "So how old is your daughter now?"

"What's that got to do with my light bill? You single?"

"I can just ball-park the age. Let's talk about lighting. Can you tell me about how many hours this light is on in a day? Think about summer and winter usage and we'll try to get an average daily bur—"

"Oh, that light I turn on when I get home, and turn it off when I go to bed."

"Uh, yeah, OK, so a couple hours a day?"

"Well, no, we don't turn it on at all in the daytime."

So about the time I'm ready to go back outside and make friends with the dog, I'm only halfway through and I've still got to get personal with this stranger.

"So, how many showers do you take in a week? How long are they?"

"Only one shower a day, usually, and I don't know, I never timed it."

"OK, how about person number two, how long are his showers?"

"Oh, that's my husband…" She sort of looks around the room. "We shower together."

"OK, seven fifteen-minute showers a week?" I try not to lead any answers but sometimes it's the only way I'll ever get out before dinner time. And the kitchen smells of meatloaf cooking in the oven.

"Yep, that sounds about right. And then there's the kids. Ya know, you guys, we get a lot of power outrages up here, I wish you could do something about it."

"Well, ma'am, as I'm just a sub-contractor, I can't speak to that, but if you call the utility, they will certainly want to know about power *outages*."

"Well, that won't do any good, we just seem to get an awful lot of power outrages up here."

"Excuse me, I'll be right back" I say. "I'm just going to go outside to get you some efficient light bulbs."

"Well, get the mail out of the box on your way back in!"

I meet up with the dog outside on my way to the car. It starts to sprinkle. In order to get away from the smoky indoor air, I fill out as much paperwork as I can outside under the open hatchback.

Well, by the time I leave, the dog and I are pretty good buddies, and I feel sorry for him by now. "I understand, buddy, good luck!" and I throw a stick before driving away.

Table 4.8 shows the energy consumption of a typical family for hot water using the following assumptions:

- There are four people in the household.
- They are all average, using 17 gallons of hot water per day.
- The hot water temperature is 130°F.
- The cold water temperature is 55°F.
- They have a 50-gallon water heater.
- The water heater has an insulation value of R-7.
- The water heater is in a 58°F basement
- The energy factor of the gas and oil water heaters is 0.55

Assessing Your Hot Water Use

How do you quantify your hot water use? The answer can help you determine how much energy you use to heat your water, decide where to cut down, and help you to properly size a new water heater. Simply put, you need to measure everything associated with your hot-water consumption routines.

After asking hundreds of people about their intimate water-using habits, I understand that family dynamics influence reality. I can't tell you how many family feuds I've started with the question of shower times. I would rather gather erroneous data than be in the middle of husband and wife telling each other how long they have to wait to get into the bathroom in the morning. Things can heat up pretty fast. Then come the teenagers with the sheepish looks on their faces when they try to tell me that their showers are only five minutes.

Yeah, right. I was never a teenager, so I don't know. I write down 15 minutes in my notes. Argue amongst yourselves, then consult the stopwatch, and be honest. A good answer requires good data.

Collecting Data

I use three simple tools to perform hot water measurements: a thermometer, a one-quart jar, and a watch with a second hand. Referring to the earlier section, "Temperature Check," on checking water temperature, take the temperature of the hot water. Get the family on board with your data collection and have them measure the temperature of their shower water, then look up the percentage mix of hot water in the shower in Table 4.9 (the average shower temperature is 104°F). Next, determine the flow rate of the shower using a watch and a container of known volume (refer back to Table 4.4), and finally time the duration of each person's shower.

When you're done gathering data on everyone's showers, add up the total number of gallons used per week per person, multiply the figure by the percent of hot water used, and you now know how many gallons of hot water are used in the shower each week.

Now take some time to think about all your other (hopefully less contentious) hot water uses and write them down. It's a good idea to measure flow rates and time each use to determine how many gallons each item consumes. Remember to adjust for hot water mix percent. Add up the totals the way you

Table 4.8: Average Hot Water Fuel Use.

Average annual water heating fuel use for a family of four	
Type of fuel	Energy used
Electricity	5,106 kWh
Natural gas	258 therms
LP gas	252 gallons
Oil	187 gallons

Table 4.9: Percentage of Hot Water Mix in Average Shower.

Percent of hot water mix for 104° shower	
DHW temp	Percent hot
104	100%
110	89%
115	81%
120	75%
125	70%
130	65%
135	61%
140	57%
145	54%
Assumes cold water temperature of 55°	

Math Box: Percent of Hot Water

You can use the following formula to calculate the percentage of hot and cold water in your warm water mix if you know three things:

• Hot water temperature = H
• Cold water temperature = C
• Warm water temperature = W

The formula compares the difference between the hot water and the warm water temperatures, to the difference between the hot and cold water temperatures. The percentage of cold water in the warm water stream is equal to:

$$(H - W) \div (H - C) \times 100 = \text{percent of C}$$

The percentage of hot water in the shower is equal to:

$$100 - \text{percent C} = \text{percent H}$$

For example: You measure the hot water temperature at 130°, the cold water temperature at 60°, and you do dishes by hand under a stream of 106° water.

$$H = 130°, C = 60°, W = 106°$$

$$(130 - 106) \div (130 - 60) \times 100 = 34 \text{ percent cold}$$

and the percentage of hot is:

$$100 - 34 = 66 \text{ percent hot}$$

Math Box: Hot Water Energy Consumption

If you want to determine how much fuel your water heater uses, you can apply some simple math to the data you've already collected. You also need to know that a gallon of water weighs 8.33 pounds. Do this by first finding energy consumption using the common energy denominator, Btus. The formula to determine the energy (in Btus) required to heat the water you use every year is this:

gallons of water × weight of water (in pounds)
× DT (temperature difference)

Example: The average person uses about 17 gallons of hot water every day. That's 6,205 gallons per year. There are four people in the family, so the total annual consumption is 24,820 gallons. Water weighs 8.33 lb. per gallon (remember, a Btu is the amount of energy required to raise one pound of water one degree Fahrenheit). You measure the cold water at 55°F and the hot water at 130°, so the temperature difference is 75°. Our formula looks like this:

24,820 × 8.33 × 75 = 15,506,295 Btus

That's how many Btus you've actually used to heat the hot water that flows from the faucets, but it doesn't include stand-by losses. To determine total energy consumed by the water heater, you now need to divide by the energy factor of the water heater. Finally, to arrive at the number of fuel units you use each year, divide the total Btus consumed by the number of Btus in each unit of the fuel your water heater uses. For example, you have a natural gas water heater with an energy factor of 0.55:

15,506,295 Btus ÷ 0.55 EF ÷ 100,000 Btus per therm = 282 therms did with showers. How do you compare with the national average of 17 gallons per day? Your hot water use probably includes at least some of the following, and maybe more:

- Showers
- Baths
- Toilet flushing
- Dish washing (hand and machine)
- Clothes washing

- Shampoo
- Shave
- Hand washing
- Food preparation
- House cleaning

You can use this information to determine the first hour rating you need from your water heater. What time of day gets the most hot water use? Add up the hot water consumption of all the things you do during that hour. The total is the first hour rating you need. Use that number as the place to start when choosing a new water heater, then compare efficiencies within that category of water heaters.

Comparing Energy Costs for Different Water Heaters

Table 4.10 compares the annual and lifetime operating costs of different water heaters assuming equivalent water usage of an average family. The chart assumes an average hot water demand of 15 MMBtus, and that they all will last 15 years with proper care. The column showing fuel consumption is adjusted by the energy factor and so takes stand-by loss into account. Your fuel costs may vary from the estimates shown.

Table 4.10: Water Heater Life-cycle Cost Comparison.

Water heater type and fuel	Fuel units used	Fuel units	Energy factor	Fuel $/unit	Annual fuel cost	Annual maintenance cost	Average installed cost	15-year life cycle cost
Electric direct-fired	4,777	kWh	0.92	$0.10	$519	$10	$400	$8,339
NG direct-fired	242	therms	0.62	$1.00	$390	$25	$800	$7,028
LPG direct-fired	265	gallon	0.62	$1.60	$683	$25	$800	$11,414
Oil direct-fired	170	gallon	0.64	$1.50	$399	$50	$1,800	$8,538
NG indirect-fired	200	therms	0.75	$1.00	$267	$10	$1,200	$5,350
LPG indirect-fired	219	gallon	0.75	$1.60	$466	$10	$1,200	$8,347
Oil indirect-fired	145	gallon	0.75	$1.50	$291	$10	$1,200	$5,710
NG on-demand	188	therms	0.80	$1.00	$234	$10	$900	$4,566
LPG on-demand	205	gallon	0.80	$1.60	$410	$10	$900	$7,200
Oil - tankless coil	273	gallon	0.40	$1.50	$1,022	$25	$400	$16,103

Water heater lifetime varies with type of unit and quality of care and maintenance
Figures are not adjusted for fuel or dollar inflation rates

Hot Water Diet

- Install an insulating jacket designed for use with hot water heaters.
- Install a low-flow showerhead.
- Reduce the temperature to 120°F or less.
- Repair water leaks. One drip every second adds up to over 1,600 gallons per year.
- Use less water while brushing your teeth, shaving, washing your face, and washing dishes by turning off the water in between uses.
- Install low-flow faucet aerators on all sinks. Try the "flip drip" type with a handy flip lever that allows you to reduce the water flow to a dribble without turning off the faucet — they're great for doing dishes or shaving.
- Wash clothes in cold water, wash only full loads, use an efficient washer.

- Avoid using the temperature boost setting on the dishwasher.
- If you go away for more than a week, turn the water heater off at the circuit breaker if it's electric, or at the thermostat if it's gas or oil.
- Insulate all hot water pipes as well as the first five or ten feet of pipe supplying cold water to the water heater.
- Flush the water heater once a year.
- Check the anode rod and replace as necessary.
- If you hear noise coming from your water heater, or if it seems to take a long time to recover, or if you run out of hot water more quickly than in the past, it's time for service.

CHAPTER 5

Heating and Air Conditioning

Introduction

FOR THE AVERAGE HOMEOWNER, a heating system may be the third-largest purchase of a lifetime after a house and car, and heating and cooling requirements probably consume the greatest portion of your home's energy. This makes improving the efficiency of your home and its heating system a good bet for significant energy and dollar savings.

I have seen too many homes where the heating system was installed (more like stuffed into an unused corner) as an afterthought. A heating system's high cost, long life, and substantial lifetime energy consumption make it worthwhile to do a little homework before deciding what will work best in your situation. In this chapter we'll discuss:

- Types of heating systems
- Heat system efficiency ratings
- Some cost-effective improvements to heating and cooling equipment and to your home's demands on that equipment
- How to choose an efficient heating or cooling system

Awareness: The Big Picture

In 1978, Americans used 6.9 quadrillion Btus (quads) to heat 77 million homes. In 2001, we used 4.6 quads to heat 107 million homes, showing the huge value of more efficient building techniques and weatherization efforts in older homes. Figure 5.1 shows the percentage of primary heating systems by fuel type.

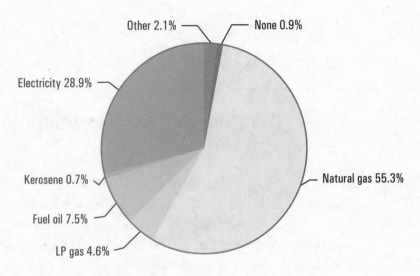

Fig.5.1: Types of US home heating fuels, 2001.

Heating-energy consumption is usually expressed in millions of Btus or, MMBtu. On average, each home in the US consumes about 50 MMBtus of energy for heating. This varies greatly by region with Florida homeowners using about 4.6 MMBtus each, while New York families average over 77 MMBtus. Over half the homes in the country heat with natural gas and about a quarter with electricity. Oil heat is most popular in the northeastern US.

In 2001, Americans spent over $50 billion on home heating fuels including:

• 3.2 trillion cubic feet of natural gas
• 116 billion kilowatt hours (kWh) of electricity
• 4.15 billion gallons of fuel oil
• 326 million gallons of kerosene
• 3.1 billion gallons of LP gas

Nationwide, residential furnaces and boilers account for nearly five percent of the total energy consumption in the US.

What Determines Home Heating Energy Consumption?

The heat load of a building is a measure of how much heat is required to be added or removed for you to stay comfortable in the building. This heating load is expressed in Btus per hour. The heating requirements of a building are affected by four major things:

- Climate
- Building efficiency
- Occupant behavior
- Heating system efficiency

In addition to heat loss, buildings also have heat gains. These are typically solar gains and those internal heat gains associated with people and all of their indoor activities. In fact, a vacant house at 55°F uses more energy for heating than an occupied one at 68°. Humans and their activities produce a certain amount of heat that reduces the load on your heating system. Each of us generates about 350 Btus of heat energy every hour, about the equivalent of a 100-watt light bulb. These heat gains are considered a bonus and are largely ignored when sizing a heating system. When sizing an air conditioner, these internal gains need to be taken into account. Let's take a closer look at the elements of heat load.

Climate

The levels of insulation needed to maintain adequate comfort levels vary with the climate. The heating energy requirements of a specific climate are defined in terms of *heating degree days*. A heating degree day (HDD) is the measure of the duration and severity of the outdoor temperature below a reference temperature of 65°F. It is conventionally assumed that once the outdoor temperature drops below 65° people will turn on the heat. For example, if today's outdoor temperature averages 30° over 24 hours, then 35 HDD have accumulated today (65 – 30 = 35). If the average temperature over an entire month is 35°, then that month will accumulate:

$$65° – 30° \times 30 \text{ days} = 1,050 \text{ HDD}$$

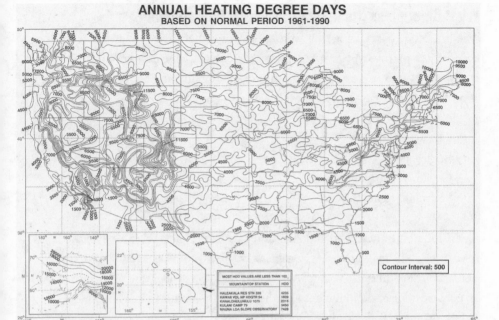

Fig, 5.2: Heating degree day map of the United States. Credit: National Oceanic and Atmospheric Administration, National Climatic Data Center.

HDD is typically expressed in annual or seasonal terms. Homes in the south experience fewer heating degree days than homes in the north. The climate in northern Minnesota typically accumulates in the neighborhood of 10,000 HDD during the heating season, while in Florida the heating season may accumulate only 500 HDD.

See Figure 5.2 for a heating degree day map of the US. Your local weather station may have more specific data for your locality. You can look up recent local climate data on the web at <www.worldclimate.com>, or at the National Climate Data Center's website at <www.ncdc.noaa.gov>.

Building Efficiency

Conduction, convection, and radiation, along with air leakage, all contribute to your home's heat loss. Heat is transmitted through the building shell, driven by the temperature difference between indoors and out, along with wind loads acting on the outside of the house. Adding thermal resistance with insulation and double pane windows reduces heat loss by all three transmission paths.

Conductive heat losses occur through the walls, roof, and insulation of a building as heat is transferred from the warmer location, through the building materials, to the cooler location. The denser the material, the greater its conductance. Air is a poor conductor of heat, metal is a good one. Insulation products are full of tiny air pockets and so reduce conductive heat loss.

Convective heat loss occurs in several ways. Wind carries away heat radiated and conducted from the house, and leads to greater air leakage within the home. Air movement created by temperature differences between materials, such as a cold window and warm air, creates convection currents. Cold air migrating into a warm, insulated wall cavity creates convection currents within the cavity, reducing the effectiveness of the insulation.

Radiation losses will occur as long as there is a temperature difference between your home and the outdoors. Heat is pressure, and pressure moves from high to low, that is, from hot to cold. Radiated heat can travel long distances, even through a vacuum. The sun is an excellent example of radiating heat.

Air leakage is driven by wind, temperature, and pressure differences within the house, and between the house and the outside. For every cubic foot of air that enters a building, a cubic foot of conditioned air escapes. Reducing air leakage is generally a very cost-effective energy improvement to make, especially in older homes. See Chapter 6 for a more thorough discussion of this subject.

Building efficiency determines the size of the heating system you need. A more efficient house allows you to use a smaller, less expensive system. A heating contractor or energy auditor can help you determine the heat requirements of your home. In Appendix D, I'll show you how to do a simple heat-loss analysis so that you can properly size a heating system yourself if you choose.

Occupant Behavior

Some like it hot. Do you open windows while the heat is on? Do you turn down the heat at night? According to the American Society for Heating, Refrigeration, and Air Conditioning Engineers (ASHRAE), humans are most comfortable when the temperature is between 72° and 78°F with a relative humidity between 35 and 60 percent. That comfort range can be extended each way depending on the individual, humidity levels, and air circulation.

The most obvious heat system interface in your home is the one you have control of — the thermostat. Think of it as a valve between your fuel supplier and your wallet. Each thermostat provides temperature control to a heat "zone" in the home. You should have enough zone control so that you are not heating seldom-used or generally cooler parts of the house while also heating a well-used living area. For example, bedrooms should be allowed to be cooler than the living room.

A programmable, automatic setback thermostat can help save energy by adjusting the temperature based on the time of day. Set it to turn the temperature down at night and when you leave for work. No need to burn fuel if you aren't home. Reducing the temperature by one degree F can save three percent of your heating energy. That's a ten-percent savings for every eight-hour period of 10° setback. A programmable thermostat remembers to turn the heat down for you, and can also adjust the temperature while you're asleep or away so you don't wake up or come home to an uncomfortable house.

Heating System Efficiency

To address this subject, we'll first need to identify different kinds of heating equipment, how they're controlled, the benefits of each, and how to improve your current heating system's efficiency. If you need a new heating system, you need to know how to look at efficiency ratings for heating equipment.

The efficiency of your current heating system can be assessed by a technician using combustion analysis equipment. Efficiency can range from about 60 percent for older equipment (and even some new space heaters), to 95 percent or higher in modern, highly controlled systems. The way the heat is distributed throughout your home can have a big effect on the system's overall efficiency.

Types of Heating Systems

A heating system consists of three main components:

Heating plant: the device that creates the heat, sometimes called a "heating appliance." Typical heating plants are furnaces, boilers, and space heaters.

Distribution system: how the heat is delivered to the living areas. A furnace distributes heat through ductwork, while a boiler circulates water through radiators.

Controls affect how the heating plant behaves and how heat delivery is regulated.

Every heating system has a personality of its own, with the requisite groans and quirks. Each provides different options for heat delivery and control, and the choice can be made by personal preference or by the constraints of the house site. Following are some of the most common heat system choices.

Furnace

In a furnace, air is heated by a fuel. The fuel can be oil, electricity, natural gas, LP gas, wood, or biofuels. Heat from the flame is transferred to air through a heat exchanger, where the hot air is fan-forced through ductwork and distributed throughout the home. This type of ducted heat distribution is called *forced air*. A fan pushes and pulls air around in a closed loop between hot air supply ducts and cold air return ducts. In between the supply and return ducts are the rooms of your home. Forced air systems are very popular (57 percent of households have them) largely because they have the benefit of sharing a common distribution system for central air conditioning, and can also provide whole-house ventilation, air filtration, and humidification. The constant air circulation offers the home a fresh feeling, and distribution registers do not take up any space within the rooms as baseboard heaters do. A furnace system does have its drawbacks, however, and they are primarily related to the distribution system.

- Ductwork can leak air and, if not sealed and insulated, what should be a forced hot-air system can feel more like a cool draft running through your home. This symptom is no reason to get rid of your furnace. Sealing and insulating ductwork can greatly increase comfort and efficiency. Insulated flex duct, however, is easy to install poorly; tight turns, sags, and kinks can all reduce airflow.
- Moving air can be noisy— the result of air speeding through a heating grate or because the ductwork carries the motor noise through it.

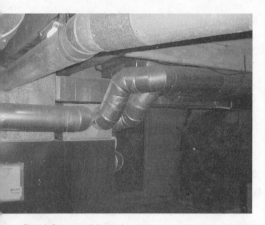

Fig. 5.3: Furnace and ductwork.

• Furnace ductwork requires more physical space than do hot water pipes for boiler heat distribution.

• Moving air with a furnace fan requires more electrical energy than moving hot water with the circulator pumps in a boiler to distribute the same amount of heat to your home.

• Furnace filters need to be changed regularly.

• Separate heat zones are generally not possible, but some control can be achieved by proper duct balancing.

• Proper design and balancing of supply and return ducts is crucial to proper performance.

• Heat registers can become blocked by rugs or furniture.

Fig. 5.4: Furnace fan control switch.

Furnace Controls

A furnace blower-motor cycles on and off in response to the thermostat and internal duct temperature. Figure 5.4 shows a furnace fan control switch called a *limit switch*. This heat-sensitive switch measures the temperature of the air inside the duct as it exits the furnace. If the air is too cold, it turns off the furnace fan. Both the high and low limit temperatures can be set according to comfort, safety requirements, and for maximum efficiency. The fan control operates independently of the burner, allowing for continued air circulation after the burner turns off so that residual heat in the ductwork is released into the house.

Boiler

In a boiler, water is heated by a fuel to (usually) 180°F and distributed throughout the house by pumps. A boiler can also create steam for distribution through radiators. The steam's pressure takes it to the radiators and as the steam cools on its journey throughout the house, it condenses and returns to the boiler as liquid water to be heated into steam again.

Heat distribution from a hot water boiler is called *hydronic distribution*. Hydronic distribution is clean, quiet, easily zoned (separate rooms have their own thermostat), and a boiler can also be used to heat domestic hot water (for your showers, dishes, etc). Hot water is circulated through pipes (generally copper or plastic) and distributed to each room by any of several means:

Figure 5.5: Boiler with indirect-fired water heater. Note the combustion air intake duct leading from outside, down to the burner on the bottom.

- Tube and fin baseboard units (mostly convection, some radiation heat transfer).
- Radiant heat tubes under or within a floor
- Upright radiators (mostly radiant, some convection heat transfer)
- Wall- or ceiling-mounted radiators with integral fan (convection, radiation)

If you are concerned about freezing due to a power failure, or your home is seasonal, the system can be filled with anti-freeze with a small sacrifice in efficiency.

Unless you choose a radiant floor system, you will lose some floor space for the distribution baseboards or radiators. Radiant floor heat distribution is becoming more popular. These systems circulate hot water through tubing built into a concrete slab, or installed underneath a wood floor. They provide a large, built-in heating surface, offering even, comfortable heat with no baseboards to get in the way or keep clean. You will pay more to have a radiant floor, and the choice is based on personal preference. Radiant floor heat is no more or less efficient than other types of distribution, though equivalent comfort levels may be achieved at lower temperatures as compared to other types. Due to the thermal mass of the floor system, radiant floors are slow to respond to thermostats. Because of this, the use of automatic setback thermostats with radiant floor systems can be problematic.

If you are building a new home and like the idea of radiant heat, you might first ask yourself what this kind of heat distribution is worth to you. Modern homes are quite energy efficient, and with a little attention, they can be made extremely efficient. You may be able to heat your entire home with a $2,500 space heater. To the other extreme, the labor-intensive installation of radiant floor heat may cost upwards of $10,000 in the same home. If you live in an older home and are considering radiant heat as a way to warm up the floors, beware that the amount of heat that can be distributed by a radiant floor is limited. You may find it more practical and cost-effective to tighten up the home and add insulation to increase your comfort level. It is best to consult with a heating contractor or energy auditor to see if a radiant floor is suitable for your house.

Boiler Controls

An *aquastat* is a kind of thermostat that responds to water temperature, allowing it to control the water temperature of a boiler (see Figure 4.9). A *modulating* aquastat (sometimes called an *outdoor reset*) on your boiler will automatically adjust the boiler water temperature based on the outside temperature. If it's not very cold, the boiler doesn't need to circulate very hot water to keep your house warm.

Circulator pumps and *zone valves* are used with boilers and respond to the thermostat by allowing hot water to flow through each individual distribution loop. The pump should operate independently of the burner, allowing continued hot water circulation after the burner turns off so that residual heat in the pipes can be released into the house.

Space Heaters

Space heaters include wood stoves, fireplace inserts, and gas or kerosene room heaters. They create heat by burning a fuel and either radiating or fan-forcing the heat into the surrounding space. Many homes use space heaters as a back-up system, for ambiance, or to heat an addition. Because there is no central (or whole house) heat-distribution system with a space heater, multiple units are typically required to sufficiently heat an average home. Space heaters are a good, low-cost heating choice if you have an open floor plan, live in a warm climate, or have a small or very efficient home. If you want a single space heater to heat your entire home, consider how the heat will move around corners, through doors, up and down stairs, and make it to the furthest rooms. As with a central heating system, it is important that space heaters be properly sized for the home. Space heaters come in several varieties including:

- Floor furnaces live under the floor: the heat rises or is fan-forced up into the living area.
- Wall furnaces are attached to a wall and circulate air between the floor and the ceiling. They can be tall and skinny or short and square.
- Room heaters such as a wood or gas stove are free-standing.
- Fireplace inserts.

Some space heaters do not require any electricity, making them a good choice if you expect the power to fail, live off-grid or electricity is costly. Space heater efficiencies are generally lower than a central heating system. Better space heaters range in efficiency from 60 to low-80 percent. Rinnai and Monitor (natural, propane gas and the latter also kerosene) are two of the more efficient brand names, with efficiencies in the mid-80 percent range. Hearthstone makes an attractive free-standing gas space heater of about 80-percent efficiency. Fireplace inserts (wood or gas) can be an economic means of converting a traditional fireplace into a more efficient (40- to 60-percent) heating source, provided they are EPA approved, sealed combustion units with tightly closing ceramic glass doors. Air-tight wood stoves range from 60 to 78 percent efficient, though wood heating equipment's efficiency is largely governed by their operation. Wood pellet stoves may be upwards of 80 percent efficient. If a woodstove is in your future, be aware that some look good in a parlor and do well with occasional use, while others can provide reliable full-time heat to an entire home. Few do both. Currently, one of the cleanest burning woodstoves is the Quadra-Fire by Aladdin. For a list of woodstove ratings, visit the US Environmental Protection Agency's website at: <www.epa.gov/compliance/ resources/publications/monitoring/programs/woodstoves/certified wood.pdf>.

Sealed-combustion space heaters are strongly recommended. This means that all the oxygen needed to combust the fuel comes from outside, not inside the house (see "Combustion Equipment Venting" later in this chapter). This is important in today's tightly constructed homes. Many space heaters are easily vented (both air intake and exhaust) through the wall, and don't need a chimney. Many new woodstoves will have a provision for external air supply to the firebox. See Figure 5.6.

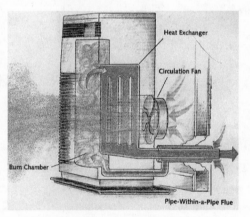

Fig. 5.6: Sealed-combustion space heater cutaway view.
Monitor Products, Inc.

Unvented space heaters (the kind that don't require a chimney) are strongly discouraged! You need air, and so does your space heater — don't be in competition with it! All heating systems produce carbon monoxide (CO) and carbon dioxide regardless of efficiency ratings and other claims. Do not allow yourself to be poisoned by an advertising campaign promising 98 percent efficiency. How does the 98-percent heater efficiency claim work? Normally, toxic flue gases are vented outdoors. These gases carry some heat away with them. If those gases were vented into your home, the efficiency of the heater would greatly increase because now *all* the heat energy, along with the toxic flue gases, ends up in your home. Most unvented heaters now come with oxygen-depletion sensors that turn off the gas supply when oxygen concentrations fall too low, along with warnings to use only in a well-ventilated area.

In addition, burning fuel releases water vapor. Much energy is embodied in this water vapor that would otherwise go out the chimney. But all that water vapor condensing on the cooler surfaces inside your house is not necessarily a good thing. For every gallon of propane, or therm of natural gas that is burned, approximately one gallon of water vapor is created.

Some readers may take issue with my concerns, but there are some very good reasons why unvented heaters are not permitted in all of Canada and some states in the US.

Combination Systems

Combination systems use a hot water heater or a boiler in conjunction with ducted heat distribution. A water heater (for small or very efficient homes) or boiler supplies hot water to a *fan coil* that lives inside a duct system. A fan coil is basically a hot water radiator, much like the one in your car. As hot water is circulated through the coil, a fan blows air over it, distributing the heat through the ductwork to the house. One advantage to this setup is that it allows a forced air system to be zoned by using two or more air handlers without the need to buy more than one complete heating plant. Using a hot water boiler also allows for the use of a more efficient indirect-fired water heater as a zone off the boiler (read more about water heaters in Chapter 4), and there is only one appliance to heat both house air and domestic hot water.

Alternatively, ground water can be used with a ground-source heat pump for heating or cooling. Water is circulated in pipes underground where it transfers heat to or from the ground (depending upon which is warmer), then through the fan coil in the ductwork where heat is again transferred from hot to cold. A reasonably steady 55°F groundwater temperature offers cooling for air conditioning in the summer and pre-heating of the furnace air stream in the winter with the use of a heat pump.

Electric Heat

In addition to fossil fuel heaters, you may find *electric resistance heat* in the form of baseboard radiators, space heaters, furnaces, radiant panels (sometimes hidden in ceilings or walls), and thermal storage units where bricks are heated by electricity and re-radiate this heat over time. With electric heat, electricity flows through a resistive heating element where the resistance to the flow of current creates heat. This is the same principle of operation as an electric light

Programmable Thermostats

Ken Sumer told me that he leaves the thermostat at 70° all the time, even when nobody is home. "Of course," he explained, "the house will cool off during the day and it will take more energy to heat it up when everyone comes home in the evening."

I looked at him, silent.

"Right?" he pleaded.

I responded by heading to the kitchen and helping myself to a pot of hot water. Ken looked quite surprised as I quietly filled the tea kettle and set it on the stove, turning the control to high. I think he was about to call for help when I said, "I don't want anything right now, but maybe in an hour or so we can sit down over a cup of coffee and talk about how to save energy."

He looked at me curiously and then to the pot of water and said, "Well, it only takes five minutes to boil the water, no sense starting it now ..." I could see it click in his head.

"Right," I said, turning off the stove. "Your house is the same way, only better because it's insulated. The tea kettle isn't, and will lose heat much faster. Your house will heat up in 15 minutes or so after you get home, so why waste the fuel when nobody's here to feel cold?"

If you really can't stand to come home to a cool house, try a programmable thermostat that will turn the heat on a half-hour before you get home. If you're asleep for eight hours, and you're at work for eight hours, that leaves only eight hours a day that you need to raise the temperature in your home.

bulb. Electric heat is 100-percent efficient when it comes to converting electrical energy input to heating energy output (not including losses at the power plant and through the transmission lines), but is probably the most expensive type of heat in most areas and should be avoided.

Efficiency Ratings for Heating Systems

A typical heating system will last 15 to 20 years or more. If yours is 20 or more years old, it is probably a good candidate for replacement. How much will you save? That, of course, depends. It depends on how inefficient the old one is and whether or not you can do anything to increase its efficiency.

Efficiency is a ratio of (heat) energy output to (fuel) energy input. If you burn one gallon of oil, you hope to get 138,690 Btus of heating energy into your home. Nothing is 100 percent efficient, and tests have been developed and standardized to measure heating equipment efficiency. When speaking about heating plant efficiency, there are two concepts to understand.

Annual fuel utilization efficiency (AFUE) is a standardized Department of Energy test of the overall efficiency of a heating appliance. It accounts for the efficiency losses described below. AFUE, measured in percent, is the figure listed on the yellow Energy Guide tags on all new heating equipment. More efficient heating systems have higher AFUE numbers. The AFUE test is equivalent to driving your car in a mix of highway and city traffic.

A boiler AFUE rating of 85 percent or higher qualifies for the ENERGY STAR label, and a furnace requires an AFUE of at least 90 percent to qualify. A new heating system may be a "condensing" type, offering greater efficiency (in the mid 90s) by capturing more heat energy from flue gases and water vapor in the exhaust. In addition, it is much easier and more economical to vent a condensing heating plant because the flue gases are cooler.

Steady-state efficiency (SSE) is a measure of how much energy is transferred from the burning fuel to the heat distribution side of the heat exchanger. Some energy is lost up the chimney and a little is lost due to incomplete fuel burning. When your contractor performs a combustion efficiency test on your heating equipment (as seen in

Fig. 5.7: Combustion testing a furnace. The probe inserted into the flue is connected to an electronic measuring device that samples flue gas and shows steady-state efficiency along with carbon monoxide and carbon dioxide levels within the flue.

Figure 5.7), he may give you a steady-state efficiency figure that is several percent higher than the system's rated AFUE. This is because the test occurs under optimum conditions and does not account for on/off cycling losses. SSE is equivalent to driving your car on the highway where it is operating at its best efficiency.

There are several ways a heating system's efficiency can be compromised.

Combustion losses occur due to incomplete burning of the fuel, and heat losses up the chimney. Combustion losses are reduced in more efficient heating systems and in systems that are properly maintained.

Off-cycle losses happen during warm-up and cool-down periods when the heating system is just starting up or has just turned off. Some heat is lost up the chimney while the burner heats the air or water up to the required temperature. Off-cycle losses can be reduced by properly sizing the heating system. Too large a heating plant will cause the furnace or boiler to cycle on and off frequently, increasing off-cycle losses. An undersized heating plant will not be able to keep up with demand on the coldest days.

Stand-by loss is heat lost through the heating plant cabinet. This is the main reason, along with exposed hot water pipes, that the boiler room is so hot. Low mass boilers can help reduce this loss.

Distribution losses occur in the hot water pipes or hot air ducts used to distribute heat around the home and are addressed by properly sizing, sealing, and insulating ducts and pipes.

Efficiency Improvements

Before you buy an expensive new heating system, consider whether it would be worthwhile to make improvements that can increase the efficiency of your current heating system. Maintenance and relatively inexpensive upgrades may be more cost-effective than a new heating plant. If you have a furnace, sealing and insulating your ducts can offer very cost-effective savings and increased comfort throughout the home.

The heating system efficiency savings in Table 5.1 shows how much fuel you can save by increasing the efficiency of your heating system by ten percent. As you can see, the savings may not justify the cost of a new ($3,000) heating plant, but less expensive efficiency improvements are certainly worthwhile.

Table 5.1: Increased Heating System Efficiency Savings.

Increase heat system efficiency 10% Annual energy savings: 6.7 MMBtus			
Type of fuel	Energy saved	CO₂ reduction (pounds)	Energy cost savings
Natural gas	67 therms	812	$84
LP gas	73 gallons	930	$131
Oil	49 gallons	1,088	$83

Savings is based on an annual heat load of 50 MMBtu and furnace AFUE of 75%.
Use your fuel cost for more accurate savings.

Maintenance

Preventive maintenance is the most important thing you can offer your heating system for maximum efficiency and long life. Here is a list of things a service technician can do to increase efficiency, reduce fuel costs, and extend the life of the heating system. You might be able to do some of these on your own.

- Clean, tune, and adjust your heating system every year if it's oil, every two years if it's gas. On oil heating equipment, one eighth of an inch of soot on the heat exchanger can increase fuel consumption by eight percent.
- During the clean and tune service, be sure to have the efficiency tested. If the service technician cannot bring the efficiency up to at least 75 percent, ask about the costs and benefits of equipment upgrades or replacement.
- Clean or replace the air filter in your furnace or space heater as needed. This may be once a month during the heating season. If the air handler (the blower fan) is used for air conditioning as well, service the filter throughout the year.
- Keep the furnace blower motor and fan blades clean.
- Seal *all* ductwork joints with a high quality (UL-181 approved) foil tape or mastic paste to eliminate leaks. Do *not* use common cloth duct tape to seal ducts!
- If the ductwork is used for air conditioning as well, be sure to keep the evaporator coils clean.
- Have the furnace supply and return ducting balanced for even airflow.

- Keep the air registers, grills, radiators, and baseboards clean and clear. Don't block heat with furniture, drapes, dirt, or other obstructions.
- Look for soot, rust, and corrosion in and around the furnace and on the floor surrounding it. Such signs require immediate service.
- Bleed trapped air from steam radiators. Noise or no heat from the radiator indicates air may be in the line.

Duct Leakage, Energy and Air Quality

Unless your furnace ducts are perfectly sealed and totally insulated, you will lose valuable energy and compromise the quality of your indoor environment. Multiple studies across the country have shown that a modest investment (about $200) in duct repairs can achieve average annual heating energy savings of 17 percent. It is estimated that US residential ductwork leakage costs consumers $5 billion each year, wasting the equivalent of the annual energy consumption of 13 million cars.

Because ductwork often runs through unheated spaces such as cold basements, hot attics, and through the interior of outside walls, heat from the ducts will be readily lost to colder areas, while heat from the attic will warm ducts carrying cool air for air conditioning. Air leaks in the supply side of the ductwork (under positive pressure) allow conditioned air to move into unconditioned spaces, while leaks in the return side (under negative pressure) can suck air from places like the attic and basement, circulating this potentially lower quality air (mold spores, insulation fibers, and dust) throughout your house. Small leaks can lead to large increases in energy costs, poor delivery of conditioned air, a dusty house, and decreased comfort.

Typical repairs include sealing all seams in the ductwork with UL-181 approved foil tape or mastic. Do not use cloth duct tape — studies show that duct tape fails after about six months when used for duct sealing. Connections between registers and floors or walls should be mechanically fastened and sealed. If wall or floor framing cavities are used for ducts, use properly sealed ductboard. After sealing, the ducts should be wrapped with at least R-5 insulation.

Another professionally applied duct sealing method is with an aerosol sealant product called Aeroseal (made by Carrier Corp.) that is sprayed into a sealed duct system. As the product finds its way out of the leaks, it expands, sealing the hole. This is very useful in sealing leaks that are buried in walls that can't be reached. You can learn more about this product on the web at <www.aeroseal.com>.

Figure 5.8 shows a typical duct system running through an unheated crawl-space. By the time the heated air in the duct makes it to the room, much of the heat has been lost to the basement. Note that none of the connections between duct sections are sealed, allowing condit-

Fig. 5.8: Typical ductwork in a cold crawlspace.

ioned air to escape from, or be sucked into these leaks. Figure 5.9 shows a properly sealed and insulated duct system. Note that both supply and return ducts are sealed with mastic, but only the supply side is normally insulated.

Duct leakage can be assessed by performing a test using a Duct Blaster®, as shown in Figure 5.10. To perform this test, all supply and return registers throughout the home are sealed. The Duct Blaster is connected to the ductwork and the Duct Blaster fan is turned on, pressurizing the entire duct system. Using pressure and flow meters, the heating contractor or energy auditor can measure the air flow through the fan. Any air moving through the fan must be leaving

Fig. 5.9 (left) : A properly sealed and insulated duct system.

Fig. 5.10 (right): Equipment required for a duct leakage test using a Duct Blaster.

the ducts through air leaks. After the ducts are sealed and insulated, the test is performed again and savings can then be quantified.

Equipment Upgrades

Here are some things that can a professional heating contractor can do to upgrade your heating system:

- Have the heating plant professionally cleaned, tuned, and tested with electronic combustion analysis equipment.
- Install an efficient flame-retention oil burner (oil heat only).
- Correct the flue draft with a properly adjusted barometric damper.
- If you have a furnace, adjust the fan thermostat (limit switch) so that air is just warm enough when the blower first turns on, and not too cold just before it turns off. This allows the home to capture as much heat as possible and reduces heat lost in the distribution system.
- Be sure that your furnace fan is moving an appropriate amount of air to properly condition your house.
- Install a time-delay relay on the boiler that allows water to circulate before the boiler comes on. In warmer weather, this warm (not hot) water may be enough to heat the house.
- Reduce the firing rate. This lowers the heat capacity and should only be done if you have reduced the heat load of the home through efficiency upgrades.
- Install adjustable radiator vents or valves on hot water or steam boilers.
- Install a modulating aquastat (or outdoor reset) on your boiler.

Comfort Improvements

People are often more motivated to action by comfort issues than by the potential for energy or cost savings. Here are a few things you can do to increase your comfort level while reducing energy costs:

- A ceiling fan will circulate warm air trapped at the ceiling allowing you to turn down the thermostat a few degrees.
- Eliminate cold drafts. Add insulation where needed.

- Increased humidity can, under certain situations, make you feel warmer at cooler temperatures. Tightening up your house can reduce dry indoor air conditions (see Chapter 6).
- If you are considering major renovations to the house, have an energy audit to see if any energy-efficiency improvements can be made at the same time.

Combustion Equipment and Fuel Safety

Central heating systems are routinely installed with an array of safety features including flame sensors and over-temperature shut-down switches. Ask your service technician to point them out to you. Some safety features may be required by state or local building codes. A properly installed gas appliance in a home with conscientious occupants will cause no trouble when prudence is first on the installation checklist. Always have a qualified service person install any type of combustion appliance and have it inspected for proper operation at least every two years. If you put in a new gas range, don't assume that hooking up a gas connector is as simple as plugging in an electric cord.

You should not need to worry that a properly installed and regularly inspected combustion appliance will cause any harm. However, do not become complacent about these powerful fuels in your home. Pay attention to the fuel-burning equipment and learn to recognize warning signals such as odor, inability to keep the burner flame or pilot light lit, and sooting (smoky, black deposits) anywhere on or around the equipment or vent system. It is especially important *never* to store flammable materials near any fuel-burning or heat-generating device. Read all labels carefully before you put anything in the same room as your heating system or hot water heater. Fumes from an accidentally spilled can of paint thinner can explode if they come in contact with an ignition source such as a pilot light.

If you worry that fuels in your home may explode or cause a fire by themselves, let me help to allay your fears. Both the proper concentration of fuel in air, *and* an ignition source are required before the fuel will ignite. Fossil fuels need to be mixed with air in order to burn, and the range of combustible fuel to air mixture is limited. For example, for natural gas, the combustible ratio of fuel to air ranges from 5 percent to 15 percent. That means that if the concentration of natural gas in air is less than five percent, there is not enough gas to sustain combustion. Likewise, if the concentration of gas is greater than 15 percent, there is not enough oxygen to support combustion. In addition to the proper fuel-to-air mixture, a fuel must be ignited with a spark, a flame, or some other source of heat. The ignition temperature of natural gas is over 1,000°F.

For LP gas the combustible range is between a two percent and ten percent mixture of fuel to air with an ignition temperature of 850°F. For comparison, the combustible range of gasoline (something most of us deal with nearly every day) is between a one percent and eight percent mixture of fuel to air with a much lower ignition temperature of 495°. If you are fueling your car, a spark generated by static electricity is enough to set the fuel vapor afire.

Draft and Backdraft

Fossil-fuel heat and hot-water equipment need air to burn fuel. In a typical appliance, this air comes from inside the house, but there are better ways to address air requirements. In all homes — especially new, tight, energy-efficient homes — it is very important to consider where the combustion air is coming from, and how the flue gases are getting out of the building. Failure to pay attention to this simple detail can result in potentially deadly carbon monoxide poisoning.

Fossil-fuel burning equipment needs a chimney or venting system to remove poisonous combustion byproducts from the house to the outdoors. It is important to make sure the chimney or venting system is in good condition and properly sized for the equipment. There are very strict codes for venting combustion appliances. Check with your local plumbing or heating contractor, or chimney sweep for an expert inspection and discussion of applicable local codes.

Two concepts will help to explain the nature and need for proper venting of exhaust gases: *draft* and *backdraft*.

Draft is the flow of air into the fuel burner and out the flue. As the fuel burns, air is drawn from the surrounding environment into the combustion chamber. The flame creates heat and the hot, buoyant, combustion gases rise up the flue leading to the outdoors. Draft can be created naturally by the combustion process, or induced by a fan in the venting system to ensure removal of combustion byproducts.

Backdraft occurs when exhaust moves backwards through the vent and into the home due to inadequate draft. It can occur if the chimney is blocked or if it is the wrong size for the equipment, if high winds force a backdraft down the chimney, or if a negative pressure is created in the area where the heating equipment exists. This negative pressure can come from exhaust fans (including clothes dryers and high-powered kitchen range fans) in the home, or other combustion equipment with a stronger draft. When the venting system cannot overcome atmospheric forces within the home, a continuous spillage of poisonous combustion gases is the result.

The problem of backdrafting has been exacerbated as new homes are built tighter to be more energy efficient, and older homes are upgraded to reduce air infiltration and heat loss. A tighter house means that fresh air is at a premium and there is a greater potential for negative-pressure problems indoors under the right conditions. I'm not suggesting you build a drafty house. Build tight enough to be energy efficient, and then control the fresh air coming in from outside with mechanical ventilation such as exhaust fans or a whole-house heat-recovery ventilation system. Mechanical ventilation strategies are explained in greater detail in Chapter 6.

You may be able to tell if your equipment is venting properly by holding a smoldering incense stick at the vent draft hood (see Figure 5.11) while the burner is firing. The smoke should be drawn up the flue. *Keep the smoke stick away from the air intake and all fuel lines!* In order to determine if the potential for backdrafting exists in your home, you will need a thorough, professional inspection including combustion analysis of all heating and ventilating equipment, along with an air leakage test to quantify how tight your house is. Air leakage issues are discussed in greater detail in Chapter 6.

Combustion Equipment Venting

In general, chimneys and vents should be straight, with tight connections between pipes or other materials, and free of sags, rust, and debris. It is important for the vent to be vertical, or at least sloped upward to the outdoors, so the hot gases can rise up and out. Elbows, twists, and turns in the vent pipe restrict and slow the flow of exhaust gas, increasing the potential for backdrafting. A single 90° bend (elbow) in a flue pipe is equivalent to an additional nine feet of straight vent pipe. The longer the pipe, the more difficult it is to establish a draft.

Combustion gases are corrosive, and any condensation or debris inside the venting system can accelerate the flue's deterioration, whether it is metal or masonry. If you have a wood heating system, offer it a dedicated chimney — do not vent any other type of fuel into the same flue because the resulting corrosive mixture of combustion byproducts will accelerate the chimney's demise. Have the chimney cleaned and inspected *at least* once a year.

When deciding how to vent your heating equipment, it is important to consider what else is happening in the house. Knowing something about air movement and pressure dynamics within your home can help you decide between one of the three common venting configurations.

Atmospheric Venting

Atmospheric venting is the most common and usually least expensive approach to equipment venting. Figure 5.11 shows a gas water heater with an atmospheric venting system. "Atmospheric" means that all the air needed for fuel combustion and flue draft comes from the surrounding environment, or atmosphere. The vent has a draft hood at the outlet of the heating appliance. The draft hood is open to the room and allows air to be drawn up into the flue, helping to create a draft. The drawback to atmospheric venting is that in modern, well-insulated, airtight homes, the outgoing draft in the flue can be overcome by the air drawn from other exhaust devices in the home, causing a backdraft situation. Additionally, atmospheric equipment allows air to pass unrestricted through the burner, heat exchanger, and vent hood, removing heat from the appliance along with conditioned air from your home, sending your energy dollars up the chimney.

Power Venting

Power venting is a type of atmospheric vent system that has a fan on the flue pipe that forces flue gases outside. Power-vented equipment tends to be more efficient, as such units normally have no standing pilot light. Instead, electronic ignition automatically lights the flame, and when gas flow is detected a gas pressure switch turns the fan on, forcing exhaust through the flue pipe. Power venting can be used successfully with unusually long or short vent pipe runs, offering a very flexible venting scheme.

Though power vents are certain to remove flue gases even through long flue runs and several elbows, air required for combustion and draft is still taken from within the house. This means that the power vent fan may create a negative pressure in the basement or utility room, possibly backdrafting other combustion appliances in the home. Another possible disadvantage is that the electric fans can be noisy and may not be tolerable if located near a living area.

Fig. 5.11: Atmospheric draft vent hood.

Figure 5.12 shows a power vent on a heating system flue pipe. The motor is seen in front, mounted into the square box above the barometric damper.

Sealed Combustion

Sealed-combustion heating equipment receives a supply of combustion air from, and vents exhaust gases to, the outdoors through a double-flue setup. There are actually two concentric pipes leading from the appliance to the outdoors, one for air intake and one for exhaust. Sealed-combustion equipment is a good choice as there is no danger of backdrafting, and conditioned air in the house is not lost to combustion or draft. Both power-vented and sealed-combustion equipment have the advantage of being vented through the wall, or if located in the basement, through the perimeter rim joist.

Fig. 5.12: Power vent draft.

An oil-fired heating appliance may use a variation of sealed-combustion known as *pressure-venting*. Pressure-venting uses the pressure created by the oil burner to draw air through a duct from the outdoors, into the combustion chamber, and out through the vent. Pressure-venting uses outside air for both combustion and draft.

The Sealed Room

If you have trouble with backdrafting of combustion equipment, there is a way to prevent it. You can build a reasonably airtight room that is aerodynamically decoupled from the rest of the house in which to put your space heating and hot water equipment. A supply of outside air is brought into the room to meet the combustion and draft requirements of the heating equipment. The air supply needs to be adequate for the specific combustion appliances you have, so it is best to consult with a heating contractor or energy auditor for proper design. Typically, you will need a hole between 3 and 12 inches in diameter for most household equipment needs.

Make-Up Air

There is a finite quantity of air in a house, and at certain times the air supply is in high demand. With a tightly constructed home closed up tight for winter, only a moderate amount of natural air infiltration occurs. When significant quantities of available air are being pulled from the house by combustion and exhaust appliances, the inside of the house becomes negative in pressure with respect to the outdoors. Where will the "make-up" air for these appliances come from?

Backdrafting at Home

The entire Sumer family was home one cold winter evening with the furnace running (using air for combustion and draft), and everyone breathing (also using air). Kenny Jr. and sister Betty were washing their clothes (one piece at a time) in hot water so the gas water heater was on — also requiring air for both combustion and draft. The dryer was venting air from the house to the outdoors. Then Betty decided to have her second shower of the day and turned on the bathroom exhaust fan. When air goes out, air must come in. Ken Sr. was cooking and the range hood exhaust fan was on full blast, pulling smoke-laden air out of the house (though of course he said the smoke wasn't his fault). The kids' lips were turning blue, and suddenly Ken couldn't keep the gas range lit. The CO sensor went off in the study where Connie was checking her e-mail.

What's happening?

The house needs air! Everything they are doing requires air and since all the windows are closed, there is no way for fresh air to get into the house. The path of least resistance has now become the chimney, full of poisonous combustion gases. The house needs a source of air to make up for what is leaving through the chimney and exhaust fans.

If the appliances are not sealed-combustion, air will move into the house from the path of least resistance. That path can be any hole in the house including an open window, the attic via a penetration in the ceiling for recessed lights, or an atmospherically vented furnace or water heater with a flue draft that cannot overcome the negative pressure in the house. In the latter instance, flue gases (including killer carbon monoxide) can enter the house.

The solution is to provide make-up air to those appliances that require air from within the house to perform their functions. For instance, the burner on an oil furnace or boiler can be set up with a kit that draws air from the outside via a PVC pipe attached to a shroud fitted over the burner. Sealed-combustion venting is also becoming more common among newer gas appliances and even wood-burning stoves.

Open fireplaces draw large volumes of indoor air up the chimney. For fireplaces, use dedicated combustion air inlets behind tightly closing glass doors to prevent removing conditioned air from within the home.

Dryers, gas ranges, and exhaust fans are more difficult to deal with in terms of providing adequate make-up air. You may simply need to open a window if many activities requiring air are occurring within the house. Or, for more control, consider a commercially available fresh air inlet such as the Aldes Fresh-80. These are filtered, four-inch wall vents that open and close by way of a draw string, allowing for a slow infiltration of fresh air where and when it is needed.

The need for make-up air can best be determined by an energy auditor who can check the home's air infiltration rate and perform a backdraft test on all combustion appliances. You should consider having these tests performed if:

- Your house feels stuffy when you come in from outside.
- Indoor relative humidity is consistently over 50 percent during heating season.
- Condensation builds up on windows.
- You notice drafts while exhaust fans are operating.
- Your carbon monoxide alarm goes off.
- Pilot lights blow out for no apparent reason.
- You notice soot build-up on or around the heat system or water heater.

If you are insulating and weatherizing your home, it will become more airtight as you go. Be aware that backdrafting problems can suddenly appear as you tighten up the house. Renovation is an opportunity to consider the house holistically, integrating energy improvements with utility upgrades while also addressing indoor air quality issues.

Carbon Monoxide

Over 800 people die of carbon monoxide poisoning each year. This colorless, odorless gas is always a potential danger wherever fuel combustion is involved. Invisible problems like a cracked heat exchanger in a furnace can be deadly. Annual inspection by a professional heating contractor reduces the chances of CO entering the home, but it is always a good idea to have carbon monoxide alarms in the home to alert you to its presence.

Carbon monoxide production is the result of incomplete combustion of fuels or other carbon-containing materials.

Some sources of carbon monoxide in your home may be:

- Faulty or improper venting of wood or fossil fuel-fired heating and cooking equipment
- The use of unvented room heaters
- Cracked heat exchanger in a furnace
- Negative pressure in the home causing backdrafting of chimneys or vents
- Blocked chimneys or vents
- Old, neglected equipment that may require adjustment
- Improper use of combustion appliances
- Operation of a gas-powered generator in a basement, garage, or crawlspace, or too close to the house

Many new homes around the country are now being built with hard-wired CO sensors throughout the building. A plug-in or battery-powered unit with a digital readout of the actual level of CO present can be more useful than one which remains silent until the alarm goes off. The sensors in carbon monoxide detectors are accurate for only about five years.

If you are exposed to carbon monoxide, you may experience flu-like symptoms such as headache, tightness across the forehead and temples, weariness, weakness, dizziness, confusion, watering and smarting of the eyes, and vomiting. As exposure levels increase, the symptoms get worse and include loss of muscular control and loss of consciousness. If you should develop any of these symptoms, get into the fresh air immediately! *Then* call for help.

In general, health risks occur with long-term exposure (eight hours or more) to CO exceeding 9 parts per million (PPM). Some of the symptoms associated with higher levels and longer exposure times include:

- 400 PPM: headache within one to two hours; life-threatening within three to five hours.
- 800 PPM: nausea and convulsions; death within two hours.
- 1,500 PPM: death within one hour.

To put these figures into perspective, 100 PPM is the equivalent of .01 percent. A home heating system may have a carbon monoxide concentration of 100 PPM inside the flue. This means that if backdrafting occurs, carbon monoxide will enter the living space. In reality, the only safe exposure to carbon monoxide is none. If your CO sensor alarm goes off, you need to find out why and repair the problem.

Here are some things you can do to reduce the danger of carbon monoxide poisoning:

- Never use an oven or stove-top burner to heat your home or RV.
- Install and maintain carbon monoxide detectors throughout your home.
- Never use an unvented gas or kerosene heater in a living or work space.
- Never cook with a propane or charcoal barbecue grill inside your home or attached garage. Even a porch can be dangerous.
- Have all fossil fuel appliances tested annually for proper operation by a qualified service person.
- Heaters used in an RV or mobile home must be approved for that use.
- Never operate a gasoline generator inside your home or attached garage.
- Don't warm up your car in an attached garage.
- Have a qualified service person verify that combustion appliances are venting properly under worst-case conditions. This would be when all combustion appliances are operating and all exhaust fans are on while the house is closed up tight, putting the house under a negative pressure.

Buying New

Whether it's next week or in fifteen years, a new heating system is likely to be in your future. To make a decision, first consider what type of distribution system you'd prefer that would be practical and appropriate for your home. Your choices for distribution are ductwork (furnace), baseboard, radiators or radiant floor (boiler), or "local" (space heater). It probably makes economic sense to keep your existing distribution system unless you really don't like the quality of heat it offers. When a new heating system is installed, it's a good time to address other issues such as heat distribution improvements (proper zoning, insulation, and duct sealing), electrical service to the equipment, and fuel supply and storage issues.

The more you rely on your heating system, the greater the payback from investing in the most efficient unit. Efficiency has an up-front cost, but also provides long-term savings. Look for the ENERGY STAR label on any new furnace or boiler you are considering, ensuring an efficient choice. When choosing a new heating system, you will want to consider:

- Comfort
- Efficiency
- Convenience
- Fuel choice
- Practicality
- Serviceability
- Reliability
- Aesthetics
- Knowledgeable supplier/installer
- Cost
- Warranty

Combustion Equipment Safety Diet

- Install carbon monoxide alarms.
- Be sure the chimney and flue pipes are clean, tight, and free of corrosion and obstructions.
- Know where underground fuel and electric lines are buried.
- Avoid running fuel lines along floors or where they can be damaged.
- Never allow copper fuel lines to come in contact with concrete or another metal, such as galvanized ductwork. Doing so will corrode the copper pipe eventually causing a fuel leak.
- Reduce the risk of chimney backdrafting. Have a heating contractor or energy auditor test for backdrafting by creating a worst-case scenario that puts your house under a negative pressure, then check for proper chimney draft.
- Be observant. Look and listen for changes in your heating system or water heater operation and noise level, your comfort inside the home, soot stains around air registers or around the heating plant, and in the exhaust coming out the chimney.
- Never use an unvented heater in an occupied space.
- Don't use the tops of your furnace, boiler, or water heater as shelves. Keep them clear all around.
- Keep flammable and corrosive materials far away from heat sources.
- When doing any work on an older system, watch for and avoid handling asbestos insulation.
- Use sealed-combustion or power venting on your next furnace, boiler, or water heater.

- Experience of service technician — new heating systems are more complex and require detailed setup procedures.
- Fuel price and trends — when I perform energy audits, I meet old-timers who remember the Rural Electrification Administration promoting cheap, convenient, electric heat. I show up 50 years later and tell them it was all a mistake. Nobody can predict the future, but it's a good bet that electricity will (for the foreseeable future) be more expensive than having fossil fuels delivered to your home.

New energy-efficient heat systems include the following features:

- Electronic ignition in gas equipment eliminates the need for a pilot light
- Condensing gas boilers or furnaces with efficiencies greater than 90 percent
- Furnaces with high efficiency, electronically controlled motors
- Sealed-combustion to ensure sufficient air supply to the burner and to reduce the potential for backdrafting
- More efficient heat exchangers, put more heat into the distribution system
- Precision fuel combustion to control the flame according to the heat load
- Low mass boilers that reduce off-cycle and stand-by losses
- Sophisticated controls that adjust the heat output according to outdoor temperature and occupant behavior

When shopping for a new boiler, look for one with a high efficiency and *low mass*. Low mass means that it doesn't hold much water inside. A low-mass boiler will hold from three to six gallons of water, as compared to ten or more gallons in a high-mass boiler. The advantage of low mass is that the boiler doesn't waste much time or energy in heating up that water reservoir to get heat circulating through your house. It also means less heat (read: dollars) lost when the boiler is not running, and less time the boiler needs to operate in stand-by mode to keep that water at 180°F, waiting for a call to action from your thermostat.

New furnaces not only use sophisticated controls to regulate their heat output, but efforts have been made to reduce their fan motor's electrical consumption. The result is the electronically controlled brushless DC motor, also called the electronically commutated motor, or ECM for short (though

ECM is a registered trademark of General Electric). These very efficient motors have controls built in to adjust speed and torque according to heating needs and pressures within the ductwork. Electronically controlled motors can reduce the electrical energy used by a furnace by approximately half.

Costs of heating systems can vary depending on the type of heating plant and especially the type of distribution you choose, along with the complexity of controls and distribution requirements. The heat distribution system will likely be the most expensive part. Get several estimates and pay a little more to have the distribution system sealed and insulated; it will more than pay for itself in the long run.

All new heating equipment will have the yellow Energy Guide tags on them (see Chapter 7) indicating the efficiency (AFUE) and estimating the annual operating cost. Higher efficiency oil heat systems will have an AFUE of 85 to 87 percent, while gas equipment is available with efficiency ratings up to the mid 90s. High efficiency (more than 90-percent AFUE) condensing equipment captures the *latent heat of vaporization*, meaning the heat that otherwise escapes through the chimney in the form of water vapor, a byproduct of combustion. An AFUE of 85 or higher qualifies boilers for the ENERGY STAR label, while furnaces require an AFUE of at least 90 to earn the ENERGY STAR.

Search the Gas Appliance Manufacturer's Association (GAMA) website (<www.gamanet.org>) for more information on specific heat and hot water efficiency ratings.

Once you decide on the distribution and the fuel, you'll want your contractor to size the heating plant and the distribution system to match the needs of your home.

Proper Sizing

Proper sizing and adjustment of controls ensures efficient operation and avoids *short cycling*. Short cycling is when the heat comes on, heats up the house in a matter of minutes, then turns off. This is a classic symptom of an oversized heating system, or a very leaky house. If your house is not well insulated, the heat may cycle on and off every few minutes trying to keep up with the heat loss of the house. This is not a very efficient way for the heat system to function as it never has a chance to warm up and operate at its best efficiency. The same thing happens if the heating system is oversized for the house: the furnace turns on and blasts a huge amount of heat into the house, warms it up rapidly, then turns off shortly after.

Short cycling is like stomping on the gas pedal to drive down your driveway, and then screeching to a halt before the end. You look to see if the coast is clear (the boiler waits until the house cools down) and then lead-foot to the corner where you jam on the brakes again. Not a very efficient way to drive your car. Your car gets its best gas mileage on the highway, and its worst in stop-and-go city traffic. Your heating system is the same. Its overall efficiency is higher when it runs continuously, rather than making frequent starts and stops. A properly sized heating system will run nearly continuously on the coldest day of the year.

The heat input of a heating plant is based on the amount of fuel being burned by the gas or oil burner. The *capacity* of the heating plant is rated in Btus per hour of heat output. The capacity should match the *design heat load* of your home. The design heat load is based on how much heat the house will lose on the coldest day of the year. Choosing a heating plant with a rated output between 100 and 125 percent of the heat load will offer plenty of heat and maximum efficiency.

It is important not to oversize the heating system as it will operate inefficiently and you will be uncomfortable. Oversizing is a consistent problem in many new homes. It is not uncommon to see output ratings 200 percent or more over what they need to be. Some heating contractors have told me that they size the systems of new homes to keep the work crew warm while they build! In addition, they would rather not have you calling them at midnight in January complaining that you are cold. So it seems a safe bet to oversize the heating system for peace of mind — theirs, not yours. You end up paying an energy and comfort penalty for this.

When replacing a heating system, don't just install the equivalent of what was there before; have your heating contractor perform a detailed heat loss calculation according to the Air Conditioning Contractors of America's *Manual J*. Doing so will ensure that the heating plant as well as the heat distribution to each room is sufficient. A basic heat-loss calculation is presented in Appendix D.

Homes are being built tighter, but heat loss calculations usually over-estimate the air leakage of a home because they are doing just that —

estimating. Air leakage can be a big factor when it comes to heat loss in a home, especially older homes. In order to determine the air leakage rate, a *blower door* test (more on blower doors in Chapter 6) must be performed by a heating contractor or energy auditor. This test not only helps in proper heat system sizing, but can also pinpoint air leakage areas that should be sealed.

Electrical Use

Most heating systems use electricity in addition to the primary heating fuel. In general, a furnace uses more power than a boiler to deliver heat to a home. This is because a volume of water can hold over 3,400 times more heat than the equivalent volume of air at the same temperature. The result is that a boiler will heat a home for less than half the electrical cost of a furnace.

Math Box: Furnace and Boiler Electrical Use

A real-world example, comparing the electric use of a furnace and boiler:

This sample furnace draws 800 watts of power, and it runs an average of six hours a day throughout a 120-day heating season. Its power consumption then is:

800 watts × 6 hours × 120 days = 576,000 watt-hours, or 576 kWh

The circulator pumps in a boiler use about 100 watts each. If you have four zones of heat, with each pump running six hours a day over a 120-day heating season you will use:

100 watts × 4 pumps × 6 hours × 120 days = 288,000 watt-hours, or 288 kWh

A very general rule of thumb points to a furnace electrical consumption of approximately one kWh per therm (or Ccf) of natural gas, or each gallon of propane or oil used. Boilers are a bit harder to apply this to, as the number of zones and pumps varies greatly.

Heating Diet

- Let in the sun! Open curtains and shades in the daytime.
- Landscape so that the sun enters south-facing windows in the winter, and provide seasonal shade and wind blocks.
- Keep the temperature as low as you can comfortably stand it.
- Maintain a consistent temperature to avoid inefficient cycling of the heating system.
- Differently used areas of the home should be on separate heat zones, each with its own thermostat.
- Turn down the thermostat while away at work or on vacation.
- Use a programmable thermostat on each heating zone. For every degree you set your thermostat down, you can save three percent of your heating energy.
- Adjust the thermostat before opening the window.
- Avoid "dueling thermostats" where the heating and air conditioning thermostats are side by side, with the heat set higher than the air conditioner.
- Keep the thermostat away from heat registers and direct sunlight.
- Don't adjust the thermostat above the temperature you want the room to be. The room will not heat up any faster.
- Seal and insulate ductwork.
- Insulate all the pipes leading to and from the boiler.
- When using insulated flex-duct avoid tight turns, sags, and kinks that can reduce airflow.
- Tighten up — seal drafty areas where outside air enters the home.
- Use insulating window curtains at night to reduce heat loss.
- Hire an experienced energy auditor with a blower door to pinpoint air leakage areas.
- Insulate roof, walls, and floor to reduce heat loss and heating system run-time.
- Keep heat registers and baseboards free and clear; don't hide heat behind furniture.
- Keep radiators, baseboards and duct registers clean.
- Close off and turn down the heat in unused rooms.
- Use a tight-closing damper on fireplace chimneys to prevent conditioned air from flowing up the chimney.
- Avoid heat system short cycling by proper sizing and adjustment of controls.
- Have the duct system properly balanced.
- Add storm windows or plastic window film.
- If the heating system is more than 15 years old, consider replacing it with an ENERGY STAR-qualified system

Off-Grid Tip: Heating During a Power Failure

How do you heat your home when the power goes out? Living off-grid presents its own heating challenges. I'm fortunate to be able to use wood as my primary heating fuel. My woodstove requires no electricity except perhaps for an optional fan to blow the heat around. A woodstove radiates so much heat, that it easily heats my 1,500-square-foot, two-story home without the need for a blower fan. The house is reasonably efficient and we burn about two and a half full cords of wood each heating season. There are many people living in old farm houses in rural areas that may use up to ten cords to keep warm. It's a lot of work to handle that much wood, and it would be worthwhile investing in efficiency to cut the wood use in half.

In addition to the wood stove, we have a propane gas heater as backup heat in case we are away and can't load the wood stove. This is also a radiant heater. It looks like a wood stove, right down to the fake logs you can see through the glass door, and requires no electricity except to run the optional blower fan. At 30,000 Btus, it keeps the house reasonably warm. If my house were larger, and I had more electrical generating capacity, I would install a boiler using circulator pumps rather than a furnace with its more demanding blower motor.

"But," you might ask, "what about me? I rely on the power company to run my furnace and I don't want to buy solar panels to run the heat if the power fails." You can use a free-standing or wall-hung sealed-combustion gas space heater that uses no electricity, but there is another option: install a backup power supply consisting of batteries, a battery charger, and an inverter. Here's how it works.

During times when electricity is available, the batteries are being charged by utility power. When the power goes out, the inverter senses the fault and automatically switches over to battery backup, feeding your circuits electricity to maintain control over systems that are essential to your home's operation. Generally, you choose which set of circuits receives power from this backup system. It might include circuits that provide power to your heating system, refrigerator, or home office. It would be possible to supply electricity to your entire home in this manner, though probably quite expensive unless your home is very electrically efficient. These systems can cost between a few hundred and several thousand dollars depending on your needs. You will need to work with a qualified renewable energy contractor and/or electrician to properly size and install the system.

Air Conditioning

In 2001, 53 percent of US homes had central air conditioning (AC), and 22 percent had room AC. All told, AC accounted for six percent of the average home's energy use. To keep cool, 72.6 million homeowners spent nearly $16 billion on 183 billion kWh of electricity, which produced about 119 million tons of CO_2.

How an Air Conditioner Works

An air conditioner, like your refrigerator, is a kind of *heat pump*, meaning that it moves heat from one place to another. Refrigerators and air conditioners don't "make" cold; they remove heat from the inside and send it outside. The warm air that blows from under your fridge or outside your AC is the heat removed from inside it. Inside a heat pump there is a refrigerant (also called a working fluid), usually a Freon-based (HCFC) compound. The refrigerant is pumped through a closed-loop system where it alternates between evaporating (absorbing heat from the indoors) and condensing (releasing heat outside). Because condensation of a liquid releases heat, while evaporation absorbs heat, this process allows heat to be absorbed by, and then removed from the refrigerant. In addition, the air conditioning process removes moisture from the indoor air, increasing your comfort level. Water vapor from the air condenses on the cold evaporator coil just as a cold drink on a hot day forms condensation on the outside of the glass. This condensation is drained outside.

Types of Air Conditioners

Room air conditioners contain the evaporator unit, which absorbs heat from the indoors, and condenser unit, which releases heat to the outdoors, in a single package. They fit into a window or wall opening.

Central air conditioners have the condenser outdoors while the evaporator lives inside the air distribution ductwork in the home. Because of this separation of components, these are sometimes called "split" systems. The ductwork is very often the same distribution network used by the central heating system and all the same measures for distribution efficiency apply. It is important to keep duct connections tight to avoid leaks, and insulate them where they venture outside the conditioned area of the home.

Where running ductwork is not practical, or where only a few rooms need to be cooled, a hybrid AC system called a Mini-Split can be used. This system uses a central, outside condenser in conjunction with several separately located evaporators inside the house.

Alternatives to Air Conditioners

Air conditioning is costly to operate. It uses quite a lot of energy — about 500 watts of power for every 5,000 Btus of cooling capacity for a reasonably efficient unit. That means that if you run a 5,000 Btu AC at maximum for eight hours, it will have consumed 4 kWh. If you run an 80-watt ceiling fan for the same time, you will have used only 0.6 kWh.

Discomfort associated with heat has three components: temperature, humidity, and convection (or air movement). Increasing your summer comfort level involves controlling these elements. In general, you can reduce the need for AC by using a few ancient ideas:

- Increase shading to prevent solar radiation from striking and entering the home.
- Increase the reflectivity of the building.
- Reduce heat- and humidity-causing activities within the house.
- Increase ventilation, especially at night to allow cool air in.

Today we can combine these basic principles with a whole lot of technology to help keep comfortable. A tight, well-insulated building envelope will help reduce the need for air conditioning. Roughly 40 percent of unwanted heat comes through your windows and another 30 percent comes by way of the roof. Shading, awnings, insulating curtains, and the proper glazing choice for your climate can reduce solar heat gain through windows. Landscape shading can be quite effective and attractive. Deciduous trees provide shade in the summer and allow sunlight through in the winter. During photosynthesis, water vapor escapes through the leaves, and passing air is cooled by the evaporation of moisture. So along with shade, trees create a cool microclimate that reduces the temperature beneath the tree canopy. During winter, trees deflect cold winds, reducing convective heat loss from the shell of the house.

Good attic insulation and a radiant barrier in the ceiling, along with reflective roof colors, will keep the attic cool and slow heat movement to the living area. If your attic is a heat trap, try adding ventilation or an exhaust fan, but only after you have insulated and air-sealed the attic floor as best you can (read more about this in Chapter 6).

Ventilation can effectively keep us cool when the relative humidity is below 70 percent. Running a fan or opening windows for ventilation will cost less than running an air conditioner, and the moving air will increase your body's evaporative cooling. A properly sized whole-house fan can remove warm air from living areas and blow it outside, while drawing fresh air in through open windows. Allow natural convection currents to move through your home by opening both lower and upper story windows, allowing hotter air upstairs to be forced out as cooler air enters from below. A window fan can encourage this air movement but be sure to take advantage of wind conditions and place the fan so that it blows in the same direction as the wind outside the house. This will increase its efficiency at moving air. Open all windows in the house so the fan can bring fresh air through all the rooms. Remove warm daytime air by operating the exhaust fan at night. In the morning, turn off the fan, close all windows and doors, and draw the shades to keep the daytime heat out.

Evaporative cooling is how your body removes excess heat by sweating. Evaporating water absorbs and dissipates heat energy. When it is humid, moisture can't evaporate from our skin and we feel hot and sticky. In hot dry climates, moisture added to the air evaporates, absorbing heat energy as it does, and so cools the air. This principle has been applied to a mechanical evaporative cooler, sometimes called a *swamp cooler* because it cools the air while also making it more humid. Evaporative cooling equipment requires no compressor and so uses about 75 percent less electricity than a conventional air conditioner, and costs about half as much to install. Though not as effective as a conventional air conditioning system, swamp coolers can provide sufficient comfort under the right conditions. Because they rely on the evaporation of moisture, they work only in dry climates where relative humidity levels are below 40 percent, and they need a steady supply of water.

Heat pumps can be used to move heat around more efficiently than conventional air conditioners. An air source heat pump can be used in moderate climates to remove excess heat from indoors to out. Geothermal heat pumps use stable ground temperature to heat and cool your home and hot water. Both of these heat pumps can be more efficient and cost less to operate than conventional air conditioners, depending on your location and climate. To learn more about heat pumps, visit the Geothermal Energy Association on the web at <www.geo-energy.org>.

Size it Right

OK, you've tried everything and you just can't bear the heat anymore. If an AC purchase is pending, buy the right one. Don't over- or under-size the AC. A unit that is too large may cool the room off faster, but may not operate long enough (it will short cycle) to remove sufficient moisture to make the room comfortable. Running a smaller unit for a longer time will use less energy to completely condition a room than running a larger unit for a shorter time. Air conditioners are rated (as is heating equipment) in Btus per hour. Central air conditioner capacity is rated in "tons." One ton is equivalent to 12,000 Btus.

As with heating systems, a central AC system must be sized correctly for the home to ensure efficient operation. A good contractor will perform a thorough *cooling load analysis* on your home to determine the required capacity for a central air conditioning system. Don't settle for a salesman's "rule of thumb" or showroom floor estimate, which is only appropriate when choosing a room air conditioner. The cooling load of a building is the number of Btus per hour the

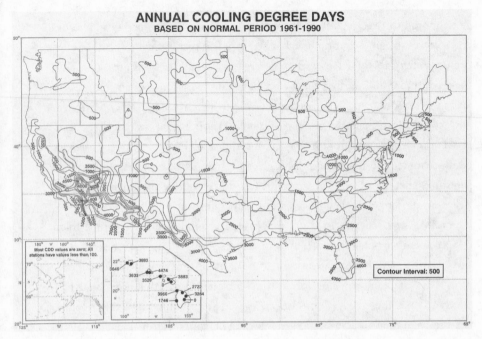

Fig. 5.13: Map of cooling degree days. CREDIT: National Oceanic and Atmospheric Administration, National Climatic Data Center

cooling system needs to remove from the home in the hottest summer weather. Cooling load is based on your home's efficiency and on a climate description known as *cooling degree days*.

Cooling degree days (CDD) is a concept similar to "heating degree days." CDD is a measure of the intensity of the summer cooling season based on the average outside temperature above the reference temperature of 78°F. It is conventionally assumed that at 78° people will turn on their AC if they have one. Figure 5.13 is a map showing average cooling degree days in the US.

It is much more difficult to predict cooling load than heating load. In addition to all the factors involved with heat-load calculations, cooling load must also consider internal heat gains such as cooking, laundry, appliances, lighting, along with solar heat gains. People are also considered part of a home's internal heat gain. Each person contributes about 200 Btus per hour of sensible heat, and about 150 Btus per hour of latent heat. These gains vary from home to home, and are generally ignored when sizing a heating system.

The *sensible heat load* has to do with removing heat associated with non-moisture-related heat sources, that is, reducing the temperature. Cooling-load calculations must also consider the energy required to remove heat-laden moisture from the indoor air. This can be due to natural humidity, the moisture created by perspiration, or the steam from a tea kettle or shower. The energy required to dehumidify the air is called the *latent heat load*, a major factor in personal comfort and a potentially big job for the air conditioner. Many new air conditioners increase their efficiency by reducing the amount of energy consumed for dehumidification. Remember that heat flows from hot to cold, and moisture moves from wet to dry. This means that in the summer you have hot, humid air beating its way into your house to replace the cool, dry air in a battle of physical laws.

Room air conditioner sizes range from about 5,000 to 14,000 Btus per hour. Table 5.2 shows the ENERGY STAR guide for sizing room air conditioners. Keep in mind, though, that each home, and each occupant's needs, are different.

When using Table 5.2 you can also make further adjustments:

- If the room is heavily shaded, reduce capacity by ten percent.
- If the room is very sunny, increase capacity by ten percent.
- If more than two people regularly occupy the room, add 600 Btus per hour for each additional person.
- If the unit is for a kitchen, increase capacity by 4,000 Btus per hour.

Table 5.2: Sizing Your Air Conditioner.

Area to be cooled (sq. ft.)	Capacity (BTUs/HR)
100 to 150	5,000
150 to 250	6,000
250 to 300	7,000
300 to 350	8,000
350 to 400	9,000
400 to 450	10,000
450 to 550	12,000
500 to 700	14,000
700 to 1000	18,000

Efficiency Ratings for Air Conditioners

Room air conditioners are rated for efficiency according to their E*nergy Efficiency Ratio* (EER). This is the ratio of cooling output in Btus divided by the power consumption in watts. A 5,000 Btu room AC that draws 500 watts has an EER of 10. When shopping for a new room AC, look for an EER of 10.7 or higher to meet ENERGY STAR standards.

Central air conditioners are rated for efficiency according to their *Seasonal Energy Efficiency Ratio* (SEER). This is the seasonal cooling output of the AC in Btus, divided by the seasonal energy input in watt-hours for an average US climate. An ENERGY STAR label requires a SEER of 12 or higher (soon to be 13). Before 1979, the SEER of central AC ranged from 4.5 to 8. If you double the SEER, you cut your AC operating costs in half. You can find a list of the most energy-efficient air conditioners on the web at <www.energystar.gov>.

More efficient air conditioners will be well worth the additional cost in returned energy savings, especially if you live in a hot and humid climate where AC is heavily used. Spend a few extra dollars on the unit with the longer warranty — you don't want to replace an expensive compressor every seven years if you can find one that will last for fifteen.

In addition to EER or SEER, AC units are rated for *sensible heat factor* (SHF). The SHF is a decimal number between 0.5 and 1 that rates the AC on its ability to remove moisture from the air. The higher the SHF, the more efficient the AC and the less moisture it will remove from the air. If you live in a dry climate, look for a high SHF. Humid climates need the dehumidifying power of a lower SHF rating of .67 to .77.

Air Conditioning Diet

At high temperatures and humidity levels, we begin to crave the comfort of air conditioning. As long as you leave your credit card at home, it will be cheaper to go to the mall and check out the latest hair styles and body art than to buy and operate an air conditioner. If moving to a cooler climate is not an option, and a trip to the mall is out of the question, and you absolutely need air conditioning, follow a strict diet to avoid a fat power bill. When you leave the house, turn the AC off. It may be convenient to leave it on all the time, but consider the energy, dollar, and environmental costs of doing so. You can probably tolerate the heat for the short time it will take to cool off the house when you get home. Everything you do to reduce heating costs, including insulation, air sealing, and duct sealing, also applies to air conditioning savings. As with heating systems, an efficient envelope allows you to reduce the size of your air conditioner. Here are some specific things you can do to keep cool at home with or without air conditioning:

- Avoid indoor heat- and moisture-generating activities.
- Reduce the amount of heat in your home by controlling heat sources such as incandescent lights, dishwashers, dryers, ovens, and solar gain through windows and insufficient insulation.
- Remove unwanted heat and moisture at its source (showers, laundry, cooking, wet basements and crawlspaces) with spot ventilation or drainage.
- Prevent heat and moisture movement from outside to the inside with air sealing and insulation.
- When discomfort is a problem, start with the least energy-intensive solution, such as a fan.
- Using a fan while the AC is operating can allow you to increase the temperature and still feel comfortable.
- Using ceiling fans instead of, or in conjunction with, the AC will increase your comfort at higher thermostat settings by moving air over your skin, creating a wind-chill effect by evaporating sweat and cooling you off.
- Shade sunny windows with landscaping, shades, curtains, or awnings.

- Open windows at night.
- Use natural ventilation instead of AC.
- When using the AC, close all windows and turn off exhaust fans (unless they are removing source heat and/or moisture).
- Upgrade older central AC systems with new, high-efficiency compressors.
- Increase your AC's lifetime and reduce its operating costs with proper periodic maintenance such as: checking the refrigerant level, condensate drain, controls, and air filters, and cleaning the evaporating and condenser coils. Clean or change filters monthly and clean the cooling coils and fan blades as needed.
- Central air conditioners rely on ductwork. This ductwork needs to be properly sealed, insulated, and balanced to provide maximum efficiency.
- Have the compressor professionally serviced at least every two years.
- Use a programmable set-up thermostat to automatically turn the AC off when you are out of the house, and turn up the temperature at night.

- Set the thermostat at 78°F or higher. On average, for every degree you set your AC thermostat up, you will about save two percent of cooling energy.
- Keep the thermostat out of direct sunlight and away from heat-generating appliances.
- Avoid using a dehumidifier when using an AC. They will both dehumidify the air, but the dehumidifier will also release heat to the indoors.
- Maintain 60 percent relative humidity for adequate indoor comfort and reduced dehumidification load of the air conditioner.
- A radiant barrier in the roof can reduce heat gains by up to 25 percent.

- Use light-colored exterior wall and roof finishes to reflect heat away.
- Use compact fluorescent lights to avoid the heat of incandescent bulbs.
- Cook during cooler evening hours, or barbecue outside.
- Avoid putting room air conditioners in sunny windows.
- Keep the compressor of a central AC in the shade, preferably on the north side of the house.
- Close off air ducts to unused rooms.
- Add insulation in the attic to keep heat out of the living area.
- Use windows designed for optimum energy efficiency in your climate.
- Have a cold drink.

And finally, here's advice that's important for the environment. The chlorine-containing CFC or HCFC refrigerant used in air conditioners is a serious, ozone-depleting chemical. It is important to prevent leaks in the air conditioner's cooling system through periodic, professional maintenance. When a service technician recharges or replaces your AC, the old refrigerant needs to be properly captured and disposed of.

CHAPTER 6

The Envelope, Please

Introduction

W E OFTEN BUY A HOME FOR ITS LOCATION ALONG WITH the aesthetic appeal of its interior and exterior. But what you *can't* see when you buy a house can cost you dearly — year after year. I often hear homeowners complain that their house is too cold in the winter, too hot in the summer, the windows are old and drafty, and the basement is wet. The expectation is that this is simply the trouble with houses in general, so the easiest solution is to use more energy to heat, cool, or dry out the house.

In this chapter we'll explore the importance of how the components of a building's *envelope* affect energy use. Specifically, we'll look at the choices you have for insulation and windows, and discuss the important issues of indoor air quality, air and moisture movement within a house, and ventilation strategies. Many efficiency choices (such as how much insulation is really needed in the walls or attic) are based on regional climates, building details, and local energy or building codes. There are many ways to build a house, and some very specific details need to be addressed in any given construction situation. It is beyond the scope of this book to address every construction scenario you may face. Appendix D leads you through a heat-load calculation in a simple building, a math-heavy exercise for the intrepid energy-geek. Other readers won't miss much by skipping over it.

Smart, energy-wise choices and actions can help make your home more energy-efficient, longer-lasting, and a healthier place to live — regardless of whether you are building a new home or considering renovations and improvements to an older one.

Terms

The envelope of your home includes everything from (and including), the paint on the inside to the paint on the outside of the walls. Framing materials, wallboard, insulation, siding, windows, doors, roof, foundation walls — anything that separates the inside from the outside — make up a building's envelope. The envelope of a home needs to keep you comfortable and protect you from the elements, be durable and aesthetically appealing — and it should do all of these things efficiently and cost-effectively. All of the envelope components, the materials they are made of, and how they are put together, affect the energy consumption and durability of the building. The envelope of a building defines its *thermal boundary*: the area separating conditioned space from unconditioned space. The thermal boundary should completely surround and enclose the home with insulation.

The *shell* of a house is sometimes used interchangeably with *envelope*. However, in this book the building shell refers only to the frame of the building, not the insulation or interior and exterior coverings of the frame.

The term *conditioned space* is used to indicate any interior space that is intentionally heated or cooled by mechanical (furnace, boiler, heat pump) or passive (sunspace) means. Conditioned space implies that energy input is required to keep that space heated or cooled. *Unconditioned areas* include the outdoors or any space in your home that is thermally connected to the outdoors (either through an uninsulated wall or by way of free air movement) such as a crawlspace, attic, or garage. An enclosed space that is unheated and uninsulated, such as a basement or crawlspace, might be described as *semi-conditioned*, because it has a thermal connection to both conditioned and unconditioned space.

Awareness

There are five main heat loss paths in a typical home. While the order may vary from house to house depending on design, construction, and operation of the building, most commonly the order will be:

- Air movement (can be one-third to one-half the total heat loss)
- Walls

- Windows
- Foundation
- Attic

Awareness of heat loss and other thermal problems within your home requires some exploration. What's behind your walls? What's in the attic and around the foundation? Is your bathroom exhaust fan vented into the attic? Is your clothes dryer vented into the basement? Do you have icicles hanging from your eaves? Icicles are not quaint *or* normal; they represent lost heating energy due to insufficient insulation or excess air movement between the house and the outside (in this case by way of the roof).

If the walls in your home have gaps in the insulation totaling just five percent of the insulated area, that five percent *doubles* the total heat lost through the walls. How can you tell what's inside the walls? A few inspection tricks can help avoid the need to punch a hole in the wall to investigate.

How much outside air moves through your home? Air leaks in a building are often the largest component of heat loss, and reducing air leakage is generally a low-cost improvement with substantial energy savings. How do you know where the leaks are? Sometimes you can see and feel them, but often it is useful to hire an energy auditor with equipment to measure and pinpoint air leakage areas in order to prioritize air-sealing efforts. In addition to heat loss from air leaks, air movement from the inside to the outside of a building (exfiltration) can sometimes lead to moisture and mold inside the walls or in the attic. This happens during the winter when warm, moist air from inside your home travels into a colder wall cavity where the moisture in the air condenses. The effect can also happen in the summer when hot humid outside air tries to make its way to a cool, dry, air-conditioned interior (remember, heat moves from hot to cold).

Later in this chapter, you'll see some infrared pictures that represent heat loss due to poor insulation and some that reveal hidden air-leakage paths. Many homeowners expect the infrared, or heat-sensing, image to be more like an X-ray, or work some other kind of magic. Infrared photos can tell you quite a bit about what's inside a wall without tearing it down, but these high-tech imaging devices have limitations. Without a knowledgeable operator, they can be almost useless. An experienced home energy inspector often uses the infrared camera to confirm what is already suspected.

When should you insulate and when should you air-seal? Think of it this way: when you go outside on a cold day, you put on a sweater. On a windy day though, a sweater won't do as much good so you put on a windbreaker too. Insulation is the sweater, while an air barrier is the windbreaker. Your home needs both. Further, these two barriers need to be aligned; that is, one needs to be adjacent to the other. Attention to details when air-sealing and insulating can alleviate many comfort issues around your home while lowering your energy bills, decreasing repair costs, and increasing your home's durability.

Contrary to popular belief, replacing your old windows is often *not* the most cost-effective solution to high heating bills. There are simple, inexpensive repairs and improvements you can make to increase the performance of your existing windows. If you do need to buy new ones, information is available on nearly every new window, so your choice can be based on energy efficiency.

Modern construction techniques allow us to build very tight, energy-efficient buildings. But can your home be too tight? Indoor air quality (IAQ) is of great concern today, since we generally spend far more time inside than out. Yet we continue to build our homes with toxic materials, and then fill them up with even more toxic stuff. A properly designed and installed ventilation system is key to moving air through your home and keeping your indoor air fresh and comfortable. An average-sized house (around 2,000 square feet) can be sufficiently ventilated using a simple bathroom exhaust fan, specifically sized and designed for this kind of service. It is important to note that most bathroom exhaust fans move only about half the air they are rated for. This is not because the manufacturer is cheating, but because installation practices are generally poor, resulting in restricted airflow.

It is important to look at the house as a whole. When you change one component, you change how other components interact. For example, if you live in an old home, and you tighten it up by sealing the air leaks, you may begin to starve the heating system of air, or create an indoor moisture problem due to poor air circulation. This was in fact a significant problem in the 1970s, the early days of weatherization programs. Many older homes with no problems other than high heating bills were tightened up to the point where stale air and trapped moisture led to mold, excessive condensation, and poor indoor air quality. If you build a new, very well-insulated, "tight" home, it will be prone to such moisture problems unless you provide for a controlled amount of air infiltration by means of mechanical ventilation. The negative pressure caused by an exhaust fan in a tight home may, in turn, create problems with backdrafting of fuel-burning equipment that requires a chimney. Backdrafting means that the flue gas (in your water heater, for example) flows backwards through the vent pipe and back into the house. One solution is to provide a source of "makeup air" for any equipment that removes air from your house. Sealed-combustion heating equipment has a built-in provision for this makeup air.

Another example of how systems interact within your home might be this: if the top floor of your house bakes in the summer, you may be tempted to get an air conditioner. But chances are that there is too little attic insulation. Adding insulation may eliminate the need for air conditioning, but your heating system may now be oversized for the winter months, causing it to run less efficiently.

Let's open the envelope now, and see what's inside.

Assessment

Before calling the window installer or insulation contractor, it's helpful to know what you have and what you need. An energy auditor or insulation contractor can tell you how much insulation you have in your walls, ceiling, floors, and basement, and make recommendations for improvements. You can do these examinations yourself if you're willing to get a little dirty and remove some of the finish materials to reveal the insulation behind the walls, ceiling, and floors.

One trick I use to inspect wall insulation is to remove a power outlet or switch cover and poke a wooden shishkebab skewer along the outside of the electrical box. By wiggling the skewer around, you might be able to pull out a few fibers of insulation. This is also a quick way to determine the depth of the walls, and therefore the thickness of the insulation. It is a good idea to turn off the power before accessing electrical boxes, and do *not* use a metal skewer for this job! If your home has had additions built on to it, check the insulation in each part of the house.

Take a look in the attic to see how much and what kind of insulation is up there already. Wear old clothes, gloves, and a respirator. The respirator is probably the most important tool for attic inspections because regardless of the type of insulation you come across, some of the material is bound to be airborne and you don't want any of it in your lungs. If you discover that the insulation is vermiculite, you should leave it alone as it may be contaminated with asbestos. Vermiculite is a brown, grey, or yellow pebble-like material and should only be handled by professionals trained in safe asbestos removal.

What is the condition of the insulation? Is it wet or moldy? Is it evenly installed with no gaps? Is there evidence of animal damage? With a tape measure, measure the depth of the insulation. Now pull some of the insulation up off the attic floor and look for the same signs. Pull it away from around any penetrations that go through the ceiling. These can include chimneys, ductwork, plumbing vents, electrical lines, light fixtures, and bathroom exhaust fans. There should be no way for air to move through the gaps surrounding them. Is the exhaust fan vented to the attic? If so, trouble is at hand. Look up at the inside of the roof for evidence of moisture or mold.

Some types of construction create an air path between interior walls and the attic. To see if your house is built that way, remove the attic insulation over an inside wall. If you can see gaps at the top of the wall, there is likely heat moving from inside the house to the attic. This connection needs to be air-sealed with sheet material (metal or rigid insulation), caulk, or expanding foam (or a combination of all three) at the seams, and covered with insulation. Remember, you want to create an air barrier (the windbreaker) as well as a thermal barrier (the sweater).

When assessing your windows, look for the number of layers of glass (also called glazing), and how tightly the windows close. If the sashes rattle against each other when closed and locked, they are good candidates for air-sealing improvement measures. If the sashes and frames are rotten, it may be time to think about replacement. If you live in a newer home with reasonably good windows, you may find that any discomfort you feel when standing next to the window is due to air infiltration around the perimeter of the window frame. If you were to pull off the trim from around the inside of a window, you might be able to see the exterior siding or even daylight from inside. Sometimes this gap is filled with fiberglass insulation but, like a sweater, fiberglass does not eliminate air movement. The fiberglass should be removed and replaced with non-expanding foam or caulk to provide a better air barrier.

How's your ventilation? There should be an exhaust fan in rooms with showers or baths. If not, moisture can condense on the walls causing mold, mildew, and rot not only on the walls and ceiling, but inside of them as well. Does your ventilation system work? You can do a quick test by holding a piece of tissue paper up to the fan while it is running. If the paper is sucked in, the fan is moving air, although this doesn't tell you how much. A well-equipped energy auditor will use a device called a *pressure pan* or *flow hood* to accurately measure fan flow rates in cubic feet per minute, or *cfm*. The importance of this test is described in the following section on ventilation.

How Much Heating Energy Do You Use?

You probably know how many dollars it costs you to heat your home, but a good assessment requires a figure that represents heating energy. To assess your heating energy use, gather all your fuel bills for the year. These bills should show the quantity of fuel purchased in therms, cubic feet, or gallons (depending on the fuel), and reflect the fuel consumption since the last meter reading or fill-up date. Add up the number of fuel units you used over the past year. If you don't save your bills, call your fuel company and ask how many gallons, kWh, therms, or cubic feet you've used over the year. If you use the same fuel for multiple tasks, some of the energy shown in your bills may be used for water heating or cooking and you'll want to subtract that from your total use. You can do this by looking at the usage during the summer months, and subtracting that figure from each month of the year. What remains is your heating energy consumption.

Refer to Table 1.2 in Chapter 1 and figure out how many MMBtus of heating energy you need to heat your home. Let's say that you use 500 therms (about 500 Ccf) of natural gas during an average heating season; since there are 100,000 Btus in a therm, your home uses 50 MMBtus.

But what does that mean? Is it a lot or a little? You can talk to your neighbors and compare, but if you want to get more specific about your home's heating energy use and assess if the heating energy you're using is reasonable for

Math Box: Quantifying Heating Energy Consumption

An energy auditor, architect, or heating specialist might define your home by how many Btus per square foot the house requires.

Let's use a 2,000 square foot home that consumes 50 MMBtus per year of heating energy as an example:

$$50,000,000 \text{ Btus} \div 2,000 \text{ square feet} = 25,000 \text{ Btus per square foot}$$

This figure can be used to compare heating consumption before and after efficiency improvements are made. The home's heating load depends in large part on the temperature difference between indoors and out. So without knowing the climate characteristics, Btus per square foot doesn't mean much unless you are simply comparing buildings in your climate region. To put the figure into perspective, we need to know something about the climate where your home is located. *Heating degree days* (HDD) are used to more specifically define the energy performance of a home with a concept known as the *Home Heating Index.* For more on heating degree days, see the *climate* section of Chapter 5 on heating and air conditioning.

The Home Heating Index (HHI) is a look at the heating requirements of a building in terms of Btus per square foot per heating degree day. This is a much more meaningful way to compare the energy efficiency of buildings. Here's an example:

If you live in a climate zone with 5,000 HDD, and your home uses 25,000 Btus square foot, your HHI is:

$$25,000 \div 5,000 = 5$$

If you live in a climate zone with 8,000 HDD, and your home uses 25,000 Btus square foot, your HHI is

$$25,000 \div 8,000 = 3.1$$

The lower the HHI, the more efficient your home. An HHI of 2 would indicate a very efficient home, while an HHI of 6 or more would be considered a definite energy hog.

your house and climate, see the Math Box on *Quantifying Heating Energy Consumption*. The exercises in Appendix D are useful to more precisely quantify energy use and loss in your home, and the answers can help you properly size a heating system. They are not required if you just want to know what's in your walls and whether or not it's enough. Charts and general concepts follow.

Insulation

As you learned in Chapter 1, heat moves from hot to cold. Any heated building will lose heat, and any building that is cooler than the outdoors will gain heat. This is a natural law of physics that you can't do anything to change. What you do have control over though, is *how fast* heat escapes from your home. The job of insulation is to slow heat transmission through the building envelope. It does this by trapping air in millions of tight little pockets embedded in a foam or fiber. When we insulate, we trade the relatively fast heat loss paths of convection and radiation for the slower movement of heat by conduction. Because insulation contains many tiny air pockets, conductive heat loss is kept to a minimum.

Air is a poor conductor of heat, but moving air will move heat. It is important, then, that no air be allowed to move through insulation; this means reducing air movement within the framing cavities creating a dead-air space. Air currents within insulation will quickly carry away any heat (by way of convection), drastically reducing thermal performance of the insulation. Insulation needs to be dense enough to slow heat loss by convection, but not so dense that the material actually conducts heat through it. Ideally, it is best not to rely on insulation to stop air movement. Rather, the insulation should be installed in an air-tight cavity to be most effective.

Before examining insulation materials, we first need to understand something about how insulation is rated for effectiveness at opposing the flow of heat.

Insulation Terms

There are a few terms that are used to describe and quantify the thermal performance of insulation.

R-value is a measure of a material's resistance to thermal conduction. All insulation products have an R-value rating. The higher the R-value of a material, the greater the insulating value, meaning that heat will move (by conduction) more slowly through the material. For layered insulating materials in building components, R-values are added together: if you have R-5 foam board over an R-11 stud-wall cavity, the nominal insulating value of the wall is R-16. The R-value number assigned to insulation products may seem arbitrary until you understand that it is based on something called U-factor.

U-factor is a measure of the thermal conductance of a material. The U-factor of a material expresses how much heat (in Btus) is transmitted through one square foot of the material in one hour when the temperature difference on opposite surfaces is 1°F. A higher U-factor indicates a greater conductivity to heat and corresponds to a lower R-value. Windows are generally rated in U-factor. U-factors cannot be added together. Note that U-factors (and therefore R-values) only relate *conductive* heat loss, not heat loss by convection or radiation. If a wall allows air to move within it, heat will be lost much more rapidly than the U-factor or R-value would suggest.

U-factors and R-values are the reciprocal of each other (1 ÷ R-value = U-factor). Therefore, a wall with an insulating value of R-19 has a U-factor of 0.0526.

Thermal bridges and *thermal breaks*. Different materials have different thermal conductivity. That is, they transfer heat at different rates. Insulation has a lower conductivity than wood or metal. A small area of a material with good thermal conductivity — such as wood studs in a wall or a metal window frame — can transfer a lot of heat as compared to the insulation within the framing cavity. A thermal bridge is a kind of thermal "short-circuit." For example, your house might have a wall with R-19 fiberglass placed between

Table 6.1: Recommended Insulation Values.

Climate	Heating system	Area to insulate			
		Ceiling	Wall	Floor	Basement crawlspace
Warm Climate [1]	Gas or oil	R-22 to R-38	R-11 to R-23	R-11 to R-13	R-11 to R-19
	E-R [4]	R-38 to R-49	R-13 to R-25	R-13 to R-19	R-11 to R-19
Mixed Climate [2]	Gas or oil	R-38	R-11 to R-22	R-13 to R-25	R-11 to R-19
	E-R	R-49	R-11 to R-26	R-25	R-11 to R-19
Cold climate [3]	Gas or oil	R-38 to R-49	R-11 to R-22	R-25	R-11 to R-19
	E-R	R-49	R-11 to R-28	R-25	R-13 to R-19

[1] southern states with air conditioning but little heating
[2] middle tier states with moderate heating and cooling requirements
[3] northern states and mountainous regions with heavy heating loads
[4] Electric-Resistance

six-inch studs located every 16 inches. Wood has an insulating value of about R-1 per inch. Within this R-19 wall then, you have an R-6 thermal bridge every 16 inches, effectively lowering the R-value of the entire wall. The heat loss caused by thermal bridging can result in cold or hot spots, condensation on interior walls or ceilings, and icicles or ice dams on roofs. The effects of thermal bridges are addressed by adding "thermal breaks" such as insulation, gaskets, or weather-stripping, that slow the conduction of heat through the thermal bridge.

How Much Insulation and Where?

Insulation is an investment in energy efficiency that will reduce your heating and cooling energy consumption and offer definite, predictable returns. However, there is a point at which it may not be cost-effective to add more insulation. How much insulation is cost-effective? That depends primarily upon your climate, heating fuel costs, and constraints of the building shell. Higher levels of insulation make sense in colder climates and where expensive heating fuels are used. Table 6.1 shows what the US Department of Energy recommends for insulation levels in different climates.

I would strongly encourage you to insulate toward the higher end of these recommendations regardless of heating fuel type. In fact, local building codes may require higher R-values for new homes than those listed in Table 6.1. My experience in verifying compliance for the Environmental Protection Agency's ENERGY STAR home efficiency label in cold climates indicates that insulating to the higher values helps to achieve the highest performance levels along with lower heating costs. Increased thermal performance leads to greater comfort levels, lower heating fuel costs, smaller and less costly heating systems, and reduced maintenance of — and reliance on — heating equipment. Too little insulation can cause condensation on walls or ceilings because cold outside temperatures will contact warm, interior finish materials. Excess moisture can cause structural or cosmetic problems within the house, render insulation a useless collection of molds, or cause health problems for the occupants. Spending what may seem like a large amount of money to upgrade insulation in a new or existing home will offer significant energy and dollar savings during the long-term ownership of your home. And because the house will probably be around longer than you, the lifetime costs and resource consumption of an efficient building will be far less than that of an average building.

Why are higher R-values recommended in ceilings? Indoor air temperature might be a few degrees warmer at the ceiling than at the floor, which results in slightly greater heat transfer through the ceiling. The truth is that attics are an easy place to pile up more insulation at a minimal cost and with a reasonable payback.

Insulation Choices

There are many types of insulating materials on the market to choose from, falling into the two broad categories of fibers and foams, each with unique advantages. These products can be used in either new or existing homes, and should be selected carefully as part of the building's envelope system.

Installing insulation properly is at least as, if not more, important than the type and level of insulation you choose. Fibers need to be well-lofted with no gaps, voids, or compressions. Foams also should be installed without gaps. Seams between rigid foam boards should be taped, and spray foams should be continuous, even, and free of voids. It is very important to prevent the

Diminishing Returns

There is a point at which the long-term energy savings gained by adding more insulation does not offer a reasonable return for the investment. However, with rising energy costs, the economics are changing in favor of greater insulation levels. Consider a Swedish housing project carried out by the Chalmers University of Technology, the Swedish Council for Building Research, Lund University, and the Swedish National Testing and Research Institute.

This 20-unit multifamily project is heated only by occupants, appliances, and lighting. The wood-framed row houses have R-71 roofs, R-63 floors, R-57 walls, and triple-glazed, krypton-filled windows. The buildings cost $7,000 more to build to this extreme energy efficient level, but they eliminated the cost of a $4,000 heating system and a lifetime of fuel bills.

movement of air and moisture through insulation, as both reduce its effectiveness. Always allow the wall cavity and insulation to dry completely before covering with wall board. Do not cover any heat-generating items such as recessed lighting fixtures, unless rated for Insulation Contact (IC rated), or insulate too close to chimneys or flue pipes, unless using fire resistant insulation. If your home is very old, the wiring should be inspected before covering it with any insulation.

Fiberglass is a man-made product that is composed of sand and recycled products such as window glass and bottles. The ingredients are melted and spun to create small fibrous strands of glass that together form "glass wool." Fiberglass is generally pink or yellow, and has become the most popular fiber-insulating material since its first use in the 1930s. Fiberglass is commonly available in long rolls or short batts in widths of 16 or 24 inches to fit between standard-width wall studs, rafter bays, and ceiling or floor joists. Different densities are available, with R-values averaging 3.2 per inch. Fiberglass can be installed by any do-it-yourself homeowner, but great attention to detail is required to fill small

Fig. 6.1: Proper fiberglass insulation.

Fig. 6.2: Poor fiberglass insulation.

voids such as those found behind and around electrical boxes, wiring, ductwork, and plumbing in walls or ceilings. If the fiberglass has a paper ("kraft-faced") or foil backing used as a vapor retarder (more on this later) that side is installed on the warm side of the framing cavity. In a heating climate, the warm side is the side of the roof or wall that is closer to the inside of the home. If you never use heat, but do use air conditioning, the paper side should be installed towards the outside.

Figure 6.1 shows properly installed fiberglass in an attic. Notice how it is flat and even, with no gaps between rows. There are two layers of fiberglass rolled out: the first is installed in between the joists with the kraft-paper facing down, and the second is rolled out on top of and perpendicular to the first. This top layer of insulation has *no* paper or foil backing. Figure 6.2 illustrates carelessly installed fiberglass batts in an attic. Note how it has been compressed along the edges, and the tops of the wooden collarties are exposed, presenting a thermal bridge in the insulation. Another layer of fiberglass should be rolled out on top of and perpendicular to the existing layer to reduce the effect of this thermal bridge.

Cellulose is a fiber insulation commonly manufactured from recycled wood or paper products, and treated with fire retardant. It is installed using machinery to blow small bits of fiber into framing cavities. Cellulose has an insulating value of approximately R-3.5 per inch depending on how densely it is packed into the cavity. Installed densities vary from about 1 to 4.5 pounds per cubic foot depending upon the type, location, and insulating needs of the particular installation.

There are several methods of installing cellulose including *damp spray*, which goes on damp and sticks to the open wall cavity. Dry cellulose fibers can be blown on top of a ceiling to a prescribed depth. The installed depth must factor in some settling of the material over time. If you decide to install cellulose in your home, ask the contractor how much settling will occur over time and whether the R-value you require (and are paying for) will be met after this settling occurs. Cellulose can also be blown into an existing finished but uninsulated wall cavity by cutting a hole in the top of the wall and inserting the blow-tube down into the wall, pulling the tube up and out as the cavity fills. Properly done, this *dense packing* blows the cellulose into a wall cavity at a high enough pressure so that no voids are left unfilled, and settling is eliminated.

Cellulose is a very versatile insulating material, offering good coverage in tight, irregularly shaped, or hard-to-reach spaces in both new and retrofit situations. Figure 6.3 shows cellulose blown into an attic, and figure 6.4 shows damp-sprayed cellulose applied to an open wall. The wall is now ready for sheet rock or other finish material.

Fig. 6.3: Cellulose insulation provides good coverage in an attic with complex framing.

Fig. 6.4: Damp-sprayed cellulose insulation.

Foam insulation products are most commonly *polystyrene* (usually blue, pink or gray) and *polyisocyanurate* (usually foil-faced) rigid insulating panels. Applied as a continuous layer of insulation over a stud-frame wall, roof rafters, or foundation wall, these foam panels provide good insulation value, reduce thermal bridging of the frame (wood, metal, or concrete), and act as an effective air and moisture barrier. Polystyrene is rated at R-4.8 per inch, while foil-faced

Fig. 6.5: Rigid foam board foundation insulation.

polyisocyanurate rates about R-6 per inch. Both should be protected from direct sunlight and abrasion, as they will disintegrate after a year or two of exposure. Seams between rigid foam boards should be taped to prevent air and moisture movement.

During manufacture, propellants are used to expand the foam to a greater volume. These propellants "outgas" from the product over time, leaving behind pockets of trapped air. In the past, foam R-values were rated when they were filled with the propellant. After outgassing, the effective R-value was reduced. New insulation products are moving towards labeling that reflects R-values after the material has stabilized.

Figure 6.5 shows polystyrene (pink board) installed around the outside perimeter of a foundation. This will eventually be covered with cement stucco, sheet metal, or other ultra-violet (sun), weather, and pest-resistant product.

Spray foams are becoming more common in new home construction due to a relatively high insulating value up to R-5.9 per inch, and the ability to form tight air and moisture barriers in the framing cavity. *Polyicynene* and *polyurethane* are the two most common spray-foam products. They are both installed using professional spray equipment requiring some skill to use well. Figures 6.6 and 6.7 illustrate polyurethane insulation. Note how it has been used in the attic to cover not only the ceiling, but also to insulate exhaust ducting from the dryer and bathroom fan. This detail will prevent condensation from building up on the metal ducts, which could cause mold and other moisture related problems if it were to drip and pool in the attic. As you can see in Figure 6.7, spray foam seals all penetrations between indoors and out.

You will also notice in Figure 6.4, that spray foam has been used to seal the perimeter of the window casing. This foam is available in small, easy-to-use spray cans at hardware stores. It comes in two varieties: minimal expanding and triple expanding. You will want to use the minimal expanding foam when filling gaps around windows and doors. The triple expanding foam should be used to fill large holes where there is no concern over bulging of materials as can happen when triple expanding foams are used in tight spaces.

Table 6.2 shows the average insulating values of different insulating materials. Look up the kind of insulation you have or need, then multiply the R-value per inch by the number of inches of material for the total R-value. Note that these figures represent the insulation values when perfectly installed. It is not uncommon to find poorly installed insulation that reduces the overall R-value to less than half its rated value.

Fig. 6.6: Urethane spray foam in attic.

Fig. 6.7: Spray foam insulation at utility penetration in basement.

Radiant Barriers

Radiant barriers reflect and slow radiant heat. Aluminum foil makes an excellent radiant barrier and several aluminized insulation products are on the market including rigid foil-faced polyisocyanurate sheets, and a versatile aluminized bubble wrap available in rolls of various lengths and widths. Radiant barriers are best used in roofs to reflect radiant heat, helping to keep the attic cool. For a radiant barrier to be most effective, it needs to face an open, calm air space. Imagine it sandwiched between the bottom of the rafters and the wall board, overlaid with strapping on which to attach the wall board creating the air space. Without a dead-air space, heat will conduct through the barrier, negating the effectiveness of the material.

Table 6.2: R-Values per inch of Common Insulation Products.

Insulation product	R-value per inch
Wood	1.0
Fiberglass batts	3.2
Hi density fiberglass	3.7
Cellulose	3.5
Extruded polystyrene (blue or pink board)	4.8
Unfaced polyiconcyanurate	5.8
Foil-faced polyiconcyanurate	7.0
Open-cell spray foam (polyicynene)	3.6
Closed-cell spray foam (polyurethane)	5.9

Credit: Oakridge National Laboratory

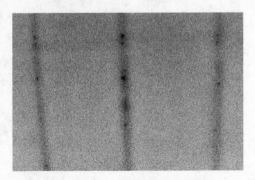

Fig. 6.8: Infrared view of a stud wall. Note the dark, colder, vertical studs and even darker sheetrock screws.

Infrared Inspection

One tool a well-equipped energy auditor may have is an infrared (IR) camera. Infrared radiation is emitted by all objects, just beyond the end of the visible spectrum. An IR camera can show where heat might be escaping from a home by visually depicting temperature differences. Figure 6.8 is an infrared photo of the thermal bridging effect of wooden studs within a common stick-framed house. In this interior photo taken during the winter, white indicates warmer areas and black indicates cooler areas. You can see that the studs behind the wall-board are cooler than the insulated cavity between the studs. They are cooler because heat is being conducted through them (away from the heated interior space) more rapidly than through the insulation. This is visual proof of thermal bridging.

Windows

What happens when you cut holes in a nice, warm, well-insulated envelope so that you can install windows? Windows occupy 12 to 15 percent of an average home's wall area, with many new homes approaching 20 percent. Because of their lower insulating value, windows lose heat much more rapidly than do walls, so it pays to install good, energy-efficient windows to reduce that loss. More windows in your walls increases the potential for both heat loss and heat gain between indoors and out resulting in larger energy consumption and possible comfort issues. Whether you live in a hot or cold climate, the right window in the right place offers a good balance of efficiency, light, and solar heat gain.

There are a number of glazing (glass) types and coatings available, and the many brands and configurations of windows offer a variety of glazing choices. The window technology you choose depends upon your climate, where the window is located in the home, and whether you have a specific use for the window such as for a greenhouse or sun space.

Glazing Options

A number of window options are available to meet specific needs in specific locations.

Number of glazing layers. Double, triple, or four-pane windows provide an insulating air gap between glazing layers. Look for a gap of between ⅜ and ½ an inch. The air space acts as a buffer zone between indoors and out, bringing the temperature of the inside layer of glass closer to the temperature of the inside of the house than a single pane window does. This increase in temperature increases your comfort level when standing next to the window because it reduces the amount of heat that radiates from your warm body to the colder window. The higher temperature also helps control condensation buildup on the window — the colder the window, the more readily condensation will appear on the warm side of the glass. Adding more panes adds more air space, increasing the insulating value and *comfort zone* (you can get closer to the window without feeling cold) of the window. Of great importance is the spacer between the glazing layers. Look for low conductance, or *warm-edge* spacers that reduce heat transfer as well as the potential for condensation buildup around the window's perimeter. Figure 6.9 shows the temperature at which condensation will form on windows, depending on outdoor temperature, indoor relative humidity, and type of window. The indoor temperature is assumed to be 70°F. The horizontal axis is degrees F and the vertical axis is relative humidity in percent.

Gas-filled windows offer improved performance in multi-pane windows by removing air from between the panes and replacing it with a low conductivity gas such as argon or krypton. This gas reduces heat conduction through the window, and because the gas is heavier than air, convective currents within the window are reduced, eliminating cold pockets near the bottom of the window.

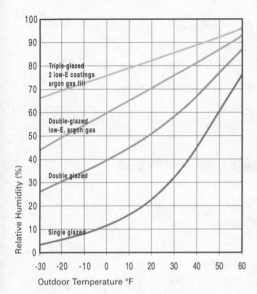

Fig. 6.9: Condensation point of different windows.

Credit: Lawrence Berkeley National Laboratory's Windows and Daylighting Group, The Efficient Windows Collaborative.

Tinted coatings offer improved cooling season efficiency in warm climates by reducing solar-heat gain without reducing visible light transmission. These coatings selectively filter out certain wavelengths of light.

Spectrally selective coatings offer optical properties that are transparent to some wavelengths of energy (visible light) and reflective to others (infrared radiation). The most common spectrally selective coatings are tints and Low-E.

Low-E (the E stands for emissivity) coatings are used on multi-pane windows. They allow visible light to pass through the window, but reflect heat energy (infrared radiation) back in between the glazing layers. The Low-E coating is applied to a single layer of glass that faces the space between two panes, or to a thin film in between panes (in the case of a triple-pane window). Typically, the window is oriented so that the glass with the Low-E coating faces the warmer zone. For example, in a heating climate the Low-E coated pane faces the inside of the house so that heat energy coming from the house is reflected back into the house. Solar heat passes through the outer glazing layer and reflects off the Low-E coating, warming the air space between panes. In cooling climates, the orientation would be reversed so that heat is reflected to the outside.

There are two types of Low-E coatings: sputtered, or soft coat is generally used in windows with low or moderate levels of solar-heat gain, while pyrolitic, or hard coat is typically used in windows with high levels of solar-heat gain. One is not better or worse than the other; it all depends on how you want your window to perform.

Window Ratings

Most windows are rated for their thermal performance by the National Fenestration Rating Council (NFRC), a nonprofit, public-private organization created by the window, door, and skylight industry. The NFRC sticker on a window indicates all of the performance criteria you need to compare window efficiencies and make an informed selection. Insulating value is only a part of the energy rating performance of windows. A sample NFRC sticker is shown in Figure 6.10. Several ratings can be listed on the NFRC sticker. The first

World's Best Window Co.
Millennium 2000+
Vinyl-Clad Wood Frame
Double Glazing • Argon Fill • Low E
Product Type: **Vertical Slider**
(per NFRC 100-97)

ENERGY PERFORMANCE RATINGS	
U-Factor (U.S./I-P)	Solar Heat Gain Coefficient
0.35	**0.32**
ADDITIONAL PERFORMANCE RATINGS	
Visible Transmittance	Air Leakage (U.S./I-P)
0.51	**0.2**

Manufacturer stipulates that these ratings conform to applicable NFRC procedures for determining whole product performance. NFRC ratings are determined for a fixed set of environmental conditions and a specific product size. Consult manufacturer's literature for other product performance information. www.nfrc.org

Fig 6.10: NFRC window label showing energy performance data.

Credit: National Fenestration Rating Council.

two are always shown, while the others are optional listings, depending on selective glazing coatings in the window and manufacturer preference.

U-factor (sometimes called U-value) ratings generally fall between 0.20 and 1.20 (remember that lower numbers are better when comparing U-factors). A single pane of glass has a U-factor of about 0.91, translating to an insulating value of about R-1.1. Most new double pane windows have a U-factor between 0.50 and 0.30 (or an R-value between 2 and 3.3). New high-tech windows with three or four glazing layers offering U-factors of less than 0.13 (R-values of up to 8 or more) are available. The extra expense of these windows is cost-effective in buildings with lots of glass, or where energy needs and/or costs are high for both heating and cooling.

ENERGY STAR criteria for window U-factors are dependent upon the climate. In the northern third of the country, ENERGY STAR guidelines call for a U-factor of 0.35 or lower (R-2.9 or higher). Along the middle of the country, ENERGY STAR specifies a U-factor of 0.40 or lower (R-2.5 or higher), and for the southern third of the US, the specification calls for a U-factor of 0.75 or lower (R-1.3 or higher).

Solar Heat Gain Coefficient (SHGC) is a measure of how much solar (heat) energy is allowed to pass through the window. An SHGC of 0.45 means that 45 percent of the solar energy falling on the window passes through it. Colder climates benefit from the use of higher SHGC ratings, while warmer-climate homes where more cooling energy is required, benefit from reduced passive solar heat gain. ENERGY STAR also offers guidelines for SHGC. In the northern third of the country, any SHGC is acceptable. In the north, you would typically want a lower SHGC on the east and west sides of the home to avoid over-heating in the summer, and high SHGC on the south side to take advantage of the low sun during the winter months. Along the central zone, ENERGY STAR specifies an SHGC of 0.50 or less, and for the southern third of the US, the specification calls for an SHGC of 0.40 or less. Lower SHGC windows will reduce the air conditioning requirements of a home in a warm climate.

Visible Transmittance (VT) measures how much visible light comes through a window. VT is expressed as a number between 0 and 1. Typical values are between 0.3 and 0.8. A higher VT means more light is transmitted. A VT of 0.58 means that 58 percent of the sun's visible light passes through the window.

Air Leakage (AL) is an air leakage rating expressed in cubic feet of air passing through a square foot of window area. Heat loss and gain occur by infiltration through small air leaks in the window assembly. Typical AL values are between 0.1 and 0.3. The lower the AL, the less air will pass through these cracks.

Condensation resistance (CR) measures the ability of a window to resist the formation of condensation on its interior surface. CR is expressed as a number between 1 and 100, with higher numbers indicating better resistance to condensation.

You can learn more about widow technology on the web at <www.efficient windows.org> and obtain ratings of new windows at <www.nfrc.org>.

Problems with Older Windows

Older windows are often maligned for being big energy wasters. Single-pane windows with loose sashes, poorly sealed trim, perhaps even with holes in the casing for ropes and pulleys, can present noticeable drafts. Before you decide to replace all your windows, try to define your window troubles in terms of comfort and durability. Obviously, a window with broken glass, little or no caulking around the glass perimeter, or broken and rotten sash or framing material should be repaired or replaced.

As for comfort issues, older windows can be drafty. Drafts are caused by air movement. Air-sealing efforts around windows can make a large contribution to your energy diet. Some windows do not close very tightly and these gaps can be the source of drafts. You may feel a draft coming from between the sash rails or from the perimeter of the window frame. Drafts are addressed by installing weather-stripping around the perimeter of the window and by installing better sash locks. Older, double-hung windows may benefit from side-mounted sash locks that pull the window tight to the sides of its frame, not just where the sash rails meet.

If you remove the inside trim surrounding the window, you can see how it was installed into the framing cavity. There is probably an air space between the house shell and the window frame. This gap represents significant air leakage and should be sealed so that air cannot move between outside and inside. If the gap is not too wide, it can be sealed with caulk, backer rod, or non-expanding foam in a can (expanding foam can cause the frame to bulge). If you have windows with ropes and pulleys, look for pulley seals to stop air infiltration there. Be aware that if you have an older home and find such air leakage paths around your windows, there are probably many larger holes in the envelope to deal with as well.

A cold window can create a convection current on its interior pane as it interacts with warm indoor air, and you may feel this as a draft that cannot be pinpointed as a perimeter draft can be. You may feel cold next to a window due to the effect of your warm body radiating heat towards the colder window. The solution here is to add a dead-air space between indoors and out. This can be done by installing double-pane windows, storm windows, manufactured interior or exterior window inserts, or a well-fitted plastic sheet covering the inside or outside of the existing window. This dead-air space acts much like the pockets of air trapped inside insulation — it raises the temperature of the interior glass, thus increasing your comfort level by reducing the heat radiated from your body towards the window. Heat loss through windows can be greatly reduced by covering them at night with heavy drapes or insulation. I have seen some very nice do-it-yourself window quilts made by sandwiching a piece of reflectorized bubble-wrap insulation in between two pieces of cloth material. This makes a window cover that can be rolled up and down as needed.

Air Leakage

Adding insulation and installing the proper windows can be a big part of increasing the overall efficiency of your home. However, it may surprise you to learn that up to a third of the energy used to condition the air in your home (much more in big, old, drafty farmhouses) can be due to uncontrolled outdoor air moving through the building envelope. Air movement can be identified as either infiltration: inward air movement generally from the outdoors into the lower parts of the house; or exfiltration: air movement from the inside to the outdoors, generally through the top part of the house. Excess air movement not only burns energy dollars, but it can also make your home drafty and either too humid or too dry.

You may have heard builders use the phrase "a house needs to breathe." In fact, a house has no requirement to breathe, but it *does* need to stay dry (except, of course, for exterior surfaces). Here is where things can get confusing for even the most seasoned builder. Too much leakiness and you get a drafty house, while too little fresh air can lead to poor indoor air quality and moisture-related problems on or within the building envelope.

It has long been thought that increased infiltration will allow the envelope to dry, and that this is why old, drafty homes seldom have moisture-related problems. Recent research has proved that this is a myth, and in fact, drafty homes were found to have at least as much mold as tight homes. By reducing air leakage, moisture movement is dramatically reduced as well.

The solution to this apparent balancing act is simply put in a new phrase from the building science industry: "build tight, ventilate right." This approach minimizes air leakage while maintaining good indoor air quality and eliminating potential moisture problems. Great attention to detail is required when air-sealing a house. Air carries moisture, and because it moves from areas with more heat and moisture to areas with less, the building envelope is the front-line defense in this battle between conditioned indoor air and outside weather.

Figure 6.11 shows the most common air leakage areas in a home. Air leakage paths are typically found in the holes drilled for electrical, plumbing, ventilation, and other utility services. Objects set into exterior walls such as electrical outlets, light fixtures, shelves, and even medicine cabinets can be leaky.

Interior soffits built into ceilings or walls with chases for duct work, plumbing, or recessed light fixtures are likely air leakage paths.

Do you have a porch roof connected to the house? This often provides an easy route for air to move through the porch roof and into the connecting wall. Areas where two different materials meet are often in need of air-sealing. A good example is where the wooden sill plate sits atop a concrete or stone foundation. In new construction a foam gasket is installed between these materials. An older home without this gasket will need caulk or expanding foam along the inside and outside perimeters. The inside of this perimeter, or rim band, is often a good candidate for total coverage with spray-foam insulation, which also acts as an air barrier. The connection between an aluminum storm window and wooden window frame is another common air leakage area easily remedied with a high quality silicone caulk.

Some construction methods present open wall- or floor-framing cavities with direct connection to the outdoors in terms of air movement. These cavities need to be air-sealed first, then insulated. Interior walls, for example, may be open to the attic allowing air to move between the inside and outside by way of the attic. Floor systems can be quite leaky as well, even in new homes. The perimeter band between floors is often a neglected air-sealing area. Air can move from outside, through gaps in siding and sheathing, enter the floor system, and reveal itself far from the source — at an interior partition wall, for example.

Leaky ductwork also can contribute significantly to the overall air leakage in your home. Furnace and air conditioning ducts are often located in attics, basements, and exterior walls. If the duct joints are not thoroughly sealed with UL-181 approved mastic or foil tape (*not* duct tape), you are paying to heat or cool outside air. Worse, the negative pressures created in duct return systems can pull potentially contaminated air from those unconditioned spaces. Read more about ducts in the chapter on heating and air conditioning.

You can discover sources of drafts in your home by using an incense stick on a windy day. Walk the smoking stick around the perimeter of each room and follow any horizontally moving smoke. Some tell-tale signs of air movement are dirty insulation or dusty cobwebs. Fiberglass insulation acts as a dust filter as air moves through it.

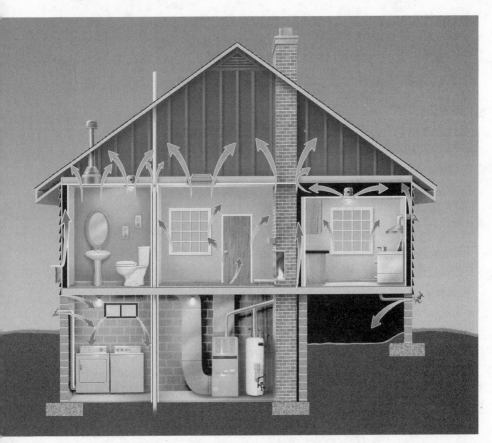

Fig. 6.11: Common air leakage paths into and out of a home. Credit: US Environmental Protection Agency.

You can reduce air leakage by tightening up your home using one or more of the many air-sealing products that are used to address specific needs. These products are available from your local hardware or home supply store and include:

- Caulk for gaps under half an inch
- Triple-expanding foam for larger gaps that are not near hot surfaces
- Non-expanding foam for use around window and door frames
- Backer rod, a flexible foam or rope-caulk crack filler sold in rolls, that can be used alone or with caulk

- Foam gaskets for use behind outlet and switch plates
- Weatherstripping in many shapes and sizes to fit windows, doors, and attic hatches
- Foam board insulation or metal flashing to close large gaps
- Metal flashing and high temperature sealant to seal chimney chases

Avoid using fiberglass insulation to fill gaps. It is porous and does not stop air movement.

Older homes can benefit greatly from air-sealing efforts. New homes generally have a continuous vapor and/or air barrier (more on these soon) installed during construction that will help reduce air leaks. New home or old, all of the same air-sealing efforts should be made. Of course it is much easier to do this kind of work as the home is being built or during renovations when walls are open, revealing possible air-leakage pathways. For example, in new construction, before any window trim is installed, all the gaps between window and door casings and the wall framing should be filled with foam or caulk to block air movement through the gap. The same should be done for all penetrations throughout the building envelope as shown in Figure 6.11. In an older home, these same measures are usually a very cost-effective way to increase comfort and reduce energy costs, even with the additional work of removing wall boards, trim, insulation, baseboards, or siding to find envelope penetrations to the outside.

Assessing Air Leakage

You can have your house checked for air leaks with a *blower door* test. This test is performed by closing up the house and placing a fan in a sealed, outside doorway. The fan exhausts air from the house, pulling it in from the outside through the cracks and leaks in the envelope. A blower door is fairly expensive and is not something an average homeowner would intuitively know how to use. A professional energy auditor can measure the flow of air through the fan using pressure and flow meters, and can easily locate air-leakage areas in the building. Blower-door guided air-sealing is an effective method of reducing energy loss due to air leaks.

Fig. 6.12: Blower door.

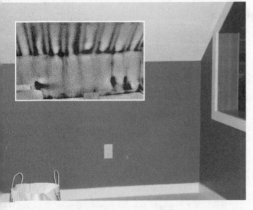

Fig. 6.13a: Top floor with knee wall. Credit: Peter Schneider.

Fig. 6.13b (inset): Infrared photo of air leakage in roof insulation with blower door running. Credit: Walter Scott.

Whole-house air leakage is typically measured in terms of *air changes per hour* (ACH). An ACH of 0.50 means each hour, 50-percent of the air in the house is exchanged through the inherent leaks in the envelope of the house. Figure 6.12 shows a photo of a blower door in place.

Using an infrared camera in conjunction with a blower door can reveal many hidden secrets in a house. Figure 6.13a shows a finished top floor with a knee wall, and 6.13b is the same area in infrared showing how insulation can be compromised when air is allowed to move through it. This problem would disappear if the roof were properly insulated and the insulation properly baffled as seen in figure 6.18. Figures 6.14a and 6.14b show typical problems at framing junctures and behind tongue-and-groove ceiling boards. A proper air barrier behind the boards and attention to air-sealing details would have eliminated this problem during construction. Darker areas in these photos indicate cooler temperatures. You can see where cold outside air is being pulled in through gaps in the trim and finish surfaces, indicating poor air-sealing of the envelope during construction.

Figure 6.15a is a photo of a second-story floor. Figure 6.15b is that same floor in infrared showing a very leaky floor system. This photo was taken during a blower door test, and so high-lights air movement paths. In this case, the perimeter of the floor was connected to the outdoors due to poorly insulated walls. Darker areas show cold air leaking into the house, and you can clearly see the warmer floor joists beneath. Needless to say, this was a very cold floor in the winter.

Envelope Improvement Assessment

Table 6.3 presents several shell improvement scenarios in a sample house. The house is of fairly typical construction where little attention was paid to energy efficiency. The table is based on a 1,500 square foot house with an open crawl-space foundation, located in a 6,000 heating degree day (HDD) climate. Here are the details of the improvement analysis:

The old single-pane windows offer a U-factor of 0.91. They cover 12 percent of the total wall area, and are responsible for 38 percent of the home's heat loss. The new windows have a U-factor of 0.35, while adding storm windows to the existing windows reduces the U-factor to 0.45.

The air-leakage rate of 0.75 air change per hour (ACH) consumes 31 percent of the home's heating budget. It is estimated that a professional air-sealing contractor can reduce the leakage rate by 40 percent to 0.45 ACH.

R-19 insulation covers all six sides of the house shell. The floor and ceiling each accounts for 7.5 percent of the

Fig. 6.14a: Tongue-and-groove ceiling. Credit: Peter Schneider.

Fig. 6.14b (inset): Infrared photo of tongue-and-groove ceiling with blower door running. Credit: Walter Scott.

Fig. 6.15a: Second story floor. Fig. 6.15b (inset): The same floor in infrared with blower door running.

Table 6.3: Annual Heating Energy Savings of Shell Improvements.

Improvement	Heat consumption (MMBtus)	Improvement savings (MMBtu)	Savings percent	Savings $ @ $1.25/therm natural gas	Estimated installed cost	Simple payback (years)	Return on investment (percent)
Base case	78.1	-	-	$976 (base heating cost)		-	-
New windows	59.7	18.4	24%	$230	$10,000	43	2%
Add storm windows	63.0	15.1	19%	$189	$2,500	13	8%
Reduce air leakage by 40%	68.5	9.6	12%	$119	$1,000	8	12%
Add 6-inches of insulation to attic	75.2	2.9	4%	$36	$500	14	7%

home's heat loss, and the walls eat up 16 percent of the heating energy. The attic improvement brings the insulating value up to R-38.

The table compares the energy and cost savings of these improvements to the base case, and includes simple payback and return on investment for each. The installed costs are estimates and may vary widely due to fluctuating material costs and variations in labor costs (see also Table 5.1 in Chapter 5 for heating efficiency-improvement savings).

As you can see, replacing windows certainly does reduce energy consumption, but air-sealing, insulating, and adding storms are more cost-effective options, especially when these improvements are combined. Replacing windows is worthwhile if they are damaged or if they are causing damage to another part of the building (e.g., leaking window sills can cause wooden framing materials to rot). If you do replace your windows, be sure to thoroughly air-seal around the new windows as they are installed. Of course, rising energy costs will increase the cost-effectiveness of all these improvements.

Air Leakage Diet

The best place to address air leaks is at their source. For example, if you feel a draft coming from around an electrical outlet you can install a foam gasket behind the cover plate to slow the leak, but this will do nothing to address the source of the leak within the wall cavity. Always try to imagine how the air is moving from the outside, through the envelope, to wind up where you notice the draft. Find the big leaks first; they're easy to spot and offer the greatest improvement opportunity. Next, concentrate on leaks to the attic, as this is where the greatest potential for moisture-induced damage can occur. Don't forget to look into suspended ceilings. Here are some ideas on how to draft-proof your home and reduce excess air movement.

- Interior partition walls that connect to attic framing should be properly air-sealed with rigid insulation, spray foam, wood blocking, metal flashing, and then covered with insulation.
- Leaky furnace ductwork located in unconditioned areas can suck unconditioned air into the ductwork, or blow conditioned air into an unconditioned space. Seal all ductwork connections with mastic or foil tape and cover ducts with insulation.
- Tongue-and-groove wood interior finishes on walls or ceilings should be installed over a continuous air or vapor barrier.
- Chimney chases, plumbing vents, or other shafts that run through the house to the outdoors need flashing or other air-stops between conditioned and unconditioned areas.
- Fireplace dampers should close tightly.
- Recessed lights provide direct access to unconditioned air above the ceiling. The top of the fixture (the part extending into the attic) should be boxed in with sheet rock, leaving at least three inches all around the lighting fixture for heat dissipation. An "IC" (insulation contact) rated recessed light fixture is one that can be safely covered by — or wrapped in — insulation without the sheetrock box. Better still, avoid using recessed lights.
- Any place where different shell or framing materials meet should be caulked, foamed, weatherstripped, gasketed, or otherwise air-sealed.
- Windows should be caulked to the sheathing during installation.
- Window- and door-casing perimeters should be caulked or foamed between the wall framing and the casing.
- Install door sweeps to stop drafts underneath the door.
- Baseboard moldings should use backer rod, caulk, or foam to block air movement between the basement or sill plate area and the living area.
- Mechanical, plumbing, electrical, gas, water, or oil lines that penetrate between conditioned and unconditioned areas should be sealed with caulk or foam.
- Exhaust fans (bathroom and range-hood fans and dryers) should have backdraft dampers installed where the vent meets the outdoors.
- Exhaust fans should be sealed to the wall or ceiling to which they are mounted so that air is pulled from the home, and not from within the framing cavity into which they are installed.
- Complex framing details where the insulation or air barrier may not be continuous need attention

to detail during construction. Tape all seams in the air barrier. Caulk or foam the gaps in between framing materials where insulation materials may not fit. A small space in a roof or wall that allows air to move, or that has no insulation can cause moisture or ice problems, in addition to energy loss.

- Cabinets built into knee walls should be weatherstripped and tightly closed.
- Obvious holes in windows, walls, ceilings, and floors should be repaired.
- Frozen pipes are usually the result of a cold draft blowing across the pipe. Seal up the draft and insulate the pipe. Avoid using electrical heat tapes as they are costly to operate, potentially dangerous, and unreliable in the event of a power failure — which is likely to happen when you need them most.

- Attic hatch perimeters should be weatherstripped, and removable insulation placed above — this is a good place to use rigid foam insulation.
- Basement sill plates should be sealed around the entire perimeter.
- The bottom plate of stud walls should be caulked to the floor deck.
- Electrical switches and outlets can be sealed to the wallboard with foam gaskets.
- Use sealed-combustion heating and hot water equipment.

Air and Moisture Movement

Air holds moisture, and when it moves, moisture moves with it. This movement will cause either wetting or drying of materials. Air and moisture movement within the house and through the envelope will affect not only energy efficiency, but also the longevity of the building and the health and comfort of the occupants. Whether you live in a new or old home, you should try to maintain relative humidity levels inside the home within the range of 35 to 55 percent. Invest in a *hygrometer* to keep you informed about indoor humidity. There will certainly be times when humidity levels are outside this range, and I am not suggesting that you and your home will fall apart if optimum humidity periodically falls outside this range.

Moisture problems may appear as apparently benign condensation on the windows, but this symptom could indicate other more severe moisture problems within the walls, under carpets, in basements, crawlspaces, or even in the attic — as well as a possibly problematic window. The issue is one of chronic versus intermittent humidity levels. Building materials can hold moisture, and they can dry if allowed. Think of your house as like a sponge. Building materials can safely store and release water, but there is a limit to a material's storage capacity. If weather conditions vary from wet to dry, these materials have a chance to release their stored moisture. However, if the drying times are too short or too infrequent, the building can run out of storage capacity and the excess moisture will cause problems.

Let's look at two ways both air and water can move, and two ways in which only moisture can move through your home.

Pressure

Heat will always move from hot to cold — that is, from high energy to low energy. In this way, heat has a "pressure," and this pressure pushes on the building envelope, driving heat energy from hot to cold and moving air around on thermal convection currents.

Like heat, moisture creates its own pressure — called *vapor pressure* — and it too is always trying to move from more to less. Vapor pressure causes humid air to migrate toward drier space. Because warm air can hold more moisture than cold air, vapor pressure generally follows heat pressure in moving from hot to cold.

Airflow

Obviously, when the wind blows air moves. If there are holes in the envelope of your house, the wind will blow outside air in through those holes. New homes tend to be more airtight than older homes due to the common inclusion of a continuous air barrier over the exterior sheathing.

A less obvious way for air to move is by way of *buoyancy*. Warm air is more buoyant than cold air, and so moves to the top of the house. When air moves in this way, it creates a draft, like the draft in a chimney. When you light a fire in a fireplace, cool air enters the fireplace, fuels the combustion process, and the hot, light (more buoyant) combustion products rise up the chimney. As the chimney warms, the draft becomes stronger. The same is true for a house.

When air leaves a building, air must come from somewhere to take its place – this is called *make-up air*. All homes leak air. As in the chimney, warm air in your home rises and finds its way out through airflow paths in the ceiling as cool air enters through the lower part of the house. This air movement sets up a convective heat flow within the house, called the *stack effect*, creating a pressure differential within the house. The upper levels will be under higher ·

pressure than the lower levels, creating a natural draft. This is not to say that all air and moisture moving within the house will follow only this path, but the stack effect should be considered when addressing air-leakage issues.

To reduce the stack effect and its energy-robbing heat loss, you must seal uncontrolled air paths in the envelope. Start at the ceiling where the warm, moist air is escaping (causing potential moisture-related damage in the attic), but don't ignore air entry paths in the basement.

Capillary Movement

Capillary movement describes the movement of water through porous materials. Capillarity is how trees and plants move water from the ground into their branches and leaves. This process can also move potentially large amounts of moisture from the damp ground into and through drier building materials. This is why it is important to prevent ground water from making contact with your concrete foundation. Concrete is very porous and moisture will readily move through it. When wet concrete is in direct contact with wooden framing materials, capillary action will move moisture from the concrete to the wood frame. Bugs, mold, and fungus love wet wood. Wet wood is not something you want in your home. A capillary break — such as a vapor barrier between the concrete and wood framing — can stop this flow of moisture.

Diffusion

Water vapor is lighter than air, and a water molecule is smaller than the oxygen and nitrogen molecules that make up air. This means that water vapor can go where air can't — even through walls. Just because you don't feel air moving doesn't mean there is no moisture movement. This kind of moisture movement is called *diffusion*. Diffusion does not contribute appreciably to moisture problems when compared to the amount of moisture that can be carried through a drafty wall.

Reducing Air and Moisture Movement

I often hear people complain that forced air or wood heat is "dry." Heat cannot be dry, nor is it wet. Heat is a measure of energy. If your house is dry during the

Permeance

A material's ability to transfer water vapor is called *permeance*, and is measured in units called "perms." Porous materials like wood, concrete, and fiberglass have high permeance and do not offer much resistance to vapor pressure, while plastic and metal have low permeance.

A *perm* is a measure of water-vapor transmission through a material over time, at a given pressure. A six-mil thick polyethylene plastic vapor retarder has a perm rating of .06, while gypsum wallboard has a perm rating of 50. You can lower the permeance of an existing wall having no polyethylene vapor barrier by applying a low-perm, (vapor-retarding) paint with a perm rating of around .45 or less. Even a good, even coat of regular paint helps.

heating season, it is likely due to excessive air leakage (more on this soon in the discussion on relative humidity). A home that holds on to moisture during the heating season probably retains heat and air just as well — meaning that the envelope does a good job at resisting the heat and vapor pressures acting on it. This also means that the air inside your home could become stagnant and stale. On the other hand, a home that is too dry is likely to be drafty and uncomfortable. In hot, humid cooling climates where air conditioning is used, the same dynamics are at play. An air conditioner removes moisture from the air and if your home is drafty, humid air will find its way inside causing the air conditioner to work harder.

In addition to insulation, a roof or wall assembly should contain materials used to slow or stop the movement of air and moisture. When you insulate a wall, you change its temperature. The temperature gradient within the insulation is going to range from the inside temperature to the outside temperature. Air will carry moisture into the wall cavity through holes in the envelope. Moisture can condense on the insulation inside the wall or ceiling if there is too much moisture or not enough insulation in the cavity to keep its temperature above the dewpoint of the air trapped in, or traveling through, the insulation. It is very important to prevent moisture from settling on the insulation within the wall as the insulating value will be reduced (wet insulation does not insulate), and because mold, mildew, and insects come with moisture. In the worst cases, structural damage occurs when the wall stays damp due to trapped moisture, unable to dry to the inside or the outside.

Some method of reducing air and moisture travel into the building envelope should be considered when building or renovating a home. Rigid foam insulation can act as a barrier to both air and moisture. Check with your contractor or energy auditor for recommendations as to the best use of air and vapor barriers in combination with the right insulation choice for your home and your climate.

Air Barriers

Air barriers are typically used on the outside of a building shell (underneath the siding) to prevent outside air from moving through the envelope. They are the windbreaker over the sweater of insulation within the walls. An ideal air barrier has taped seams and is sealed to all building penetrations, wrapping the entire house in an airtight membrane. A good, tight air barrier is the best way to reduce both air leakage and moisture problems in your home.

Vapor Barriers

The term "vapor barrier" is a bit misleading. Few materials are absolutely impermeable to vapor, so "vapor retarder" has become the more accepted term, although they are used interchangeably in many books on construction and energy. Vapor retarders are used on a wall or ceiling frame to slow the migration of moisture into the framing cavity where it can damage the insulation and other building materials. Vapor retarders are typically placed on the more humid side of the building frame. For example, in northern climates where homes are heated most of the year, the vapor barrier is installed on the inside of a building to prevent warm, moist, indoor air from migrating into the cool, dry wall cavity where condensation can occur within the wall. In hot, humid climates (such as the southeastern US) dominated by air conditioning rather than heating load, the vapor barrier may be placed on the outside of the wall or ceiling frame to prevent humid outdoor air from entering the stud cavity or rafter bay. In warm, dry climates, no vapor barrier may be required at all, but an air barrier is always a good idea.

The most common vapor retarders used in modern construction are the paper or foil backing on insulation, and plastic sheeting (polyethylene) stapled to the building frame. Never use more than one vapor retarder, as moisture can become trapped between them with no way to dry out. No vapor retarder is 100-percent waterproof, nor can they be perfectly installed. At best, a well-installed vapor barrier will greatly slow the diffusion of moisture, but there will always be a way for moisture-laden air to enter a wall or ceiling cavity. Given that moisture will enter the wall, it must then be allowed to dry out of the wall. A good builder will admit this and design for minimal moisture migration into the envelope, provide proper drainage of water away from the building, and allow for drying of the building envelope once it does get wet. This is accomplished with strategic placement of air and vapor barriers that allows moisture to dry to the inside or to the outside of the building, depending on local climate conditions and how the house is operated.

The sun is a driving force when it comes to both heat and moisture. When your siding, trim, or window frames get wet from rain, and then the sun comes out, the sun's heat (pressure) may evaporate some moisture, but it will also drive moisture deeper into the siding, and even into the sheathing or wall framing. Remember that both heat and moisture move from areas of more to less. If there is no way for the moisture to dry out of the wood, mold and decay will be the result. Always provide a way for moisture to drain and dry between the siding and sheathing of a house, and to dry out of building materials so that it does not become trapped.

Peeling paint can mean trapped moisture. If moisture from within the house migrates outward, it can penetrate the back of the siding and cause paint to peel off the front. Back-priming the siding can help, but designing the building for proper drainage and drying will help prevent moisture from becoming trapped within a wall system.

If you have a crawlspace or basement with a dirt floor, it is important to prevent moisture in the ground from migrating into the building. This is most easily accomplished by putting a heavy (at least six-mil thick) polyethylene

Wet Basements and Cold Drinks

When you open your refrigerator on a summer day, humid air rushes in and deposits moisture on the cold things in the fridge. The same thing happens when you take a cold drink out of the refrigerator. Condensation represents the absorption of heat energy as moisture is squeezed out of the air that comes in contact with the cool drink container.

Now let's look at your basement. Foundation walls are made of water-absorbing concrete, or leaky stonework. The ground behind the walls is moist, and ventilation in most basements is poor. In addition, basements are underground and tempered by the cool earth. Given that most basements are cool and damp, how do you control the humidity? The most common answer I hear is, "Open the windows in the summertime to let it dry out." Now that you know about the physics of relative humidity you can see why this is bad advice. Allowing warm, humid, summertime air to enter a cool, damp basement will do nothing but encourage even more moisture to condense on cool walls and other surfaces, making the basement even wetter. Cold air simply cannot hold as much moisture as warm air. Often, this process of ruining one's home is accelerated by the use of fans to blow the outside air in. This effort to maximize drying accomplishes the exact opposite of your intentions, depositing gallons of water with nowhere to go. It doesn't matter which way the fan is blowing either. If you exhaust air from the basement, air will be pulled in from somewhere to take its place. Only if that replacement air is warm and dry will the basement eventually dry out. The best way to achieve a dry basement is to eliminate moisture at its source, preventing it from entering in the first place.

vapor retarder on top of the dirt. If you need to walk on this floor on a regular basis, you will need to protect the plastic from damage by covering it with gravel or other suitable material.

Relative Humidity and Moisture Control

Air holds moisture, and how much moisture it holds at any given time is defined as *relative humidity*. Relative humidity (RH) is a measurement indicating the amount of water vapor a volume of air *is* holding compared with the maximum amount of water vapor it *can* hold at a given temperature.

The study of air and moisture dynamics is called *psychrometrics*. This subject can be quite complex, but you can get the general idea of relative humidity by thinking of it this way: a volume of warm air can hold more water vapor than the same volume of colder air. This is because cold air is denser than warm air. As air temperature rises, its energy level increases, causing the molecules to bounce off each other faster, increasing the distance between molecules, expanding the air. The greater space between air molecules makes room for more water vapor molecules. When it's hot and humid, our body's cooling mechanism, perspiration, becomes less efficient because it's more difficult to evaporate sweat into moist air.

As you know, homes are not airtight — they leak — and where do they leak to? The outdoors. Air sneaks in through the cracks in the house, and every time a door is opened to outside. If there is no make-up air for heating and ventilation equipment, the air infiltration rate increases as the house is put under a slight negative pressure. The outdoor air may be 35°F and 70 percent RH, but once the air infiltrates your home and warms up, that same air at 70° now has a relative humidity of 19 percent. As the temperature rises and the air expands, the relative humidity decreases, and the air feels dry.

Humidity levels also have an affect on human health. Too little moisture can negatively affect breathing, promote virus growth, and dry your skin. Many viruses thrive in low-humidity environments. Too much moisture can cause the growth of mold and mildew, causing allergies or illness. A 1999 Mayo Clinic study found that mold was the cause of nearly all chronic sinus infections. Dust mites are a major human allergen, thriving where humidity is greater than 55 percent and the temperature is over 70°F.

In a new home, most of the products used in construction will contain some moisture. It will invariably rain during construction, and concrete requires large amounts of mix-water which can take years to fully dry. The moisture drying out of these construction materials (up to two gallons per day during a home's first year) will likely end up inside the house. Some provision should be made to remove this moisture.

Do you consistently see condensation on the inside of your double-pane windows? Does mold grow easily in dark corners or around the bathtub? Are there mysterious stains on the walls or ceilings? Is your siding warped or peeling paint? Do you have an allergic reaction when you walk into your musty smelling house? If so, you may have an indoor moisture problem. Carpets and wallpaper can hide some very beautiful, but unhealthy, molds.

If you could squeeze all the water out of the air in your home, it would total less than two gallons. The relative humidity inside your home will change dramatically with small changes in actual water quantity. The activities of a typical family of four can generate about three gallons of moisture every day. The American Lung Association's Health House Project measured respiration and perspiration moisture rates of about three pints per person per day. Breathing is one of the great joys of life, but we cannot breathe well without fresh air. If your home is too humid, you will need to eliminate the moisture source and/or add fresh-air ventilation to remove the moisture. Controlling moisture requires identification of its sources — damp basements, leaky roofs, plumbing leaks, plants, showers, laundry, cooking, dishes, aquariums, new or seasonally wet construction materials, and breathing. I would discourage the use of a dehumidifier unless absolutely necessary as dehumidifiers can be costly to operate. If you do operate a dehumidifier, be sure to look for the ENERGY STAR label indicating a high level of energy efficiency.

By tightening your home to keep outside air out, you get to hold on to your expensive, conditioned air. Moreover, if you eliminate air leaks, remove unwanted sources of moisture, add dedicated combustion-air inlets to heating equipment (as explained in Chapter 5), and a mechanical ventilation system, you can effectively control your home's humidity level, reducing maintenance costs while improving the health of your family *and* your home.

Indoor Air Quality

The US Environmental Protection Agency (EPA) ranks poor indoor air quality among the top five environmental risks to public health. The EPA also reports that the level of air pollution inside a home can be two to five times higher —

Ken's Car

When I explained all these moisture matters to Ken Sumer, he said, "Yeah, I have a condensation problem in my car in the winter. I turn on the heat and all the windows fog up. I keep meaning to bring it to the shop to have it fixed."

"Well, it's not winter, but show me," I said. We walked to the car and Ken set the heater controls to recirculate the air within the car.

"Heats up faster that way," he said.

"What, the engine, or you? When you recirculate air within the car, you're just breathing your own exhaust. The windows fog up because of the moisture you exhale and your perspiration. The hotter you make it in the car the worse the problem will be, because the temperature difference between the inside and outside of the windows encourages condensation. Just flip the lever over to 'fresh air' and bring in fresh, drier air from outside."

This scenario is identical to what can occur in a home that does not get enough fresh-air circulation. Condensation occurs when warm, moist air comes in contact with a cold surface. Moisture and pollutants need to be removed from inside your home and replaced with fresh air. This air exchange should occur at a rate that supplies enough fresh air to occupants, but without being excessive — which can over-dry the home and lead to increased heating-fuel consumption.

and occasionally 100 times higher — than outdoors! This indoor air quality problem can lead to breathing difficulties and other health problems. To make things worse, some surveys have indicated that Americans spend up to 90 percent of their time indoors, and many homeowners do not change the air filters in their air conditioners or furnaces as often as recommended.

Indoor air quality is becoming a concern as new homes are being built tighter. A tight home is good for energy efficiency, but when a home becomes too tight with no provision for fresh air exchange, health problems can be the result. Many synthetic materials are used in modern building products, as well as the materials used to finish and furnish homes. Buildings can be diagnosed as "sick," and people are finding themselves to be acutely sensitive to common chemicals used in building products. Potential air quality hazards in a home include:

- Dust
- Mold
- Radon
- Bacteria, viruses, pollen, and dust mites
- Tobacco smoke contains about 4,000 chemicals, including 200 known poisons, such as formaldehyde and carbon monoxide, as well as 43 carcinogens
- Lead dust
- Pesticides
- Pet dander
- Carbon monoxide
- Formaldehyde (used in adhesives, building materials, carpets, upholstery)
- Volatile organic compounds (VOCs) released when using combustion equipment, adhesives, cleansers, perfumes, hair sprays, solvents, paints, carpets, air fresheners, plastics, and preservatives

Poor indoor air quality can cause or contribute to the development of chronic respiratory diseases along with headaches, dry eyes, nasal congestion, nausea and fatigue. These ailments are best avoided by:

- Eliminating the use of offending products and using non-toxic (to the earth and humans) building materials and household cleansers
- Removing the toxin at its source
- Cleaning the air through proper ventilation and/or an air-cleaning system
- Maintaining indoor humidity levels at or below 50 percent
- Keeping furnace and central air conditioner filters clean
- Having your home tested for radon
- Keeping your smoke and carbon monoxide detectors operational

The best way to achieve good indoor air quality and energy efficiency is to build a tight envelope and control the amount of fresh air delivered to the house with a mechanical ventilation system.

Ventilation

Achieving energy efficiency, moisture control, and good indoor air quality within a home requires attention to details. You must control moisture and pollutants in the building, and prevent airflow through the envelope. That said, you must recognize that we do not live in a perfect world, and that we do not build air-tight homes out of waterproof materials.

Older homes are not known for energy-efficient construction techniques. They were generally poorly insulated and quite drafty. These drafts introduce plenty of fresh air into the home, but also carry away substantial amounts of costly conditioned air. Since the 1970s, new homes have become far more energy efficient, and older homes have benefited from weatherization efforts. With the growing knowledge gained and shared by the building science industry, new homes use better construction techniques, are better air-sealed and insulated for energy efficiency, and incorporate mechanical ventilation systems to ensure good indoor air quality.

The general idea behind "build tight, ventilate right" is to build a tight envelope and control the amount of fresh, outside air allowed into the house by using a mechanical ventilation system such as an exhaust fan or air-to-air heat exchanger. Although a hermetically sealed house would be ideal in terms of energy efficiency, living in such a home would not be pleasant. If the house was too tight, both occupant and building would suffer ill effects. So how does one ensure a sufficient supply of fresh air so that no occupant health problems or physical damage to building materials occurs? How much air is enough?

The optimum rate of natural air exchange within a home that is a good compromise between indoor air quality and energy efficiency is generally accepted to be 0.35 air changes per hour (ACH). The accepted minimum ventilation requirement is 7.5 cubic feet per minute (CFM) of fresh air per person. The actual rate of air movement is measured by performing a blower door test on the home. If the air leakage is measured at 0.35 ACH or less, consider your home "efficient." If the air leakage rate is much higher, and if all

Close Call

When I was building my house, I lived in a large tent on the land. In the tent were a gas cook stove and a gas refrigerator. Around October, it started to get cold. I went in the tent, zipped it all up and began to cook dinner with a friend. Fifteen minutes later, the stove went out.

"I hope I'm not out of gas," I thought.

I got out the matches to re-light the stove, but the matches wouldn't light. "Must be wet," I said.

So I got out a propane torch with an automatic ignition and that wouldn't light either. "Must be empty," my friend said.

Then there was a roar from the fridge flame as it suddenly went out. My friend and I looked at each other, shrugged our shoulders in confusion, and then it dawned on me. I opened the tent door and fired my torch outside. The matches worked outside too. We looked at each other to see if our lips were blue from lack of oxygen. No symptoms — at least that we were aware of. I had no idea that a tent could be so airtight! Had we not gone outside immediately, we would not have felt or noticed any pain as we slowly, painlessly succumbed to carbon monoxide poisoning. Fortunately, we lived to learn a valuable lesson about tight buildings and good indoor air quality.

I use and recommend only sealed-combustion equipment and have several carbon monoxide detectors in my home. The detector batteries are replaced every year, and the detectors themselves are replaced every five years, which is the average lifetime of the electronic sensors inside carbon monoxide detectors.

If, for some very strange and perhaps misguided reason you decide to use a vent-free heater in your home, be sure you have a few carbon monoxide sensors around. Also, be sure that the heater is equipped with an "oxygen depletion sensor," which will stop the flow of fuel should ambient oxygen levels become too low. Many of these vent-free heaters come with a warning to use only in well-ventilated areas, though I have

not yet seen a well-ventilated area that is worth heating. You can read
more about heating equipment in Chapter 5.

the home's appliances are sealed-combustion (exhausted to outside, with make-up air also provided from outside), then we can safely tighten up the house to save some heating and/or cooling energy without creating air quality or backdraft problems.

Mechanical Ventilation

Natural ventilation is inconsistent and does not guarantee air movement through the house. Some days your house might feel stuffy while other times it might be drafty. If a blower door test measures 0.35 ACH in your home, there may be quiet weather days when the actual air leakage is zero, while stormy days may allow twice the measured amount or more.

For air to move through an open window or a small leak in the envelope requires that the wind blow or that some other force (such as temperature or vapor pressure) create a pressure difference between indoors and out causing air to move. For this reason, fresh indoor-air requirements are best met through a mechanical ventilation (motorized fan) system rather than simply opening a window or relying on prevailing weather conditions. Mechanical ventilation puts the house under a negative pressure, forcing air to move into the home from outside.

Mechanical ventilation systems can be divided into three general categories:

Spot ventilation such as a kitchen range-hood or bathroom exhaust fan, removes stale air at the source, and brings fresh air inside by creating a negative pressure within the house. This negative pressure causes outside air to be pulled into the house by way of the path of least resistance, such as an open window, a fresh air inlet vent, or natural leaks in the house. A high CFM fan (downdraft range fan or commercial range-hood) used in a very tight house with a fossil fuel heating or hot-water system that is *not* sealed-combustion can present a problem. In this case, the path of least resistance may be the chimney or flue, causing combustion by-products to backdraft into the home.

In a typical home under 2,000 square feet that is reasonably (but not overly) tight, a high quality, well-installed bathroom exhaust fan with a capacity of around 100 CFM can provide adequate ventilation to the house without creating backdraft problems.

Multi-port ventilation operates much like spot ventilation but has multiple, ducted air inlets from different rooms leading to a single central exhaust fan. Spot and multi-port ventilation are "exhaust-only" systems, and both systems create a negative pressure in the house. Forcing stale air out forces fresh air in as the pressure difference between inside and outside try to maintain a balance. With exhaust-only ventilation, air will move, but will move in an uncertain path.

Balanced ventilation offers separate exhaust and supply ducting, and so removes stale air from inside while introducing fresh air from outdoors. This is the best option for effectively ventilating a home because it removes stale air at the source, and puts fresh air where the people are. It is called balanced because an equal amount of air is supplied to the house as is exhausted from it.

A *heat-recovery ventilator* (HRV) is the most efficient type of balanced ventilation system. An HRV allows heat energy to be transferred between fresh incoming air and stale but conditioned outgoing air as they both pass through a heat exchanger. This heat-recovery process minimizes the energy costs of introducing fresh outside air into the home. HRVs have the following advantages over other types of ventilation systems:

- A heat exchanger transfers heat between the outgoing and incoming air without mixing the two streams. This energy transfer works in both heating and cooling seasons.
- Effective ventilation occurs evenly throughout the entire home.
- Ventilation is directed to where occupants are.
- Whole-house air filtration is possible, offering additional health benefits.
- Because it is a balanced system, negative pressure is not created; therefore there is no potential for ventilation-induced backdrafting of combustion equipment, such as may happen in a tight home with an exhaust-only ventilation system.

- The home can be air-sealed for a natural ventilation rate of well below the 15 CFM per person (or 0.35 ACH) natural infiltration threshold, offering maximum energy savings while still providing adequate fresh air to occupants.
- Enhanced indoor air quality leads to greater occupant comfort.

Another type of HRV is called an *enthalpy recovery ventilator*, or ERV. An ERV allows for the transfer of water vapor (and therefore recovers latent as well as sensible heat) by way of a desiccant wheel revolving between incoming and outgoing air streams. An ERV may be the right choice if the home tends to be too dry, or if the home is air-conditioned. Beware though: a dry home is probably one that is over-ventilated — either intentionally or not — because ventilation (natural or mechanical) removes moisture from the home. The use of an ERV allows air conditioning equipment to be downsized because it will transfer moisture from humid incoming air to the drier exhaust air stream, thereby reducing the dehumidification load of the AC.

There are few instances where an HRV would be inappropriate to ventilate a home (even an old, drafty one) and many builders are opting to install them as a matter of course because they can almost guarantee against moisture-related callbacks.

Installation

When installing a ventilation system, be sure to use well-sealed, rigid vent ducting — not the flexible, spiral-wound, dryer vent commonly found in hardware stores. Flex-vent is easy to install poorly by bending it too tightly or making it too long or too short, while sagging can allow for the collection of water in low spots. Figure 6.16 shows this situation in an attic. The two vents in the figure are coming up from a clothes dryer and a bathroom fan on the floor

Fig. 6.16: Poorly installed flex-vent. There is water trapped in the bottom of these vent hoses. One hose is used as a dryer vent, the other as a bathroom fan vent.

below. Both vents *will* eventually fill with water and the dryer vent *will* become clogged with lint as well, possibly creating a fire hazard.

Most bathroom exhaust fans only move about 50 percent of their rated capacity in CFM. Much of this reduction is due to flex-vent materials, too many elbows, leaky connections, unsealed gaps between the fan box and ceiling sheetrock plane, and improper or faulty exhaust ports. Be sure to vent the fan outside, not into the attic where warm, moisture-laden air from the house will undoubtedly cause problems. Avoid venting the fan into the roof soffit as this restricts the airflow and moisture will be drawn back into the attic. Use mastic or foil tape (*not* duct tape) to seal pipe and vent port connections. Be sure the vent pipe is mechanically fastened (not just taped) to the outlet port both on the fan and where it leaves the house. The vent pipe should slope slightly downward towards the outside to allow accumulated moisture to drain. If you decide to install an HRV it is best to have an experienced professional install the ductwork, as special tools and great attention to detail are required to achieve maximum performance.

Operation

Exhaust-only ventilation can provide adequate whole-house ventilation when properly installed and used. A quiet, low-wattage fan, coupled with a programmable 24-hour timer is a good, basic system for an average-size house. The fan's run-time depends on how tight the house is. Start with a timer setting that allows the fan to run 20 minutes out of every hour while the house is occupied. Adjust the running time up or down from that setting depending on the results. If you have consistent condensation problems on your windows when it's not too cold outside, watch the condensation level decrease with increased fan-operating time. Your goal is to achieve an indoor relative humidity of between 35 and 55-percent.

Choose a fan with a low sound rating (under 1.5 sones), and low power use (under 40 watts). If the fan is noisy when it's on, or you notice its power consumption in your electric bill, you will be less inclined to use it. In addition to a timer, the fan can operate from a *dehumidistat*, a switch that senses the moisture level in the room and automatically turns the fan on. Dehumidistats are commonly used in bathrooms in conjunction with HRV systems.

Attic Ventilation

You might be wondering about the use of attic fans to remove hot air from your house. Attic fans are designed to remove hot air from the attic, and work best if there is enough air available from outside the attic — meaning outside the *house* — to make up for the air being removed by the fan. What you want to avoid is moving conditioned air from the living space below into the attic, wasting energy and possibly moving excessive moisture into the attic. A properly designed and sized attic ventilation system will ensure that overheated air is removed from the attic only, and that all makeup air comes from the outdoors.

Ice Dams and Icicles

Imagine a snowy, New England village with quaint, old farmhouses, wood smoke rising from their chimneys and icicles dangling from the roof reaching nearly to the ground. This scene may warm the heart, but the insides of those homes are anything but warm. Icicles are *not* quaint! They are the result of poor insulation and/or air leakage paths between heated spaces and the roof. Icicles lead to ice dams, especially around dormers, roof valleys, and other hard-to-insulate areas. When snow melts on a roof, then re-freezes in an ongoing process, the result is an ice dam. Ice can push its way under roofing material, causing water leaks and potentially great damage to the home.

The easiest solution is to install a heating cable on the roof to melt the ice and drain it away. This solution does not address the source of the problem though, and is also the most expensive remedy in the long run. Icicles and ice dams indicate wasted energy, and you need to stop the leaking heat. I saw one project where several very long heat tapes were used to keep icicles from forming on a school roof. At issue was the safety of people walking next to the building, underneath a potential killer icicle. When the problem was finally addressed from an energy standpoint, with insulation and air-sealing improvements made, the result was no icicles, reduced heating costs, and substantial electrical savings that paid for the cost of the efficiency improvements in about two years.

Icicles and ice dams may be due to poor roof drainage and sun melting the snow, but more often the problem is due to heat moving rapidly away from

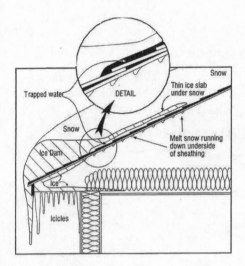

Fig. 6.17: How ice dams form. Credit: Canadian Mortgage & Housing Corporation (CHMC), Attic Venting, Attic Moisture, and Ice Dams, 2001.

inside the house. The source of that heat loss may be poorly insulated ductwork in the attic, poor ceiling or wall insulation, or air leakage from indoors to the roof. A common problem that occurs where knee walls are used is that heated air migrates from the first floor ceiling up into the knee wall cavity where the roof is not insulated, while cold air can infiltrate the cavity through the soffit vent. Another problem is interior walls that connect to the roof or attic space, thermally connecting the heated space with the roof, warming the roof and melting the snow. I've seen far too many attics where the insulation does not cover the entire ceiling due to voids, gaps, or the failure to extend all the way over the top plate of the wall below. Insufficient or improperly installed ceiling insulation allows heat to leak from the house and melt snow on the roof, as do any unsealed penetrations into the attic. Thermal bridging caused by rafters and complex roof-framing details that are difficult to insulate can also lead to ice dams. Good planning while framing the roof and attention to insulation and air-sealing details will help avoid roof heat-loss problems, keeping the roof cool so as not to melt snow. Figure 6.17 shows a classic example of why ice dams form.

All of these scenarios expose the cold roof to warm indoor air. Heat leaves the house, and with little to stop it, rises up to the roof, melting the snow. Melted snow turns to water, and if the water can't drain away rapidly, it freezes and turns to ice. When water turns to ice it expands, and this expansion is more powerful than most roofing materials can withstand. The ice can literally migrate into the soffit or attic.

Roof Venting

Your contractor may talk to you about "roof ventilation" and how it can help reduce the potential for ice problems. While this can be true, roof ventilation is a tricky subject. Conventional wisdom states that roof ventilation is required to remove heat and moisture from within the roof framing and attic, while keeping the roof "cold," meaning closer to the outside temperature than the indoor temperature, thus with no snow melting. A properly vented roof will move outdoor air into a vented soffit, up along the roof slope through a vent channel between the roof deck and the insulation, and out through a ridge vent or gable-end vent.

Fig. 6.18: Good insulation detail in a flat ceiling.
Credit: US Environmental Protection Agency.

The insulation should be baffled or otherwise isolated from the venting airflow to prevent air movement within the insulation. If air moves through insulation, heat is carried away, and the insulation is rendered useless. A rigid, corrugated foam sheet is commonly used to create this venting channel, which you can see in Figure 6.1; it's the sheet running up the slope of the roof in between each rafter. A poor example of a vent channel is seen in Figure 6.2, where an attempt was made using a piece of cardboard. Cardboard can be used, but to ensure sufficient ventilation it needs to be installed in every rafter bay without being compressed. In a flat ceiling, an insulation baffle is required at the eave-end of the rafter bay to prevent air from moving into the end of the insulation, and to prevent insulation from blocking the soffit vent.

Figure 6.18 shows a properly insulated and baffled flat ceiling. A sloped, or cathedral, ceiling would follow the same approach, but in addition to the wind baffle, a vent channel is created between the roof deck and the insulation. Note also that the ceiling insulation extends over the top plate of the wall, eliminating a potential heat-loss path.

Figure 6.19 shows an infrared photo of the icicles resulting from insulation installed without a baffle, allowing air to move freely through it. The photo was taken outside the north wall of a house — you can see the horizontal siding leading up to the vented soffit along the top, with icicles dangling from the roof.

Fig. 6.19: Infrared photos of icicles.

White indicates warmer areas in the photo, and you can see the horizontal white stripe behind the icicles indicating the warm soffit vent. Heat is lost from the house and moving air carries heat away from the insulation, warming the snowy roof and creating icicles. Just to the left of the icicles, you can see that the white (hot) area has diminished (the heat loss is not as great), and there are no icicles.

If you live in a cold region, take a look at the roofs in your neighborhood the next time it snows. If you can see vertical stripes, you are looking at the thermal bridging effect of the rafters. If you see ice dams and icicles, or places on the roof where all the snow has melted, you know that a serious insulation or air-sealing problem exists.

Like all air movement, the airflow path from soffit vent to ridge vent requires a pressure difference. You can expect heat loss from the house to drive this air movement as heat is lost through the attic insulation, warming air in the attic, causing it to rise and exit via the ridge vent, drawing makeup air in through the soffit vents. This airflow also removes any moisture that may be in the attic area, reducing the potential for condensation buildup within the attic.

The trickiness in roof ventilation arises when one asks the question: "Why is all this heat and moisture in the attic anyway?" The answer often lies in poor insulation and air-sealing between the attic and the source of the heat and water vapor — the house. Roof venting originally arose as a moisture-control strategy for cold climates. In theory, a perfectly air-sealed ceiling, along with enough insulation, should allow a roof to remain cool and dry, with no ice dams or condensation, and without the need for ventilation. In practice, building with this level of detail is challenging, but most certainly attainable.

Diet for a Warm, Dry, Healthy Envelope

- Drain moisture away from the house with gutters, foundation drains, and sloped landscaping.
- Remove moisture at its source.
- Run bathroom exhaust fans during, and ten minutes after, each shower.
- Prevent air and moisture from entering framing cavities by creating a good, tight air barrier between indoors and out.
- Allow moisture to dry out of the envelope.
- Keep basement windows and doors closed in the summer. Warm, humid, summer air entering a cool basement will cause condensation there.
- Avoid gaps in the insulation. Gaps totaling only five percent of the insulation's surface area will vastly increase the heat load.
- Make sure corners and edges of ceilings, walls, and floors are properly insulated — this is often where heat leaks are found.
- If the foundation is uninsulated, it will be cost-effective to add insulation, given that the average ground temperature is around 50 to 55°. Alternatively, if the basement is not heated, you can insulate the basement ceiling to keep heat upstairs in the conditioned area.
- A foil-faced radiant barrier under the roof will reflect heat away from the home in summer, and back into the home in the winter.

- Air-seal and insulate ductwork.
- Have wiring in your old home inspected by an electrician to ensure it can be safely covered by insulation.
- Provide good air circulation throughout the house, especially in kitchens and baths.
- Provide effective, adequate, whole-house ventilation to remove moisture and heat, control indoor humidity levels, and bring fresh air into the home.
- When cooking, use a range-hood exhaust fan (vented to the outdoors) to remove moisture and pollutants.
- There may be several gallons of water in a load of wet clothes — be sure that clothes dryers and bathroom exhaust fans are vented to the outdoors, not indoors or into the attic, where condensation problems can occur.
- Install storm windows or tight-fitting plastic over single pane or drafty windows. This will raise the temperature of the interior glazing surface, reduce condensation on the window and increase the comfort level near the window.
- Cover windows at night with heavy curtains or window quilts. Open the curtains during the day.

How to Perform a Heat-Load Calculation on Your Home

Those who want to learn how to calculate building heat losses should refer to Appendix D for the inevitably math-heavy instructions. *Heat load* is a measure of how many Btus per hour are needed to heat or cool a building. Its two main components are heat loss by transmission, and by air leakage. In Appendix D we will first define your house in terms of heat loss and then look at these components separately.

CHAPTER 7

Buying New Appliances

How to Buy a New Appliance

IN THIS CHAPTER WE WILL IDENTIFY SOME OF THE KEY ISSUES you face when considering the purchase of new appliances. There are some general criteria common to many appliances, and some specific details to look for depending on which fuel the appliance uses. Of course, many household appliances use electricity, but you should be ready to decide on the most cost-effective fuel source for a new heating or hot water system.

We have all probably experienced "sticker shock" — that jump in your chest when you look at the price of a new car or the quote to replace the furnace that blew up on a cold January night. The sticker price of an item is its *first cost*. After you buy it, you pay to use and maintain it. I want to impress upon you that buying an energy-consuming appliance is an investment with very real impacts on household finances beyond the purchase price. Often, the appliance with the lowest first cost will have the highest lifetime cost. The environmental impacts of your choices are very real, too.

To illustrate this concept, we will compare the *return on investment* offered by different appliances that do the same job, and perform a simple *life-cycle cost analysis* to help determine the overall lifetime cost of the appliances you are considering. I'll use refrigerators as an example throughout this chapter, but you can apply the same concepts and formulas to any energy-consuming appliance. Before we get to the math though, there are other easy ways to shop for new energy-efficient appliances.

Energy Guide Tags

One piece of information is uniformly provided on nearly every new appliance that uses any kind of energy. Take some time when you shop to look closely at the yellow Energy Guide tag, which tells you exactly how much energy that appliance consumes (in fuel-specific units), estimates the annual operating cost, and compares it to other appliances of a similar type. These tags are due to the efforts of the Federal Trade Commission.

The energy consumption and cost printed on the tags are based on average energy cost and usage patterns, and are probably different from your actual fuel cost and usage. These figures are useful in that they offer a relative comparison of energy consumption and cost between similar models based on a standardized test for each category of appliance.

Looking at Figure 7.1, let's take a tour of the Energy Guide tag. The upper left corner lists the type of appliance. In this case it says you are looking at refrigerator. The upper right lists the size and model number. The heart of the tag is the bar graph in the middle. It shows the range of energy use for similar models, identifying the lowest energy user (more efficient) on the left, and the highest energy user (less efficient) on the right. Somewhere along the bar will be an arrow and a number that indicates the fuel consumption of the item you are looking at. The numbers are presented in fuel units. For example, if you're looking at an electric appliance, the units will be in kilowatt-hours (kWh). If it's a heating system or water heater, the units will be in gallons of oil or LP gas, or therms of natural gas. The important thing to remember is that the more efficient appliances will use less energy and the arrow indicating the actual consumption will be towards the left end of the bar. In this case, the arrow does not appear because the power consumption is actually below the most efficient refrigerator rated at the time.

Above the bar graph is printed the actual number of fuel units you can expect to use each year under test conditions — 485 kWh of electricity for this model. Below the bar graph is an estimate of what you can expect to pay to operate the refrigerator each year based on the average fuel consumption listed above the bar graph.

On the bottom of the tag is the fine print. It tells you that the price of electricity used to arrive at the annual operating cost was $0.0867 per kWh.

$$485 \text{ kWh} \times \$0.0867 = \$42$$

You probably don't pay the fuel price shown, as it represents a national average at the time the rating occurred. To estimate your annual operating cost, multiply the number of fuel units used by your cost per unit of fuel. Be aware that these numbers are for comparison only, and in most cases you will probably use the appliance differently than the testing organization did to arrive at its figures. The last sentence on the tag sums up this point: "Your actual operating cost will vary depending on your local utility rates and your use of the product."

Some effort is being made to make these labels easier to read, so the presentation of information on these tags may be different from the example shown.

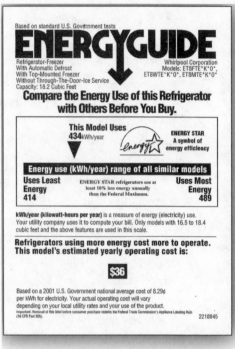

Fig. 7.1: Energy Guide label.

The ENERGY STAR Label

The ENERGY STAR program was introduced by the US Environmental Protection Agency (EPA) in 1992 as a voluntary labeling program designed to identify and promote energy-efficient products in order to reduce carbon dioxide emissions. When you buy an ENERGY STAR qualified appliance, you can be sure that you are getting one of the most efficient units available. ENERGY STAR is about more than energy savings though; other criteria, such as expected lifetime, are also reviewed.

In 1996, the EPA partnered with the US Department of Energy to promote ENERGY STAR. The ENERGY STAR program now covers residential heating and cooling equipment, major appliances, office equipment, lighting, consumer electronics, windows, televisions, VCRs, water coolers, ventilation products, dehumidifiers, and even whole buildings. EPA commercial partnerships include over 1,200 manufacturers labeling more than 13,000 products and over 1,600 builders that have constructed over 57,000 new homes. As of the end of 2002,

750 Million ENERGY STAR products had been purchased, saving Americans more than $5 billion in energy costs and reducing pollution by an amount equivalent to that produced by 10 million cars.

The ENERGY STAR label for buildings is based on a performance-rating system that allows owners to evaluate the efficiency of their building relative to others. This performance rating is a comprehensive evaluation of a building's overall efficiency. You can have your home rated by a certified energy-rater or rating organization. Energy Rated Homes is one such organization with affiliates in many states and a list of certified energy raters on the web at <www.natresnet.org>. You can also call your state energy office, or visit the National Association of State Energy Officials on the web at <www.naseo.org> to find out who to call in your state. In addition to providing an energy rating, many rating organizations and home performance contractors have trained and certified energy specialists on staff who can offer a comprehensive energy audit and make specific recommendations about improving the efficiency of your home.

According to the EPA, if all consumers, businesses, and organizations in the United States made their product choices and building-improvement decisions over the next decade with ENERGY STAR standards in mind, the national annual energy bill would be reduced by about $200 billion. In addition to energy and cost savings, we would realize a sizable reduction in air pollution and the chemicals blamed for climate change. If the appliance you're looking at is ENERGY STAR qualified, it will have a logo on it that looks like that in Figure 7.2.

There are some very good appliances that are not yet rated by ENERGY STAR. These appliances are often manufactured by smaller companies, or have no ENERGY STAR rating criteria. Some appliances that are difficult to make more efficient include electric dryers, electric water heaters, and manual defrost refrigerators. For more information, call the ENERGY

Fig. 7.2: ENERGY STAR logo. Credit: US Environmental Protection Agency.

Energy Improvement Loans

Banks today are often willing to finance energy efficiency improvements and even renewable energy-powered homes through the energy star loan program. Ask your lender about an Energy Efficient Mortgage that uses the energy savings of a new energy efficient home to increase the buying power of consumers and capitalizes the energy savings in the appraisal. Existing homeowners may also be able to take advantage of this service by financing energy upgrades of an existing home. Contact your lender, or visit these websites for more information:

ENERGY STAR <www.energystar.gov> and follow the *resources* link. The Residential Energy Services Network <www.natresnet.org>.

STAR hotline at 1 (888) STAR-YES [1 (888) 782-7937] or visit them on the web at <www.energystar. gov> where you can find a list of every product with an ENERGY STAR label.

Checklist for Choosing a New Energy Efficient Appliance

- Plan ahead. Don't wait for an emergency to buy a new appliance — you are more likely to buy out of desperation than make an informed choice.
- Learn all you can about the appliance before you shop from reputable sources such as *Consumer Reports*.
- Check the lists on the ENERGY STAR website.
- Research the brand's warranty and repair details.
- Go shopping with brand names and model numbers from your research.
- Study the yellow Energy Guide tag attached to the appliance.
- Ask the salesperson to show you the more energy efficient ENERGY STAR-rated models with power consumption toward the lowest end of the scale. If they are not in stock, ask to see a catalog that may contain other models. Manufacturers' catalogs and websites can help you find the right model.
- Don't be shy about educating the sales staff.

Financial Incentive

When you buy a new appliance, think of it as making an investment. You want to spend money on something that will cost you less to operate than what you already have, or than compared with other choices to accomplish the same task. The bottom line is far greater than the purchase price, and your choices can impact your finances for years to come.

When buying a new appliance, most of us look for the item with the features we want at a price we can afford. All energy-consuming appliances have up-front costs (the price we pay at the store) and operating costs. Operating costs include those associated with energy consumption and equipment maintenance and repair. Perhaps one model costs a little more to buy, but uses less energy. Before buying new appliances, take a few minutes to compare products and crunch some numbers.

Following are a few simple exercises that can really pay off. Don't be afraid of the math; it's not hard and it's worth your time to be able to save a few hundred dollars over the life of the product. The following concepts and formulas apply to anything you buy that uses any kind of energy.

Simple Payback

How much time will it take to pay off that new appliance in energy savings? *Simple payback* (in years) is found by dividing the installed cost or purchase price of the appliance by the annual energy-cost savings. The lower the operating costs, the shorter the payback period.

The simple payback Math Box gives an example using two different new refrigerators I am considering as a replacement for an older, less efficient unit. They are both the same size and offer the same features with similar warranties.

Return on Investment

I may not wait to buy that new fridge. By replacing my old refrigerator with the ENERGY STAR model, I can start saving $86 per year right away! If you were investing in the stock market, you would expect your stock to increase in value and you would want to know what to expect in return for your investment. You can (and should) figure your annual return on investment (ROI) of a new appliance as well. ROI is calculated using the same numbers as simple payback,

Math Box: Simple Payback

My old refrigerator uses 1,500 kilowatt-hours per year and probably has a few years left in it before it completely fails. If it breaks down, I won't want to put any money into repairing it. I want to be ready and know exactly what to buy and where to buy it. I really don't like emergencies.

Fridge #1 costs $550 to buy, and according to the Energy Guide tag consumes 850 kWh per year in electricity.

Fridge #2 costs $750 to buy, and according to the Energy Guide tag consumes 450 kWh per year in electricity. It has the ENERGY STAR label.

To determine what each unit costs to operate, multiply the price you pay for electricity by the refrigerator's power consumption.

I pay 8.2 cents per kWh for electricity. My old fridge is costing me:

$0.082 per kWh x 1,500 kWh per year = $123 per year in power.

Fridge #1 would cost $69.70 per year in power (0.082 × 850), and Fridge #2 would cost only $36.90 per year to operate.

Fridge #1 then *saves* me $53.30 per year in power ($123 – $69.70), while Fridge #2 would save $86.10 per year.

Purchase price and energy cost are all we need to know to determine Simple Payback. Here is the formula:

Purchase Price ÷ Annual Energy Cost Savings
= Simple Payback (in years)

The payback for replacing my old refrigerator with fridge #1 then is:

$550 ÷ $53.30 = 10.3 years.

The payback for replacing my old refrigerator with the more efficient fridge #2 is:

$750 ÷ $86.10 = 8.7 years.

Even though fridge #2 costs more to buy, it has a shorter payback period due to its superior efficiency.

but the formula is slightly different. It is the annual cost-savings offered by the new appliance divided by its installed cost or purchase price. The answer is expressed as a percentage, so the lower your operating costs, the higher the percentage of return. You receive a return on the investment until the investment matures; in this case the maturity is the length of the simple payback period. In other words, after a period of time your energy savings have paid for the new refrigerator and you pocket the savings.

Math Box: Return on Investment

ROI is telling you what percentage of the purchase price you get back every year as a function of energy savings. Here's the formula:

Annual Cost Savings ÷ Installed Cost of the Appliance × 100 = ROI

The reason you multiply by 100 is because the answer is expressed in percent. If I choose the ENERGY STAR refrigerator, I will need to spend $750 to reap an $86.10 annual savings. My annual ROI then is:

$86.10 ÷ $750 × 100 = 11.5% annual return on investment

Compare that percentage with what your money might earn in a simple savings or money market account. Energy efficiency is a great investment — even compared to Wall Street!

Math Box: Lifetime Costing

Fridge #1 costs $550 to buy, and consumes $69.70 per year in electricity. It comes with a one-year warranty.

Fridge #2 costs $750 to buy, and consumes $36.90 per year in electricity. It has an ENERGY STAR label and comes with a three-year warranty.

My old refrigerator is costing me $123 per year in power, and I expect maintenance to become a large part of its operating expense fairly soon.

Whichever model I buy, I plan on keeping it for at least 15 years. I really *don't* like shopping, and when I do shop, I like to think of the things I buy as long-term investments, rather than a "consumer purchase."

Over 15 years, Fridge #1 would cost me $1,045.50 in power ($69.70 per year × 15 years), while Fridge #2 will consume $554 worth of electricity.

Over its 15-year lifetime, fridge #1 will cost me:

$550 (purchase price) + $1,045.50 (electricity cost) = $1,595.50.

The cost of electricity is 66 percent of the total lifetime cost of refrigerator #1 ($1,054 ÷ $1,595).

Over its 15-year lifetime, fridge #2 will cost me:

$750 (purchase price) + $554 (electricity cost) = $1,304.

The electricity cost of refrigerator #2 is only 42 percent of the total lifetime cost.

Lifetime Costing

Just how much does an appliance cost you over its entire lifetime? A life-cycle cost analysis can help answer this question by comparing lifetime operating and maintenance costs, along with the purchase price of each piece of equipment you might be considering. The idea is to estimate how much you think it will cost you each year to own the appliance. The lifetime costing Math Box uses our refrigerators as an example, building on the previous Math Boxes.

Buying the more expensive but more efficient refrigerator saves $291.50 over the cost of the cheaper unit during its lifetime. You can expect electricity prices to rise a few percent every year, so the actual lifetime cost of each fridge will also rise proportionally, making Fridge #2 an even more attractive long-term investment. Buying efficiency is a hedge against increasing future energy costs. In addition, the ENERGY STAR fridge comes with a longer warranty. This indicates to me that the manufacturer has more confidence in its product and it will probably require less maintenance. Paying a little more up front can save a lot over the appliance's lifetime.

There may be other costs associated with owning and operating home appliances, which might include shipping, installation, maintenance, repairs, and finally, disposal at the end of its life. These costs must be factored into the lifetime cost analysis to arrive at a realistic figure. It is difficult to predict what repairs will be required in the future, but in the case of heating equipment you already know that you should pay a local heating contractor an hour's worth of labor every year for preventive maintenance such as annual tune-ups and filter replacement. Add annual maintenance costs to the annual operating cost as you did with energy costs.

Cost of Efficiency

The cheapest kilowatt-hour is the one you don't have to buy. This is a concept sometimes referred to as *negawatts* (or negative watts), and it applies to equipment that uses other fuels as well. One of the primary points of this book is that energy-efficient products are an investment. It is cheaper to invest in efficiency than to buy power. If you spend an additional $200 for the more efficient refrigerator, you will save 400 kWh per year for 15 years, totaling 6,000 kWh over the life of the refrigerator. You have purchased efficiency at a cost of $0.033 per kWh ($200 ÷ 6,000kWh), far cheaper than the cost of purchasing power from your electric company. If you pay $0.082 per kWh for the next 15 years, you will save $492 in power costs. For every dollar you spent on efficiency, you saved $2.46 in reduced power costs ($492 ÷ $200).

Off-Grid Economics

If your goal is to supply your home with electricity from the sun or wind, the economics of efficiency become even more dramatic. Buying and operating your own electric power plant can be quite costly, so it is important to analyze the long-term costs and benefits of all your energy uses. The energy source itself (sun or wind) may be free, but the infrastructure for gathering and storing that energy is not. Efficiency is the first step toward sustainability, and this is especially true when planning your off-grid home and its energy requirements.

Let's continue with the refrigerator example from above and add in the costs associated with supplying electricity from the sun to operate each unit. To operate the refrigerators we will need solar panels to generate the electricity and batteries to store it for use at night. For this analysis though, we will keep things simple and concern ourselves only with the cost of the solar panels required to power the refrigerators to illustrate the point about the cost-effectiveness of efficiency.

Here's the relevant information we know so far:

• Fridge #1 costs $550 to buy, and consumes 850 kWh/year in electricity.
• Fridge #2 costs $750 to buy, and consumes 450 kWh/year in electricity.

They each have a capacity of 19 cubic feet.

Look over rows one through eight in Table 7.1. These rows compare general information about each refrigerator. Rows nine and ten were discussed in the previous section on financial incentives. Rows eleven through fourteen present the new information we will need to consider using solar energy to power our refrigerators.

First, we need to know how many hours of sun fall on the solar panels. These are daily, peak sun hours (usually between 10 a.m. and 2 p.m.) averaged over a year and include days when the sun doesn't shine. In this case, we'll assume the sun shines brightly on the solar panels an average of four hours per day.

Here's where the first bit of math comes in. If fridge #1 uses 2.33 kWh (2,330 watt-hours) per day, and we have four hours of sun per day, then we need to generate:

$$2{,}330 \text{ watt-hours} \div 4 \text{ hours} = 582 \text{ watts.}$$

Table 7.1: Refrigerator Comparisons.

General Information		Fridge #1	Fridge #2
1	kWh per year	850	450
2	kWh per day	2.33	1.23
3	Cubic feet	19	19
4	kWh per year per cubic foot	44.7	23.7
5	Price	$550	$750
6	Price per cubic foot	$28.95	$39.47
7	Electricity cost ($ per kWh)	$0.082	$0.082
8	Annual operating cost	$69.70	$36.90
15 year lifetime cost			
9	Lifetime electric cost	$1,046	$554
10	Lifetime fridge cost	$1,596	$1,304
Solar power variables			
11	Average daily sun hours	4	4
12	PV power needed (watts)	582	308
13	Solar module price per watt	$6.00	$6.00
14	Solar array cost	$3,493	$1.849
Total installed cost of solar powered refrigerator			
15	Total cost	$4.043	$2,599

This analysis does not include equipment maintenance or additional solar power costs (such as batteries, panel mounts, labor).

582 watts of solar-electric generating power will be needed to keep fridge #1 running, and to store enough electricity (in batteries) for nighttime power use. Solar panels are not free, even though the sunlight falling on them is. To buy solar electric panels, you might pay $6 per watt. For example, a 50-watt solar panel costs about $300 to buy new. The refrigerator requires 582 watts of solar panels, at a cost of $3,493. When the purchase price of the refrigerator is added in, you will be faced with an up-front cost of $4,043 to get your fridge going, as shown on line 15. Compare this to the more efficient fridge #2, which has a total installed cost of $2,599. This refrigerator costs only $200 more to buy, but saves over $1,440 in total system costs if you are going solar. There are some refrigerators that are extremely efficient and extraordinarily expensive. Decide

what your priorities are, then perform a life-cycle cost-analysis to see the financial impacts of your choice.

How Much Energy Do You Use?

Your Energy Consumption Profile

The average American uses about 350 million Btus of energy each year. That's the equivalent of just over 60 barrels of oil. Add up your own annual energy consumption by filling in the blanks, and then doing some simple math.

Transportation

How many miles do you drive your car every year? _____

How many miles per gallon (MPG) does your car get? _____

Divide the number of miles you drive by the MPG to determine the number of gallons of motor fuel you use every year: _____

Multiply the number of gallons of gasoline or diesel fuel used by the number of Btus per gallon listed in Table A. 1 to determine how many Btus of energy your car consumed. If you use diesel fuel, use the Btu-per-gallon figure for home heating oil. _____

Example: You drive 20,000 miles every year in a car that averages 25 MPG.

20,000 ÷ 25 = 800 gallons of gasoline.

800 gallons × 115,000 Btus per gallon = 92,000,000 Btus.

Dividing by 1,000,000 = 92 MMBtus used every year for transportation.

Home Fossil Fuel Use

How many gallons of home heating oil do you use every year? _____
Multiply the number of gallons by 138,690 to find the number of Btus consumed. _____

Divide by 1,000,000 to get MMBtu. _____

How many therms of natural gas do you use every year? _____

Multiply the number of therms by 100,000 to find the number of Btus consumed. _____

Divide by 1,000,000 to get MMBtu. _____

How many gallons of LPG do you use every year? _____

Multiply the number of gallons by 91,690 to find the number of Btus consumed. _____

Divide by 1,000,000 to get MMBtu. _____

Table A. 1: Energy Content of Home Fuels.

Fuel	BTU/unit	Unit
Natural gas	100,000	therm/Ccf
Liquid petroleum gas (LPG)	91,690	gallon
Gasoline	125,071	gallon
Kerosene	135,000	gallon
Coal	21,000,000	ton
Wood	20,000,000	cord
Electricity	3,413	kWh

Note: Energy content per unit of fuel may vary due to additives, impurities, and source.

Electricity Use

How many kilowatt hours of electricity a year do you use? _____

Multiply your kWh per year by 3,413 to get Btus consumed. _____

Divide by 1,000,000 for MMBtu. _____

Example: You use 8,500 kWh per year.

8,500 kWh × 3,413 = 29 million Btus.

How did you do? If you're average, your home plus your car will have used about half of your energy budget as shown in Table A. 2. The remainder is used by the commercial and industrial sectors to manufacture and sell the products you buy.

Table A.2 lists average energy consumption per person by state. Variations are due primarily to industrial activity.

Table A 2: Energy Consumption Per Capita by State

State	MMBtu	Rank	State	MMBtu	Rank
Alabama	459	10	Montana	467	7
Alaska	1122	1	Nebraska	361	24
Arizona	255	46	Nevada	340	28
Arkansas	472	6	New Hampshire	279	41
California	253	49	New Jersey	318	38
Colorado	285	40	New Mexico	365	23
Connecticut	256	45	New York	235	50
D.C.	327	31	North Carolina	320	37
Delaware	370	22	North Dakota	577	4
Florida	255	47	Ohio	384	20
Georgia	359	25	Oklahoma	410	14
Hawaii	204	51	Oregon	335	29
Idaho	414	13	Pennsylvania	310	39
Illinois	320	36	Rhode Island	264	44
Indiana	460	9	South Carolina	384	19
Iowa	391	17	South Dakota	326	32
Kansas	396	16	Tennessee	378	21
Kentucky	462	8	Texas	574	5
Louisiana	827	3	Utah	326	33
Maine	422	12	Vermont	278	42
Maryland	267	43	Virginia	324	34
Massachusetts	254	48	Washington	389	18
Michigan	328	30	West Virginia	407	15
Minnesota	351	26	Wisconsin	345	27
Mississippi	437	11	Wyoming	879	2
Missouri	323	35			

Your Greenhouse Gas Profile

Based on your energy use, how much carbon dioxide do you produce? Total US CO_2 production in 2000 was 6.4 billion tons from all sources — about 22.5 tons for each one of us. Table B. 1 shows where it came from:

The US Environmental Protection Agency's *Inventory of US Greenhouse Gas Emissions* reports emissions criteria for the fuels listed in Table B. 2.

Your Personal Greenhouse Gas Profile

Fill in the blanks below, then do some simple math to determine how much carbon dioxide is produced as a result of your energy consumption.

Table B. 1: US CO₂ Production, 2000.

Source	Tons CO$_2$	Percent
Home electricity	3.01	13%
Other home fuel use	1.48	7%
Transportation	7.42	33%
Commercial	3.82	17%
Industrial	6.75	30%
Total	22.49	

75% of commercial and 49% of industrial CO₂ emissions were from electricity. Electricity production accounted for 41% of all CO₂ emissions.

Transportation

How many miles do you drive your car every year? _____

How many miles per gallon (MPG) does your car get? _____

Divide the number of miles you drive by the MPG to determine the number of gallons of motor fuel you use every year. _____

Multiply the number of gallons of gasoline or diesel fuel you use by the pounds of CO_2 per gallon listed in Table B.1 to determine the number of pounds of CO_2 produced by your car. _____

Example: You drive 20,000 miles every year in a car that averages 25 mpg. $20,000 \div 25 = 800$ gallons of gasoline.

Table B. 2. Greenhouse Gas Emissions Criteria.

Type of fuel	Pounds CO_2/unit	Unit	Pounds CO_2/MMBTU
Oil, diesel	22.4	gal	161
NG [1]	12.1	therm	117
LPG	12.7	gal	139
Kero	21.5	gal	160
Gasoline	19.6	gal	156
Anthracite coal	3,852	ton	227
Bituminous coal	4,931	ton	205
Sub-bituminous coal	3,716	ton	213
Lignite coal	2,792	ton	215
Wood [2]	3,814	ton	222

[1] 1 therm + 100,000 BTU = 100 cubic feet.
[2] 1 full cord = ~1.5 - 2 tons depending on species.
Burning wood does not produce a net atmospheric CO_2 gain.
Wood contains 7250 BTUs/pound @ 0% moisture.
Source: www.eia.doe.gov.oiaf/1605/factors.html

800 gallons × 19.6 pounds per gallon = 15,680 pounds (7.84 tons) of CO_2.

Home Fossil Fuel Use

How many gallons of home heating oil do you use every year? _____ Multiply the number of gallons by 22.4 to find the number of pounds of CO_2.

_____

How many therms of natural gas do you use every year? _____
Multiply the number of gallons by 12.1 to find the number of pounds of CO_2. _____
How many gallons of home LPG do you use every year? _____
Multiply the number of gallons by 12.7 to find the number of pounds of CO_2. _____

Electricity Use

How many kilowatt-hours of electricity a year do you use? _____

Multiply your kWh per year by the average number of pounds of CO_2 per kWh for your state as listed in Table B. 3. _____

Example: you use 8,500 kWh/year and you live in Louisiana.

8,500 kWh × 0.18 pounds (Louisiana) CO_2 per kWh = 6,391 pounds (3.2 tons) of CO_2.

States with higher numbers rely more heavily on fossil fuels, while those with lower numbers use more nuclear or renewable energy. Idaho is near zero because about 90 percent of its electricity is produced by hydro. Vermont's low figure is because a large portion of its electricity is nuclear. Southern and Midwest coal-burning states have higher CO_2 emission rates.

Table B. 3: Carbon Dioxide Emissions – Average per kWh by State

State	lbs/kWh	Rank	State	lbs/kWh	Rank
Alabama	1.31	24	Montana	1.43	30
Alaska	1.38	27	Nebraska	1.4	29
Arizona	1.05	13	Nevada	1.52	33
Arkansas	1.29	21	New Hampshire	0.68	6
California	0.61	5	New Jersey	0.71	7
Colorado	1.93	43	New Mexico	2.02	47
Connecticut	0.94	12	New York	0.86	11
Delaware	1.83	40	North Carolina	1.24	18
Florida	1.39	28	North Dakota	2.24	50
Georgia	1.37	25	Ohio	1.8	39
Hawaii	1.66	36	Oklahoma	1.72	38
Idaho	0.03	1	Oregon	0.28	4
Illinois	1.16	15	Pennsylvania	1.26	19
Indiana	2.08	48	Rhode Island	1.05	14
Iowa	1.88	42	South Carolina	0.83	9
Kansas	1.68	37	South Dakota	0.8	8
Kentucky	2.01	46	Tennessee	1.3	23
Louisiana	1.18	17	Texas	1.46	31
Maine	0.85	10	Utah	1.93	44
Maryland/D.C.	1.37	26	Vermont	0.03	2
Massachusetts	1.28	20	Virginia	1.161	16
Michigan	1.58	34	Washington	0.25	3
Minnesota	1.52	32	West Virginia	1.98	45
Mississippi	1.29	22	Wisconsin	1.64	35
Missouri	1.84	41	Wyoming	2.15	49
			US average	1.325	

Note: These state-level electricity emissions factors represent average emissions per kWh generated by electric utilities for the 1998–2000 time period. They do not include emissions from power produced by non-utility generators. The Voluntary Reporting of Greenhouse Gases Program believes these factors provide reasonably accurate default values for power generated in a given state.
Source: http://www.eia.doe.gov/oiaf/1605/e-factor.html

Appliance Use Chart

Table c. i consists of a appliance use chart; simply look up the appliance you want to know about and use the default usage figures. Note that I have made some assumptions about how many hours you might use each appliance in an average month, and you won't use everything on the list throughout the year (air conditioners, for example). Your power consumption will vary depending on how you use each item, so you will need to adjust for your actual usage.

The first column of the chart identifies the appliance, the second shows the power demand in watts, the third column gives an estimate of the monthly hours the appliance is in use, while the fourth offers an adjustment for cycle factor. Perhaps the most useful column is the fifth, showing average monthly power consumption of the appliance so that you can work with this chart while looking at your monthly power bill. The last column is an average annual use for each appliance, assuming that it is used year-round. This may not be true in all cases, such as with air conditioning.

If you have items that are not on the chart, or if you wish to more closely calculate your actual consumption, you will need to know two things:

1. The power demand, in watts, of the appliance. You can use the default wattage listed in the chart, the wattage information listed on the appliance, or the metered wattage.
2. The monthly hours of operation. Multiply watts times the time in use to arrive at monthly watt-hours consumed by the appliance, then divide by 1,000 to arrive at kWh per month.

Table C.1: Appliance Use Chart

Appliance	Average Power in Watts[1]	Average Use in Hours/Month	Cycle Factor[2]	Consumption in kWh/Month	Average Annual Power Use in kWh
Air Cleaner	60	730	100%	44	526
Air Conditioner – 12,000 BTU	1200	150	100%	180	2160
Air Conditioner – 5,000 BTU	500	150	100%	75	900
Air Conditioner – Central	3000	300	75%	675	8100
Answering Machine	10	730	100%	7	88
Aquarium – Filter Pump	15	730	100%	11	131
Aquarium – Heater	75	730	75%	41	493
Aquarium – Light	25	240	100%	6	72
Battery Charger, automotive, 6 amp	125	8	100%	1	12
Blender	400	1	100%	0.4	5
Boiler Circulator Pump	100	240	100%	24	288
Bread Maker	650	3	100%	2	23
Bug Zapper	40	90	100%	4	43
Clock – Digital alarm radio	5	730	100%	4	44
Clothes Dryer – Electric (1 hr/load)	5000	20	75%	75	900
Clothes Dryer – Gas (1 hr/load)	300	20	100%	6	72
Clothes Washer – Top Loader	300	20	100%	6	72
Clothes Washer – Front Loader	200	20	100%	4	48
Coffee Grinder	110	1	100%	0.1	1
Coffee Maker (100 Watt-hrs to brew 6 cups)	1000	31	75%	23	279
Computer – Desktop	90	90	100%	8	97
Computer – Desktop, standby	20	730	100%	15	175
Computer – Laptop	20	60	100%	1	14
Computer – Laptop, standby	10	730	100%	7	88
Computer Printer, inkjet, while printing	10	4	100%	0.04	0
Computer Printer, laser	400	4	100%	2	19
Computer Scanner, with light on	16	4	100%	0.1	1
Crock Pot	300	12	75%	3	32
Deep Fryer	1450	4	100%	6	70
Dehumidifier (damp basement)	800	730	30%	175	2102
Dishwasher – temp boost + heat dry	1700	20	100%	34	408
Dishwasher – temp boost, no dry	1400	20	100%	28	336

Appliance	Average Power in Watts[1]	Average Use in Hours/Month	Cycle Factor[2]	Consumption in kWh/Month	Average Annual Power Use in kWh
Dishwasher – no temp boost or dry	500	20	100%	10	120
DVD player	15	24	100%	0.4	4
Electric Blanket	100	240	50%	12	144
Engine Block Heater	500	80	100%	40	480
Electric Fence	10	730	100%	7	88
Fan – Attic	375	240	100%	90	1080
Fan – Bath	75	30	100%	2	27
Fan – Ceiling	80	240	100%	19	230
Fan – Window	150	240	100%	36	43
Fax Machine (in standby)	5	730	100%	4	44
Fax Machine (in use)	150	10	100%	2	18
Food Processor	400	4	100%	2	19
Freezer (see p. 295)	varies		100%		
Furnace Blower	800	120	100%	96	1152
Garage Door Opener (0.5 HP)	450	1	100%	0.5	5
Garbage Disposal	400	1	100%	0.4	5
Griddle	1200	8	100%	10	115
Hair Curler	15	3	100%	0.05	1
Hair Dryer	1500	5	100%	8	90
Heat Lamp	250	30	100%	8	90
Heat Tape (7 watts per foot)	140	240	100%	34	403
Heater – Baseboard, 6 feet (250 watts per foot)	1500	240	100%	360	4320
Heater – Portable	1500	60	100%	90	1080
Heating System – Oil Burner Motor	130	240	100%	31	374
Hot Plate	1200	8	100%	10	115
Hot Tub (indoor – average power)	5000	50	100%	250	3000
Hot Tub (outdoor – average power)	5000	75	100%	375	4500
Humidifier	125	240	100%	30	360
Iron	1100	4	100%	4	53
Knife – Electric	40	1	100%	0.04	0
Lights (vary) average 10% of your electric use, or about 1,000 kWh per year			100%		0
Microwave	1600	10	100%	16	192
Microwave (standby)	7	730	100%	5	61
Mixer Hand/Stand	200	2	100%	0.4	5

Appliance	Average Power in Watts[1]	Average Use in Hours/Month	Cycle Factor[2]	Consumption in kWh/Month	Average Annual Power Use in kWh
Motors & Pumps[3]					
Oven	2600	12	75%	23	281
Oven – Broiler	2600	4	100%	10	125
Oven – Gas, glowplugs only	200	4	100%	1	10
Oxygen Concentrator w/compressor	400	365	100%	146	1752
Popcorn Popper – Hot Air	1400	4	100%	6	67
Popcorn Popper – Oil	575	4	100%	2	28
Radio/tape player (portable)	10	60	100%	1	7
Range – Large Surface Unit	2400	20	100%	48	576
Range – Small Surface Unit	1300	20	100%	26	312
Range – Self-Cleaning Cycle	2600	4	100%	10	125
Refrigerator (see p. 295)					
Satellite Dish Receiver	25	730	100%	18	219
Sauna (minimum power)	5000	10	100%	50	600
Saw, chop or circular	1000	0.5	100%	1	6
Sewing Machine	90	1	100%	0	1
Shaver	15	7	100%	0	1
Stereo	75	270	100%	20	243
Swimming Pool Pump (5 months)	800	730	100%	243	2920
Telephone – Cell	5	730	100%	4	44
Telephone – Cordless	2	730	100%	1	18
Telephone – Cordless, w/ answering machine	7	730	100%	5	61
Television	100	120	100%	12	144
Toaster – 2 slice	1100	3	100%	3	40
Toaster Oven	1200	4	100%	5	58
Trash Compactor	400	4	100%	2	19
Vacuum Cleaner – Central	1600	16	100%	26	307
Vacuum Cleaner	750	16	100%	1	144
Vaporizer – Cold Air	30	160	100%	5	58
Vaporizer – Steam	500	160	100%	80	960
VCR	15	24	100%	0.4	4
VCR (standby)	5	730	100%	4	44
Waffle Iron	1200	2	100%	2	29
Water Cooler/Heater dispenser	varies	730	30%	125	1500
Water Heater[4]	4500	92	100%	414	4968

Appliance	Average Power in Watts[1]	Average Use in Hours/Month	Cycle Factor[2]	Consumption in kWh/Month	Average Annual Power Use in kWh
Waterbed – king size, no cover	400	730	35%	102	1226
Waterbed – queen size, no cover	300	730	35%	77	920
Well Pump[3]	800	20	100%	16	192

Notes:

[1] This is an average power rating figure only. Your appliance may draw more or less power.

[2] Adjust the actual hours used by the cycle factor. For example: A light bulb is on 100% of the time that you can see it is on. A dryer may cycle on and off based on the thermostat setting. The "on time" of a dryer may be 75% of the total time the timer is set for. In this case, you would multiply by 0.75

[3] To figure motor wattage, find the Horsepower (HP) rating on the motor tag. A reasonable assumption is that 1,000 watts is equal to 1 HP. Multiply HP by 1,000 to find watts. Example: 0.25 HP = 250 watts

[4] See chapter worksheet

There are an average of 730 hours in a month and 8,760 hours in a year.

Table C. 2: Refrigerator/Freezer Comparison Chart

Freezers	Annual kWh	Monthly kWh	Daily kWh
Upright, 17 CF, Auto Defrost, 1980	1342	112	3.7
Upright, 17 CF, Auto Defrost, 1990	1082	90	3.0
Upright, 17 CF, Auto Defrost, 2003	685	57	1.9
Upright, 17 CF, Manual Defrost, 1980	917	76	2.5
Upright, 17 CF, Manual Defrost, 1990	608	51	1.7
Upright, 17 CF, Manual Defrost, 2003	479	40	1.3
Chest, 18 CF, Manual Defrost, 1980	897	75	2.5
Chest, 18 CF, Manual Defrost, 1990	610	51	1.7
Chest, 17 CF, Manual Defrost, 2003	426	36	1.2
ENERGY STAR chest freezer, 17 CF, Manual Defrost, 2003	360	30	1.0
ENERGY STAR upright freezer, 17 CF, Auto Defrost, 2003	616	51	1.7
Refrigerators			
18 CF, top freezer, 1980	1181	98	3.2
18 CF, top freezer, 1990	845	70	2.3
18 CF, top freezer, 2003	486	41	1.3
22 CF, Side-by-side, 1980	1619	135	4.4
22 CF, Side-by-side, 1990	1146	96	3.1
22 CF, Side-by-side, 2003	675	56	1.8
ENERGY STAR 18 CF, Top Freezer	442	37	1.2
ENERGY STAR 22 CF, Side-by-side	590	49	1.6

Heat-Load Calculations for Your House

A s mentioned in Chapter 6, *heat load* is a measure of how many Btus per hour are needed to heat or cool a building. Its two main components are heat loss by transmission, and by air leakage. We'll look at these components separately, but first we need to define your house in terms of heat loss.

Before starting this section, please review the information on U-factor and R-value in Chapter 6.

The House

For simplicity, let's use a small, six-sided, stud-framed box and call it a house. The box is 16 feet wide, 24 feet long, and 8 feet tall. This gives us a 384-square-foot house with a volume of 3,072 cubic feet. We'll put our wall studs, along with our floor and ceiling joists two feet on-center and insulate the box with R-11 fiberglass inside the framing cavities. In order to determine the heat loss of the box, we need to first figure out the surface area of all six sides.

We have two walls that are 8 × 16, two that are 8 × 24, and a roof and ceiling that are each 16 × 24. Multiplying these areas out and adding them together gives us a total surface area of 1,408 square feet through which heat is lost through the envelope of the house.

Transmission Heat Loss

The basic formula for heat loss in Btus per hour is:

$$\text{U-factor} \times \text{Area} \times \text{Temperature Difference (delta-T, or } \Delta T)$$

Or, in short:

$$U \times A \times \Delta T$$

We've insulated to R-11 and we know that U-factor is 1 ÷ R, so

$$1 \div R\text{-}11 = U\text{-}0.0909$$

What is the temperature difference? Let's make it cozy. 72°F on the inside, 20°F on the outside. Our difference, or ΔT is:

$$72° - 20° = 52°$$

Putting the equation $U \times A \times \Delta T$ together, gives us:

$$0.0909 \times 1,408 \times 52 = 6,655 \text{ Btus per hour}$$
required to keep our box house warm.

There is more to our box, though. Remember the stud wall? Every stud represents a "thermal break," or an uninsulated area that conducts heat better than through the insulated area. A kiln-dried two-by-four actually measures 1.5" × 3.5", and wood has an R-value of around 1 per inch. So we have an R-3.5 value in all that wood which needs to be taken into account.

Our eight-foot (96-inch) -tall, 2 × 4 studs are two feet on center, and the house has a perimeter of 80 feet. That gives us 40 studs offering a thermal break through the walls.

1.5" × 96" × 40 = 5,760 square inches or 40 square feet of stud area in the walls.

Now add the roof and floor, which have 12 joists each, 16 feet (192 inches) long, or 48 square feet of framing material in the ceiling and floor. That adds up to a total area of 88 square feet in our structure with an R-value of 3.5 or a U-factor of 0.286. We need to subtract that 88 square feet from our total box area and do two separate $U \times A \times \Delta T$ calculations. First find the area:

1,408 − 88 = 1,320 square feet of area insulated to R-11, or U-0.0909.

Then apply the heat loss formula:

$$0.0909 \times 1,320 \times 52 = 6,239 \text{ Btus per hour}$$
heat lost through the insulated cavity.

Plus the framing material heat loss:

$$0.286 \times 88 \times 52 = 1,309 \text{ Btus per hour lost through framing.}$$

Our total heat loss is now up to 7,548 Btus per hour.

How about windows and doors? Let's add one window on each side plus a door. We'll use ENERGY STAR-rated windows with a U-factor of 0.35. They are each 15 square feet. Our door is 20 square feet with an R-value of 7 (U-0.143). First we'll subtract the 80 square feet of window and door area from our R-11 box area to get our new box U-factor of:

$$0.0909 \times 1,240 \times 52 = 5,861 \text{ Btus per hour.}$$

Now for the windows:

We have 60 square feet of ENERGY STAR windows having a thermal value of U-0.35.

$$0.35 \times 60 \times 52 = 1,092 \text{ Btus per hour of heat loss through the windows.}$$

Plus the 20-square-foot door:

$$0.143 \times 20 \times 52 = 149 \text{ Btus per hour.}$$

Our home has a total heat load of:

• R-11 walls and ceiling = 5,861 Btus per hour
• Stud walls, floor and ceiling joists = 1,309 Btus per hour
• Windows = 1,092 Btus per hour
• Door = 149 Btus per hour

Total = 8,411 Btus per hour of heat are lost through the envelope.

An alternate method of performing a heat-load calculation is to add up all the component UA values (U-factors multiplied by the area in square feet) to arrive at the total unit U-factor.

For example:

- The R-11 walls have a U-factor of 0.0909 and a total area of 1,240 square feet. The UA for this wall component is 112.7.
- The studs and joists total 88 square feet with a U-factor of 0.286, so the UA = 25.1
- Windows occupy 60 square feet with a U-factor of 0.35 for a UA of 21.
- The door's UA is 2.9
- Total UA for the house is 161.7

Multiplying total UA by the temperature difference gives us a heat load of 8,408 Btus per hour (this is off by three Btus from the previous calculation due to rounding errors). What else can this number do for us? First, it will give us average U-factors and R-values. You could not have done the above calculations with R-values as they cannot be added together for different component areas as UA values can. R-values can only be added together if they are part of the same building component such as putting R-10 rigid insulation on top of R-30 fiberglass in the ceiling, offering a total of R-40. To calculate the average U-factor of an area, the formula is:

$$U \times A \div \text{Total Area}$$

or, commonly: $\qquad\qquad\qquad$ UA/A

For example, our home has a total surface area of 1,408 square feet and a UA of 161.7. This gives the building an average U-factor of:

$$161.7 \div 1,408 = 0.115$$

and so an average R-value of:

$$1 \div 0.115 = 8.7$$

UA formulas are most useful when adding up different parts of a similar component with different insulation values. For example, if a ceiling is insulated to R-30 in one area and R-38 in another, the UA of each part of the ceiling can be added together to arrive at an average U-factor. If half our example building was R-20 and the other half R-40, you might think that the average R-value is R-30. It is, in fact R-26.7.

Heat Loss Through Air Leakage

Nothing is airtight. Our example home is fairly well put together though, and our energy auditor measured the air leakage rate with a blower door at .30 air changes per hour. This means that every hour, 30 percent of the heated air in the house exchanges with cold outdoor air due to natural leaks in the house. All this fresh, cold air needs to be heated, and we can predict how much heat will be required by determining the volume of air to be conditioned.

Our box is:

$$16 \times 24 \times 8 = 3{,}072 \text{ cubic feet}$$

With an ACH of 0.30, how many cubic feet of air are exchanged every hour?

$$3{,}072 \text{ cubic feet} \times 0.30 = 922 \text{ cubic feet of heated air lost every hour}$$

Air has a *heat capacity* of 0.018 Btus per cubic foot per °F. The heat capacity of a material tells us how much energy (in Btus) is required to raise the temperature of one cubic foot of that material 1°F. Air has a heat capacity of 0.018 meaning that it takes 0.018 Btus of heat energy to raise the temperature of one cubic foot of air by 1°F. Water has a heat capacity of 62.4, so it takes 62.4 Btus to raise the temperature of one cubic foot of water (7.48 gallons, or 62.4 pounds) 1°F.

To every cubic foot of cold, incoming air, we need to supply 0.018 Btus for every degree of temperature difference. In our case, that works out to be:

$$0.018 \times 922 \text{ CF} \times 52° = 863 \text{ Btus per hour}$$

That brings our total heat losses up to 9,274 Btus per hour. This is the total heat load of the house, and if 20° is the coldest temperature we'll ever see outdoors in this climate, that's how big our heating system needs to be.

Sizing the Heating Plant

Now that we know the heat load of the house (9,274 Btus per hour) and the region's design temperature (20°F), we can choose our heating system. This is such a tiny place that a small gas space heater will do the job nicely. If we install a space heater rated at 10,000 Btu output, with an efficiency of 80%, it will consume fuel at the rate of:

$$10,000 \div 0.80 = 12,500 \text{ Btus per hour}$$

On this 20° day the house will require:

$$9,274 \text{ Btus per hour} \times 24 \text{ hours} = 222,576 \text{ Btus.}$$

To keep the place warm, the heater will run for:

$$222,576 \text{ Btus} \div 10,000 \text{ Btus} = 22.25 \text{ hours.}$$

If it's an LP gas heater, it will have consumed:

$$222,576 \text{ Btus} \div 91,690 \text{ Btus per gallon} \div 0.80 = 3 \text{ gallons of fuel.}$$

Finally, if our cabin is in a climate of 5,000 heating degree days, how much heat energy would the building require over the heating season? Here's where we can use our average UA from above.

Total seasonal heat load is:

$$UA \times HDD = \text{Btus per hour}$$
or
$$161.7 \times 5,000 \times 24 \text{ (hours per day)} = 19.4 \text{ million Btus.}$$

Our cabin needs 264 gallons of propane gas over the heating season.

Head-load calculations get more involved as we consider more building details. A wall section may have more studs for window framing, siding, sheathing, insulation, and plasterboard, all affecting the overall thermal value of the wall and the heat load. To determine air leakage, it's best to have a blower-door test performed, but you can use these defaults as a general guide:

- 0.50 ACH is an average place to start.
- 0.40 ACH if you live in a new home.
- 0.20 ACH if you know it's an extremely tight home (i.e., built with stress-skin panels or double-stud walls).
- If the house was built before 1960, it might be closer to 0.75 ACH.
- An old, drafty farmhouse might measure 1 or 2 ACH.

Index

About the Author

P AUL SCHECKEL IS A SENIOR PROJECT MANAGER for the award-winning Vermont Energy Investment Corporation. As an energy efficiency specialist, he has performed thousands of home energy audits, Energy Ratings, and inspections in all kinds of homes, engaging homeowners on a personal level about all aspects of energy efficiency and renewable energy. He is certified as an Advanced Energy Auditor, Home Energy Rater, Rating Supervisor, Building analyst, Shell Specialist, and Heating Specialist.

Paul has operated a solar energy installation company, and was a partner in the Vermont Electric Car Company. Their "E-96" was the most efficient car in its class in the 1992 American Tour de Sol electric vehicle rally, and later became the first electric car to be built and sold in Vermont.

When not working or writing, Paul can usually be found immersed in a project designed to reduce personal energy consumption to a bare minimum. His wife, June, teases him about measuring energy by the teaspoon. They are raising their first "off-grid-kid" in the solar powered house they built, and drive a car powered by vegetable oil.

If you have enjoyed *The Home Energy Diet*, you might also enjoy other

BOOKS TO BUILD A NEW SOCIETY

Our books provide positive solutions for people who want to
make a difference. We specialize in:

Sustainable Living • Ecological Design and Planning
Natural Building & Appropriate Technology • New Forestry
Environment and Justice • Conscientious Commerce
Progressive Leadership • Resistance and Community • Nonviolence
Educational and Parenting Resources

New Society Publishers

ENVIRONMENTAL BENEFITS STATEMENT

New Society Publishers has chosen to produce this book on recycled paper
made with 100% post consumer waste, processed chlorine free, and old
growth free.

For every 5,000 books printed, New Society saves the following resources:[1]

36	Trees
3,261	Pounds of Solid Waste
3,588	Gallons of Water
4,680	Kilowatt Hours of Electricity
5,928	Pounds of Greenhouse Gases
26	Pounds of HAPs, VOCs, and AOX Combined
9	Cubic Yards of Landfill Space

---

[1]Environmental benefits are calculated based on research done by the Environmental Defense
Fund and other members of the Paper Task Force who study the environmental impacts of the
paper industry.

For a full list of NSP's titles, please call 1-800-567-6772 or check out our web site at:

www.newsociety.com

NEW SOCIETY PUBLISHERS